INSPIRE

INSPIRE

The Universal Path for Leading
Yourself and Others

ADAM GALINSKY

HARPER
BUSINESS

An Imprint of HarperCollins*Publishers*

HarperCollins books may be purchased for educational, business, or sales promotional use. For information, please email the Special Markets Department at Spsales@harpercollins.com.

FIRST EDITION

Designed by Emily Snyder

Library of Congress Cataloging-in-Publication Data has been applied for.
ISBN 978-0-06-329467-7

24 25 26 27 28 LBC 5 4 3 2 1

To the GO Family (Jenn, Asher, and Aden):
You INSPIRE me every day!

Contents

Introduction

THE JOLT WAS so forceful and so abrupt that Captain Tammie Jo Shults felt like a Mack truck had slammed into the aircraft. "My first thought was that we *had* been hit—that we'd had a midair collision." The aircraft immediately went into a snap roll to the left, but she and her first officer, Darren Ellisor, instantly caught it and leveled the wings. But as they did so, a roar rushed into the cockpit. Suddenly, they couldn't see, they couldn't hear, they couldn't breathe.

Southwest Airlines Flight 1380's left engine had experienced catastrophic failure and exploded. But the situation was even more dire than Shults initially realized: debris from the turbine had smashed the left window in row fourteen. The air rushing through the shattered window was causing the deafening roar, the loss of pressure, and the desperate need for oxygen. Even worse, a passenger had been fatally sucked halfway out the window. Shults realized that she and her copilot were now confronted with "an unscripted combination of emergencies . . . hydraulic lines were cut, fuel lines were cut, and we were dealing with drag that we hadn't ever practiced dealing with."

Time was critical. At their current altitude in a depressurized plane, Shults and Ellisor had only sixty seconds before they would suffer from oxygen deprivation. But Shults's first move was to stay the course: it was Ellisor's turn to fly the plane, and she signaled to him with a head nod and a release of her hands that he was still in control.

To the passengers on board, it seemed like they were free-falling. Passenger Marty Martinez recounted the terrifying sense of doom, "I literally bought WiFi as the plane was going down because I wanted to be able to reach the people I loved . . . thinking these were my final moments on earth." His colleague sitting next to him began typing out a goodbye message to his family. Martinez noted it wasn't just the passengers who appeared to be panicking, but also the flight attendants.

Despite the panic in the main cabin, Shults and Ellisor were in control and already orchestrating a reasonably paced descent. Once they reached a safe altitude, they needed a place to land, and fast. It was Ellisor who noticed how close Philadelphia was. Shults quickly agreed that it was an ideal airport given its long runway and medical resources.

At this point, Shults uttered ten simple words over the intercom that completely transformed the psychological state of the passengers: "We are not going down. We are going to Philly."

Although her message was simple, it was also deeply reassuring. She later noted, "Only a few minutes had passed since the explosion, but a few minutes can seem like an eternity in a life-threatening situation . . . Afterward, the passengers shared how that one simple message made all the difference. It changed the attitude inside the aircraft . . . panic began to subside . . . terror was replaced with possibility."

As the plane approached the tarmac in Philly, Shults retook control of the plane. But there was a problem: when Shults went to make the final right turn to line the plane up with the runway, nothing happened. She was stunned, so stunned that the cockpit microphone recorded her asking for guidance—"Heavenly Father?"—as she desperately tried to figure out what she was missing. She then made the risky decision to ease the throttle back while standing on the right rudder.

The plane turned before it was too late.

At 11:23 a.m. on April 17, 2018, Flight 1380 was safely on the ground in Philadelphia. But Shults wasn't done navigating her plane or protecting her passengers. She purposely parked the plane right by the fire trucks on the tarmac and even made sure that the trucks were on the damaged side of the plane. Shults also instinctively understood that some of her passengers might leap out onto the wings if they were feeling desperate to get off the plane. To reduce the risk of injury, she turned the flaps to forty degrees to offer a little slide.

When Shults entered the cabin, she proceeded to greet her passengers. This wasn't unusual for Shults, as she would often walk down the aisle during lengthy delays or unusual circumstances. This time she moved more slowly, deliberately looking each passenger in the eye and asking if they were okay. Like her simple update, her attentive journey down the aisle resonated with her passengers, and the larger public. Shults later said, "I've found it intriguing that people covering the story have been more interested in how I treated people after the flight than in what it took to fly the crippled airplane safely to the ground."

When Shults was being physically evaluated a little while later, the EMT asked, "How do you get through security?" When Shults seemed surprised, he continued, "With those nerves of steel . . . you don't even have an elevated heart rate, you're completely calm."

Southwest generously offered the crew an extended period of paid time off, but Shults was back flying only three and a half weeks after the emergency landing. Beyond helping her return to the normalcy of everyday life, she understood her actions would be an important signal to others: "I also thought it was important for my family, and anyone else who was watching, to see I still had confidence in flight, in Southwest Airlines, and in Boeing aircraft." She knew by flying again, she could help prevent "any falsehoods about the incident from taking root."

When Shults later reflected on the successful landing, her mind drifted back to the moments before the flight took off. Unlike many flights, the plane was fully prepped a few minutes before the passengers boarded. Given the extra time, Shults assembled her crew in the galley. This was the first time the crew had worked together and Shults looked for points of connection. She and Ellisor realized that they both had

seniors in high school, and they bonded over finding the right graduation gift. When Shults mentioned her idea of gifting the Book of Proverbs,
the three flight attendants began to share their own connections to the
Bible. Rachel Fernheimer was excited about her new version, which had
room to journal on the side. Kathryn Sandoval mentioned she was in a
study of Psalms, and Shults shared that she was also participating in a
similar study.

Shults credited this informal conversation as critical to the well-
coordinated responses of the crew: "When you talk about things deeper
than the weather—your family, your faith—the things that matter to
you, even if they're different, it tends to create a bond. The few minutes
we had together before the flight, talking about things that were important to us, created a foundation of trust that we critically needed after
the engine failed."

ON JANUARY 13, 2012, 3,206 passengers and 1,023 crew members were
on the *Costa Concordia* for a seven-day Mediterranean voyage. That
evening, the ship suddenly deviated from its course to sail closer to the
Isle of Giglio. It is debatable why Captain Francesco Schettino brought
the ship so precariously close to shore. He claims he wanted to salute
other mariners. Prosecutors would later claim that the married Schettino was trying to impress his mistress, a Moldovan dancer, who was on
board. What isn't debatable is what happened next: the *Costa Concordia*
struck the Scole Rocks, a reef eight meters below the surface. The collision was so forceful that it tore a 160-foot hole in the port side of the
ship. Water quickly engulfed the generators and engines, causing an
electrical blackout.

Had Schettino taken immediate action, it's likely that every passenger and crew member would have been safely rescued. But that's not
what happened. Instead, Schettino focused on a different kind of damage control. When talking to the boat's crisis coordinator, he tried to

deflect blame by claiming the accident resulted from the electrical problem, rather than vice versa. And he would later try to put the shipwreck
squarely on the helmsman. Even as the ship began to sink, Schettino
was spending his mental energy on getting his story straight. He asked
the boat's crisis coordinator, "What should I say to the media?. . . . To
the port authorities I have said that we had . . . a blackout."

Because of his focus on saving his reputation, Schettino delayed reporting the accident to the Italian Search and Rescue Authority. And
even when he did contact them, he dithered for twenty minutes before
he came clean on the accident and the dire situation. As a result, the
evacuation didn't begin for more than an hour after the ship was ripped
apart by the reef. And, even then, many passengers claimed they didn't
hear the evacuation orders.

While passengers and other crew were scrambling to find safety,
Schettino himself was already safely in a lifeboat. But Schettino took
no credit for his lifeboat feat, claiming he unintentionally "fell" into the
lifeboat due to the ship's tilt. And you might have missed seeing Schettino in the lifeboat, given he was no longer in his captain's uniform.
Somehow, Schettino found time to change into a suit before fleeing from
his sinking ship.

The following transcript reveals the conversation that Schettino
had with a member of the coast guard, Gregorio De Falco, while sitting
in the lifeboat.

> DE FALCO: Listen, this is De Falco from Livorno. Am I speaking
>   with the captain?
> SCHETTINO: I am Captain Schettino, Chief.
> DE FALCO: Listen, Schettino. There are people trapped on board.
>   Now, you go with your lifeboat. Under the bow of the ship,
>   on the right side, there is a ladder. You climb on that ladder
>   and go on board the ship . . . and tell me how many people are
>   there. Is that clear?

SCHETTINO: At this moment the ship is listing.

DE FALCO: Get back on the ship and tell me how many people there are, tell me if there are children, women and what type of help they need. And you tell me the number of each of these categories. Is that clear?

SCHETTINO: Please . . .

DE FALCO: There is no "please" about it. Get back on board. Assure me you are going back on board!

SCHETTINO: I'm in a lifeboat, I am under here. I am not going anywhere. I am here.

DE FALCO: What are you doing, Captain?

SCHETTINO: I am here to coordinate the rescue . . .

DE FALCO (INTERRUPTING): What are you coordinating there! Get on board! Coordinate the rescue from on board! Are you refusing?

SCHETTINO: No, I am not refusing.

DE FALCO (YELLING): You get back on board! That is an order! There is nothing else for you to consider. You have sounded the "Abandon Ship." Now I am giving the orders. Get back on board. Is that clear? Don't you hear me?

SCHETTINO: I am going aboard.

DE FALCO: My rescue craft is at the bow. Go! There are already bodies, Schettino. Go!

SCHETTINO: How many bodies are there?

DE FALCO: I don't know! . . . Christ, you should be the one telling me that!

SCHETTINO: Do you realize that it is dark and we can't see anything . . . Look, Chief, I want to go aboard but the other lifeboat here has stopped and is drifting. I have called . . .

DE FALCO (INTERRUPTING): You have been telling me this for an hour! Now, go aboard! Get on board and tell me immediately how many people there are!

SCHETTINO: [No response]

DE FALCO: Listen, Schettino, perhaps you have saved yourself
from the sea, but I will make you pay for this. For **** sake,
go back on board!

Schettino ended up paying a price for his actions. He was convicted
of multiple crimes and ordered to spend sixteen years in prison: ten
years for multiple manslaughters, five years for causing a shipwreck,
and one year for abandoning the passengers at the time of the sinking.

TAMMIE JO SHULTS and Francesco Schettino were both captains of
their own vessels. And they both faced similar crises as they contended
with gaping holes in their vehicles. But they couldn't be more different.
Beyond their obvious dissimilarities in gender and nationality, what
really distinguishes these two captains is how they acted during a crisis.

Shults was inspiring. Schettino was infuriating.

Inspiring leaders, like Shults, transform a crisis into a routine and
ordinary course of action. The explosion and subsequent damage to her
plane were not foreseeable by Shults, yet she was fully accountable and
in complete control during the crisis that ensued.

In contrast, infuriating leaders, like Schettino, pervert and twist the
routine until it turns into a crisis. Schettino should have anticipated how
being so close to the shore could cripple his ship. And then he refused to
take any responsibility for the crisis that he had created.

Inspiring and infuriating leaders do not only exist in times of crisis.
They are part of the everyday fabric of our lives as they transform common-
place moments into psychologically remarkable ones.

I want you to think about a Shults from your own life, to reflect on
someone that inspired you. Your inspiring figure can come from anywhere in your life: a relative or religious leader, a teacher or a coach, a
boss or a peer.

What characterizes this feeling of being inspired? When I have
asked people across the globe to describe the feeling of being inspired,

XVI   INTRODUCTION

they frequently use words like *bright, light,* and *warmth.* Others describe it as a mix of *awe, admiration,* and *wonder.* And many recognize it as a wellspring of *hope* and *possibility.*

Now I want you to pinpoint the *cause* of that feeling. What was it *about* this person that made you feel inspired? Try to identify the precise attribute they possessed that inspired you.

I call these people Inspiring Leaders. As a noun, inspiring leaders represent the people in our lives who motivate and guide us to become a better version of ourselves. As a gerund, it captures how each of us—through our own behavior, words, and presence—can inspire others. These two meanings serve as a guide for growing and spreading the seeds of inspiration across the globe.

Now, I want you to think about a Schettino from your life. The Schettinos in our lives also have the capacity to change us inside. But people often use words like *hot, red, searing,* and *boiling* to describe the infuriating leaders of their lives. These leaders create a seething cauldron of rage and resentment. I want you to really feel that fury. Notice how overwhelming it is, how consuming it is. Now identify the root of that infuriation. What was it *about* this person that really made your blood boil?

I've conducted this exercise—reflecting on the Inspiring and Infuriating Leaders in our lives—with thousands of people from across the globe. My research has led to three insights about leadership, and more broadly about human nature.

At first blush, Shults and Schettino couldn't seem more different. But they are more connected than we might think. In fact, Shults and Schettino are mirror images of each other, standing on opposite ends of a continuum. That is the first key insight from my research: *Inspiring and Infuriating Leaders exist on an enduring continuum.*

The second insight is that the thousands of examples I have collected around the globe can be reduced to three key factors along this inspiring-infuriating continuum. Schults and Schettino revealed these three dimensions during their crises.

Shults was *visionary*. She was able to see the big picture and give her passengers a reassuring *why* when the plane was rapidly descending: "We are not going down. We are going to Philly." In contrast, Schettino was narrowly focused on minimizing his responsibility and deflecting blame.

Shults was an *exemplar of desired behavior*. She was a calm, courageous, and competent protector. Her nerves of steel never wavered. Schettino instead cowardly abandoned his ship.

Shults was a *great mentor*. She empowered her copilot, Ellisor, by letting him continue flying the plane, and after they safely landed, she was quick to credit him for suggesting they land in Philly. She took the time to get to know her flight attendants. She even made sure her passengers were emotionally okay after the ordeal was over. Conversely, Schettino selfishly put his own well-being above that of his passengers and crew. He never even expressed any remorse or empathy, declaring at his trial, "I cannot feel responsible."

These three factors—visionary, exemplar, mentor—represent how we see the world, how we are in the world, and how we interact with others in the world. We can inspire others through our words, our actions, and our interactions.

The third insight is that the three dimensions that make up this enduring inspiring-infuriating continuum are universal. The exact same characteristics emerge in every culture and country across the globe. There is not a single inspiring or infuriating attribute that is unique to a specific country or region. Of course, how each element gets expressed may vary by country or culture, but the attributes themselves and the continuum they represent are part of a universal tapestry. Being inspired and infuriated by others is rooted in the very architecture of the human brain.

The three dimensions of inspiring leader are universal because each one fulfills a set of fundamental human needs. Visionary fulfills the human need for meaning and purpose. Exemplar fulfills the human need for protection and passion. Mentor fulfills the human need for support and status.

MY DISCOVERY—THAT INSPIRING and infuriating leaders exist on an enduring continuum that is made up of three universal factors—carries a profound implication: *Each and every one of us has the potential to be inspiring*. Because there is a universal and systematic set of inspiring attributes, those skills can be taught, they can be nurtured, and they can be developed.

The universal continuum is philosophically interesting and practically important. Theoretically, it answers the enduring question about whether inspiring leaders are born or made. My research shows that we are not born as inspiring or infuriating individuals. Rather, it is our current behavior that either inspires or infuriates. Our words, our actions, and our interactions create either a wellspring of hope and possibility or a seething cauldron of rage and resentment inside others. Shults's reassuring words created immediate hope while her compassion lingered with her passengers. Schettino, in contrast, filled De Falco with a rage so intense that he thirsted for retribution.

Although there is a universal tool kit for inspiring others, the process isn't easy; life often slants us toward the infuriating end of the continuum. We are too often a Schettino. But the continuum also offers hope. When we find ourselves drifting to the infuriating end, we already have a clear path back to the other side. We can—with the right reflection, the right preparation, and the right intention—move from being a Schettino to being a Shults.

IN THE PAGES that follow, I will show how understanding the universal path of inspiring others can help address the most pressing problems and dilemmas we face daily: How do I negotiate so I can create more value for myself and others? How do I make wise decisions that produce innovative ideas? How do I allocate scarce resources fairly? How do I navigate an increasingly diverse world?

To answer these questions and guide you toward the inspiring end of the continuum, I integrate the scientific and the personal. *Inspire* is deeply scientific. Building on my quarter century of research and hundreds of scientific articles, I unpack the empirical basis of what it means to be inspiring, the systematic levers that create a vicious cycle of infuriation, and the scientific pathway for staying on the inspiring end of the continuum. These data-based principles will guide you to have a more positive impact on others and build a more inspiring world.

But *Inspire* is also deeply personal. I not only present compelling examples from across the globe, but I also share illustrative stories from my own life. My hope is that *Inspire* is also personal for you, that it helps you embark on a journey through your past and present to forge a brighter future for yourself and for those around you.

Inspire isn't just about leadership. It's really about life. I have been surprised by how many people have used its principles to inform and transform their personal relationships. A CEO told me *Inspire* made him a better spouse. A Fortune 100 board member shared that it made her a more motivating parent. A student confided that it helped him become a more dependable friend.

Before we start, I want to emphasize two ideas that are so critical for our journey together. First, as leaders, we do not have a choice of whether we have an impact or not—neutrality is not an option; we will either inspire or infuriate. However, we do have control over the *type* of impact we have. We always have a choice of whether to inspire or infuriate.

Second, leaders are not born, they are made. Because there is a scientific basis to inspiring others, each of us can learn, nurture, and develop the capacity to be inspiring. That means every single one of us has the potential to inspire others.

You can be a Shults. You can be a more inspiring version of yourself. Let's learn how.

PART I

Reimagining Inspiration

CHAPTER 1

The Leader Amplification Effect

WHEN I SAT down for the first class of my doctoral program at Princeton University, I was so nervous. There were only eleven new doctoral students in the psychology department, and I was intimidated by the brainpower of my fellow students. But I was also eager to prove that I belonged.

My first class was with Daniel Kahneman, who would become the only psychologist to win the Nobel Prize in Economics. About an hour into the three-hour class, I saw my chance to say something insightful, and I eagerly raised my hand.

I still remember, thirty years later, the exact transformation in Danny's demeanor as I delivered my insight. He scrunched up his face, vigorously shook his head, folded his arms, and spat out, "That's not right at all."

Danny and the class moved on, but I didn't. I was frozen in place. I could barely breathe. I felt completely mortified. His words, "That's not right at all!," reverberated inside of me. It would take me weeks before I could speak in Danny's class, let alone in any class.

About six weeks into the semester, Danny passed me in the hallway and nonchalantly said, "Adam, I really enjoy reading your reflection papers. You are a great writer." Before I could even respond, Danny had already turned the corner. I felt so elated by his comment that I literally skipped down the hallway.

These two very different Danny Kahneman interactions represent the opposite ends of the inspiring-infuriating continuum. Danny was infuriating in his fleeting yet forceful dismissiveness. In contrast, he inspired me to be an even better writer with his casual compliment.

But these two interactions also represent another key phenomenon, one I have labeled the *leader amplification effect*. When we are in a position of leadership, all our words and expressions—positive and negative—get amplified. Because of his position, his dismissive comment became HUMILIATING CRITICISM, while his compliment became GLORIOUS PRAISE. In each case, his comment was amplified by his authority, multiplying its impact. Although Danny's comments were offhand and inconsequential to him, they were so impactful to me that I vividly remember each one more than three decades later.

When we have power or authority, our words and behavior matter more. They even matter more when they are ambiguous.

"I NEED TO TALK TO YOU."

IMAGINE WAKING UP to this text from a friend. Those six words are straightforward, but the message itself is ambiguous. It's unclear whether the news is good or bad, or whether it involves you or not. It might make you worry, but probably just a little.

Now, imagine that text came from your boss. Suddenly, those six words—I NEED TO TALK TO YOU—scream off your screen, ominous and portentous. You are convinced that it's bad news and it's coming for *you*. The words may be ambiguous, but your reaction is now crystal clear: you are consumed by worry.

When I was a young assistant professor, I came face-to-face with these six words and the leader amplification effect. As an assistant professor, I was in the ultimate middle power position: I had more power than the doctoral students who depended on me for resources and letters of recommendation. But I had less power than the senior faculty members who would one day vote on my promotion.

One morning, the elevators opened at 9:00 a.m., and I saw a doctoral student, Gail Berger, and said, "Gail, I need to talk to you. Come by my office at 3:00 p.m." Later that afternoon, I was surprised when Gail walked into my office in a fearful crouch. I was particularly perplexed because I just wanted to go over Gail's research materials with her. And I was extremely befuddled by what Gail did next. She slammed her fist on the table and shouted, "Never do that to me again!" "Never do what?" I stammered. "Never ask to meet with me without telling me *why*. Do you know how much work I got done in the last six hours? Zero! All I could think of is 'Is Adam mad at me, is someone else mad at me, am I going to lose an important resource?'"

At first, I thought that Gail was just being neurotic (it turns out that Gail *is* a little neurotic ☺). But the very next day, I got an email from the most powerful person in my department saying she needed to talk with *me*, and I entered her office in the same fearful crouch as Gail.

It's not just the phrase "I need to talk to you" that sends people scurrying. Sometimes it's receiving any communication at all from a leader. Consider what Victoria discovered after she got promoted to a leadership position. Given her new role, she was so busy with meetings that she didn't have time to write or respond to emails until the end of the day. To stay on top of her inbox, she would send a whole slew of emails in the evening because this was the time that was convenient for her to respond to all the communication that had accumulated throughout the day. She didn't expect or even want anyone to respond that evening. But that's not what happened. Upon receiving an email from the newly powerful Victoria, her employees would reply *immediately*. By receiving her emails in the evening, people thought they had to respond *now*.

When we are leaders, our criticism, praise, and ambiguous commands get amplified. But so does our silence.

DEAFENING SILENCE

ON FEBRUARY 17, 2014, United Airlines Flight 1676 was traveling from Denver to Montana when it suddenly and dramatically fell one thousand feet in twelve seconds. That's like jumping off the Eiffel Tower. An infant flew out of her mother's arms, miraculously landing unharmed in a nearby seat. A flight attendant wasn't so lucky: she hit the ceiling so hard that she was knocked unconscious and remained so for the rest of the flight.

What happened next is remarkable, because what happened next was . . . nothing. The pilots never said a word. All the passengers heard was silence.

My twin brother was on that flight. In the days that followed, he told me how terrified he was by this silence and how desperately he craved communication from the pilots in charge:

> The lack of information from the cockpit caused my fear to spike.
> My mind began to try to fill the information void. I imagined that
> perhaps the pilot had been injured during the turbulence. I wondered if the wings, or perhaps the engines, had been damaged by
> the violent shaking of the plane. I raced to understand what was
> going on. Without any communication from the cockpit, I felt
> unsafe, and I was left to search for possible answers to fears that
> would have and should have been allayed by the pilots.

He described the lack of updates as *deafening silence*.

It turns out this wasn't a one-off occurrence. When I was sharing this story with an audience of consultants visiting from Europe, they broke out in energetic chatter. Apparently, a similar event had happened on their plane to New York, and the details were eerily similar. When the plane precipitously dropped hundreds of feet, a baby flew back one row but was safely caught by one of the consultants, a flight attendant was injured, and the pilots again said *nothing*, not a word. As a result, they were all seized by terror.

We can all understand that the pilots were likely overwhelmed dealing with issues triggered by the sudden and precipitous descent. But silence, like "I need to talk to you," is *ambiguous*. Silence steers people down the portentous side of the mountain. When our leaders remain silent, we fill the void with worst-case scenarios. This is why silence is often so infuriating.

Now contrast this silence with Tammie Jo Shults and her reassuring communication after an exploded engine burst a hole in the plane's cabin, "We are not going down. We are going to Philly." Those simple words were transformative, moving people from abject fear to hope and possibility.

IMBUING THE INCIDENTAL WITH IMPORTANCE

WHEN BARRY SALZBERG became CEO of Deloitte Global, a consulting company of more than 330,000 employees, he was puzzled by the fact that every major meeting always had bananas. Even though he had spent more than thirty years at Deloitte, he wondered if bananas were an important symbol of Deloitte that he had somehow overlooked. Or did someone important really like bananas? When he finally asked his assistant why there were bananas at every meeting, she replied: "Because *you* love bananas!" Apparently at his first executive meeting as CEO, he walked in, seemingly perked up when he saw bananas, and ate one before the meeting started. Because his assistant was paying such close attention to his behavior, she coded this action as signaling an undying and enduring love of bananas. She then went to great lengths to ensure that bananas were present at every meeting he attended.

Barry's banana adventures highlight how seemingly random, coincidental behavior gets imbued with meaning and purpose when we are a leader. Notice that Barry didn't say a word; he simply picked up a banana and ate it with a touch of enthusiasm. When we are leaders, even faint facial expressions can send others scurrying. A few years ago, Ashley Martin, then a doctoral student at Columbia University, was practicing a research presentation she was going to deliver at Harvard and Stanford Universities. Because she was interviewing for a faculty position, the stakes were sky-high and so was her anxiety. As she presented her research, her anxiety intensified when she noticed a look of displeasure on my face. No matter what she did, my face didn't seem to express anything but disapproval. My frown convinced Ashley that her presentation was just awful. She was wrong: I thought it was great! Sure, I had some suggestions for improvement, but I felt she was on the right track. So, what happened? Because I was a parent of two boys under two, my annoyed look was simply the product of fatigue. But my faculty status led Ashley to pay close attention to my expressions, and she interpreted my frown as *caused* by her presentation.

A COROLLARY OF the leader amplification effect is the *parent amplification effect*. As parents, our words and actions, even offhand ones, get amplified with our kids. Even if we are unaware of the impact of our incidental comments, their effects can linger throughout our child's lifetime. Consider how a casual comment from her mom led one of my former doctoral students, Erica Bailey, to abandon one of her childhood passions. Both she and her sister played piano when they were kids. When Erica was around twelve years old, she overheard her mom say to a friend, "Both girls are great at piano, but Abby has a real knack for it." Erica was so incensed at the suggestion that her sister had more natural talent that she never played piano again!

Not appreciating the parent amplification effect almost cost me one of my greatest joys. Every morning since he was old enough to walk, my son Asher has crawled into bed and snuggled tightly with me. At one point when he was seven, I noticed that when he came to our bed, he wouldn't come near me. After a few days, I asked why and he said, "Because *you* don't want to snuggle with me!" When I tried to convince him that it wasn't true, he wouldn't listen. I was so confused until I remembered that a few days earlier Asher had come into our bed earlier than usual on a night when I had gone to bed later than usual. Because his early morning snuggling was disrupting my much-needed sleep, I abruptly left the bedroom to get more sound slumber elsewhere. He interpreted my bedroom departure as a complete and total rejection of his snuggling! By explaining and apologizing for my abrupt departure, we were able to resume our morning ritual and the shared joy it brought us.

THE DRIVERS OF THE LEADER AMPLIFICATION EFFECT

THE FIRST DRIVER of the leader amplification effect is the simple fact that leaders attract *attention*.

Shakespeare's famous phrase "all the world's a stage" is especially true for leaders. When you are a leader, you are constantly onstage. That means those around you are attending to your every move, listening intently to your every word, studiously interpreting your every expression, analyzing your every interaction. Our words, expressions, and behaviors generally send signals of meaning and intention. But attention amplifies those signals, making them louder, bolder, and stronger. Attention turns hope into HOPE and fear into FEAR.

The second driver of the leader amplification effect flows, in part, from the *power* that leaders wield. Because leaders typically control resources that others want, others feel dependent on them. This dependency steers those with less power to pay close attention to everything a leader says and does. When you have power, people search for positive or negative intentions in all your words, and even in your silence. That's what happened to me with Danny Kahneman; because I was dependent on him for my grade, I was highly sensitive to both his criticism and his praise. That is what happened with Gail; because she was dependent on me for resources, both material and reputational, she was highly attentive to any ominous possibilities. And that's what happened when Barry Salzberg's assistant cornered the banana market; because he was her boss, she paid close attention to his preferences.

Power doesn't flow solely from positions of leadership but stems from controlling valued resources. Consider that professors are generally in more powerful positions than computer technicians at most universities. But when a professor's computer is having issues, the technicians are now in control of this valuable resource, and the faculty member is dependent on them to fix it. At a former university, when my computer needed a repair, it would often go into a black hole, reappearing at a random future date. This was upsetting to me, not because the technicians were slow, but because I was left in the dark. I worried that they had forgotten about my computer, or that it was lost, or it was unfixable. That experience helped me realize that receiving silence is inherently disempowering. As soon as we send a communication—a phone call, an email, a text—we are now in a low-power position, dependent on the other person to respond.

A third driver of the leader amplification effect is being part of an *audience*. My research with Garriy Shteynberg of the University of Tennessee discovered that simply observing the same stimulus with an audience intensifies our reactions compared to viewing that stimulus alone. We used the term *shared attention* to describe the situation where more than one person is viewing the same object. In our experiments, simply sharing attention with fellow group members made scary images scarier and happy information more joyful. In one study, we used charitable advertisements that were designed to produce sadness. Because shared attention intensifies sadness, we found that ads viewed with others received more donations than when the same ads were viewed alone.

Attention, and the fact that leaders are always in the spotlight, is at the core of the leader amplification effect. *Power* is a second driver of attention. *Being part of an audience* is a third driver of attention. The combination of being in the spotlight, having power, and presenting to an audience *amplifies* the impact of our behavior and words on others.

One of my consulting engagements highlights how the combination of attention, power, and audiences intensifies reactions. I was hired by a company to give a series of workshops to both its senior leaders and its younger associates on three different continents in less than ten days.

What precipitated my breathless trek around the world? It was a disastrous town hall. Two things happened at this company-wide event that shook the company. First, when people gave ideas, they were mostly greeted with dismissive pleasantries such as "That's interesting." People wanted their ideas to be engaged with, but instead, they were ignored. Even worse, some comments were met with no response at all; the town hall just moved along after an awkward but deafening silence.

Second, one of the senior executives got defensive about a point and expressed open scorn toward the employee who made it. His contemptuous reaction was amplified not only by his position of power but by the shared attention of the company-wide meeting. Watching this senior executive lose his temper in front of the whole company wasn't just humiliating to the individual targeted by the executive's wrath, it was traumatizing to everyone who was in the audience. After the town hall, no one felt comfortable sharing their perspectives—now it was the employees' silence that was deafening. The company had to intervene by having me fly around the world and share ideas on the topic of psychological safety and how to help employees feel comfortable speaking up.

IN THE SPOTLIGHT BUT FEELING INVISIBLE

BECAUSE LEADERS COMMAND attention, have power, and communicate to audiences, their behavior, words, and expressions get amplified. But here's the thing: when we are leaders, we are often unaware that we are on a metaphorical stage. Although leadership puts us in the spotlight, it can ironically make us feel invisible. As a result, leaders are often oblivious to the profound impact they have on others.

Danny Kahneman was completely unaware that his words had such a powerful effect on me. When I shared my classroom experience in a *New York Times* article two decades later, he emailed me, "The problem of power is one that I have learned about for the first time, really, in the last few years. In my consulting job, because I believe (perhaps wrongly) that I am willing to take criticism from them, I started out as uninhibited in my comments on their work as I memorably was to you." For Danny, his comments were casual and without significance. For me and many others, they were transformative. Similarly, Erica's mom had no idea that her offhand remark had led Erica to quit playing piano until I shared the story at Erica's graduation.

I have too often been oblivious to the leader amplification effect, even though I have studied the phenomenon. I had no idea that my "I need to talk to you" comment would send Gail into a tornado of worry. And I was unaware that my facial expressions were so alarming to Ashley during her practice talk. Even on days when I am *literally* teaching about the leader amplification effect, I can be blind to its effects. In the fall of 2022, I taught for the first time since becoming a vice dean at Columbia Business School. When I entered the classroom for my first session, there was a problem: the projector was emitting a high-pitched squeal. When multimedia support informed me there was nothing they could do before class started, I sternly told them that I found their response to be unacceptable. Although the noise interfered with class that day, I received good news that evening: the multimedia team had worked all day on the issue and had found a way to solve it! I was so grateful that I sent a note lauding their efforts and deeply expressing my appreciation.

A few weeks later, the chief operating officer of the school Katie Conway came by my office to remind me that I was always wearing "a dean's hat," even when I was only teaching. I retorted, "Uh yeah, duh, I know." She said, "Really? Do you?" She then shared with me that my forceful words on that first day of teaching had left one of the multimedia members in tears. When I criticized her, I wasn't a random professor who was merely disappointed. Now, I was a DEAN who was *yelling at her*. I was stunned and ashamed that I had caused such emotional turmoil. I now realized that it was *my behavior* that was unacceptable! The one saving grace was that my praise and gratitude when the problem was fixed were also amplified.

This example is deeply ironic: I was *literally teaching* about the leader amplification effect and yet I was completely oblivious to its presence. I forgot that as a vice dean I was always in the spotlight and my behavior would have a greater impact. Whether I liked it or not, I was no longer just a professor.

This example also highlights the amplifying echoes of our actions as leaders. Audience members take their interactions and observations with them and share their reactions with others. The word of my classroom anger spread all the way to my bosses. And that's what also happened in the disastrous company town hall; everyone knew the story even if they weren't there. As leaders, we are the subject of gossip and, as a result, the amplifying impact of our behavior will spread even to those who missed our performance.

A FAILURE OF PERSPECTIVE-TAKING

LET'S GO BACK to the six hours of terror I induced in Gail when I said, "I need to talk to you." Why didn't I tell Gail why I needed to speak with her? Because *I knew* the topic wasn't bad or scary, I thought it would be obvious to Gail. But I was cursed by my knowledge and failed to appreciate that, from Gail's perspective, she was in the dark. Once we know a piece of information, it becomes difficult for us to adjust to the fact that others may not be privy to that same knowledge. Both the curse of knowledge and underappreciation of the leader amplification effect are failures of the same psychological process: perspective-taking.

Here's a simple problem that highlights the complexities of perspective-taking. What number is on the table? It's a trick question because the answer depends on perspective. From *your* perspective it's sixteen, but from the perspective of my former research assistant Roslyn Raser, the number is ninety-one.

Perspective-taking failures are a general problem, but my research with Joe Magee shows that they are particularly pronounced when we are in positions of leadership. Part of the failure is purely cognitive. Because we often have more demands on our attention as leaders, we have less time and resources to consider all the perspectives of those who follow us. But perspective-taking failures are also driven by our power: because leaders are less dependent *on* others, we have fewer incentives to consider the perspectives *of* others.

My research with Joe Magee has found that power *causes* a loss of perspective-taking. When we randomly place some of our participants into positions of power and others to be their subordinates, the powerful leaders suddenly become oblivious to the perspective of others. Our research shows that the association with power and poor perspective-taking is driven by simply having power, and not because people who are bad perspective-takers may end up in positions of power.

SOLVING THE LEADER AMPLIFICATION EFFECT

so, how do we solve the leader amplification effect? It requires the two things that leaders, because of their power, often lack: awareness and perspective-taking.

Awareness involves recognizing that as a leader we are always in an attentional spotlight and, as a result, our behavior and words *will* have an impact. The awareness that our words, expressions, and behavior will deeply affect others helps us to take their perspective. Awareness and perspective-taking can solve every dilemma we discussed in this chapter.

Danny Kahneman's withering rejection of my insight, "That's not right at all," is a criticism that still haunts me to this day. Reflecting on that experience led me to start biting my own critical tongue in public and looking for more private moments to share my thoughts. It also led me to stop sharing constructive criticisms the same day that a graduate student publicly presents their research. I realized that my future-oriented comments, no matter how constructive, immediately deflated their joy of successfully completing this stressful task. Now I celebrate their accomplishment by only offering praise immediately after the talk, and I wait a day or two to offer any ideas for improvement.

There are other times when we, as leaders, need to keep our thoughts to ourselves. In my second year of teaching, a student told me how infuriating he found my ongoing political asides and how they had reduced his engagement and learning. From then on, I stopped making political comments in the classroom as I realized they were inherently divisive. Similarly, my dean, Costis Maglaras, confided in me that one disappointment of becoming the dean was that he could no longer tease or joke around with his colleagues. Costis had been a regular member of the faculty prior to becoming the dean, and he loved sharing slightly sarcastic but cheerful comments. But now, everything he said was interpreted like a biblical passage, even by his friends. He found it impossible to offer the type of offhand remarks that he delighted in making. As dean, he realized that nothing is ever offhand.

Let's go back to my interaction with Gail and her suggestion that I tell her *why* I wanted to meet. Originally, I said, "Gail, I need to talk to you. Come by my office at 3:00 p.m." I could have said, "Gail, let's meet to review your materials. Come by my office at 3:00 p.m." Notice that wording would have cost me nothing—both messages are literally thirteen words. To offer her that reassuring why, I needed to overcome my curse of knowledge and understand that she couldn't read my mind and know my intentions weren't scary.

After learning about the leader amplification effect, Michael Robinson, the vice dean for engagement at Columbia Business School, changed the emails he sends to MBA applicants to stop inducing panic in them. Michael frequently communicates with applicants about the status of their application, and he realized that because of his admissions role, sending an email that simply read, "I need to touch base with you, please give me a call," could potentially send an applicant into a tizzy. Now, when he sends an email, he tells applicants the specific reasons why he needs to touch base with them or he reassures them that there isn't a problem.

Armed with knowledge of the leader amplification effect, each of us can commit to giving people a *why* when we want to meet, especially when the reason isn't scary. And even if we are too busy to do so, we can find other ways to offer reassurance. When the employees of a multinational company asked their president if he would simply tell them *why* he wanted to meet with them, he refused, stating that he didn't have the time or inclination to explain his every request. After a back-and-forth negotiation, he finally agreed to type two extra characters into his texts when his request to meet wasn't a big deal: a colon and closing parenthesis, i.e., a ☺. The smiley face solved the problem of ambiguity and prevented the leader amplification effect from running rampant.

Awareness of the leadership amplification effect reminds us to invite people inside our heads. That's what I learned from my experience with Ashley Martin. She didn't know that it was my sleep-deprived state, and not her presentation, that was causing my frown. By becoming aware that I had produced panic in Ashley, I was able to prevent similar terror in the future. Two years later, I was at another practice presentation, this time for Jon Jachimowicz, who was giving his own high-stakes job talk at Harvard University. Although I was again a sleep-deprived zombie, I consciously tried to smile or keep a neutral expression. And I let Jon know *before his talk* that any tortured expressions on my face would be due to lack of sleep and not his talk. He found my heads-up deeply reassuring.

Awareness that our behavior may be sending unintended signals can help us install daily hacks to prevent panicking others. Let's go back to Victoria and her evening emails that would send her team scurrying to reply. Once she appreciated the impact that her evening emails were having on her employees, she changed *when* she sent them. She still wrote them in the evening when it was convenient for her to do so, but she scheduled them to be delivered the next morning when it was less stressful for her employees to receive them.

Remember the terrifying silence of the pilots on my brother's flight versus Tammie Jo Shults's reassurance that her plane wasn't going down but headed to Philly? Awareness and perspective-taking can help us offer support instead of silence. By recognizing the inherent anxiety in delayed responses, we can reassure people in times of uncertainty by keeping them in the loop. That's what the computer support department did to go from the worst department in customer satisfaction to the best. Their big innovation was daily updates. When a faculty member dropped off their computer, they had to be updated of its current status every afternoon, even if there was no new information. These daily updates let people know their computer wasn't lost or forgotten or unrepairable. I personally found these daily check-ins deeply reassuring, and it's easy to see why: they helped keep uncertainty and anxiety at bay.

The simple yet powerful elegance of updates isn't just about their frequency but also about their reach. Many leaders do a decent job of keeping their closest colleagues and direct reports in the loop. But then they leave the rest of the organization in the dark, unaware of their decisions or their thinking. By ensuring that we update the broader community, we eliminate any rising tides of anxiety caused by being out of the loop.

LEVERAGING THE LEADER AMPLIFICATION
EFFECT TO INSPIRE OTHERS

AWARENESS AND PERSPECTIVE-TAKING mitigate the negative consequences of the leader amplification effect. But they can also help us leverage it to inspire others.

Consider my elation at Danny's offhand praise of my writing. Because of his position, his simple compliment became glorious praise. When we become more intentional and more frequent with our praise and gratitude, we fill others with confidence and motivation. The next time you notice a less powerful person hit a task out of the park, let them know it! Or the next time someone goes above and beyond, make sure to express your appreciation. Your expressions of praise and gratitude may even inspire people for years to come. Danny's offhand compliment of my writing has nourished me for more than three decades.

When I give presentations on *Inspire*, I ask audience members to make a leader amplification commitment. I tell them to reach out to three less powerful people and express praise or gratitude for something that person has recently done. And I ask them to be specific because generic platitudes can come across as inauthentic, and even a little bit infuriating. The more precise our praise or gratitude is, the more impactful it will be.

One morning I was giving a talk to a group of CEOs and presidents. At 10:15 a.m., I asked them to make this leader amplification commitment. As we headed into a coffee break at 10:30 a.m., one of the CEOs raised his hand and said, "I already sent my three emails and I already received three joyful replies. Each person gushed that I had just made their week and one of them immediately began to plan a celebratory dinner with their spouse." This example highlights two important points. First, it confirms a finding from my research that powerful leaders are often impulsive—this CEO couldn't even wait for the break to send his emails! But more importantly, it demonstrates that it doesn't take much time to offer praise or gratitude.

That's what Joseph Stagliano discovered when he became president of retail community banking at NBT Bank. He turned recognizing his employees into a fast and efficient habit. Joseph starts his day with a cup of coffee and a few birthday emails to any employee celebrating that day. Seems simple, right? Well, Joseph has over 1,200 employees under his watch. That means he's sending almost five of these emails every single day! And Joseph doesn't just say "Happy Birthday." He takes the time to add a couple of unique details about the person. Now it seems impossible, right? But here is one example, "Happy birthday! I hope you have a great weekend! How did track and bowling go?" As you can see, the email is simple and straightforward. But the replies are extensive and expressive, overflowing with gratitude, as the employees offer deeper details about their passions. By clearly showing knowledge of the person, the impact of this simple birthday message was immense. But Joseph says it takes him less than ten minutes per day. As we will discuss later, with a simple structure and a little effort and practice, we can design daily habits to help us more efficiently inspire those around us.

Here is one final recommendation: amplify your inspiring ampli-
fications. How? By sharing your praise of others with their leaders.
When you work with someone who really excelled at a task, you can
let their boss know how much you appreciated their efforts. Taking
the time to write a note of praise or gratitude to one's supervisor
further amplifies the value of their contributions. My mom frequently
amplified her appreciation by letting managers know of the wonderful customer service she received from a particular representative.
Maybe that's what drew me to my wife, Jenn—she also frequently
reaches out to supervisors to inform them of the heroic efforts of one
of their employees.

TO SOLVE THE leader amplification effect and minimize its negative consequences, we need to recognize that as leaders, we are always onstage
and in an attentional spotlight. Whenever we are in a position of authority or power, or held in high regard, others will be attending to our
every move. Nothing we do will ever be offhand. Second, the attention
we receive as a leader amplifies all our behavior and expressions—from
frowns and criticisms to smiles and praise, and even silence. Thus, we
need to be aware of our expressions from moment to moment, both
verbal and nonverbal, *and* we need to take our audience's perspective to
appreciate how those expressions might be impacting them.

But there's good news: we can harness the leader amplification effect
for good. By intentionally praising or gratefully thanking others for their
efforts, we give them rocket fuel. When we leverage the leader amplification effect, we become truly INSPIRING.

CHAPTER 2

Universal Inspiration

O N JANUARY 25, 2006, I flew to Los Angeles for a conference. When my plane landed a bit past midnight, I turned on my phone and it immediately buzzed to life. I knew something was up when voicemail after voicemail carried weary voices telling me to call them back "no matter how late."

When I returned my twin brother's call, he told me the tragic news: my dad had been hit by a car and killed while walking to a basketball game.

As you can imagine, I was a mess. I felt trapped as our plane slowly inched its way to the gate. My body, uncontrollably shaking, desperately wanted to escape this metal cage and the presence of others.

There were two saving graces that night. The first was my friend and colleague Roderick Swaab. He comforted me in my seat and guided me off the plane. He canceled his own conference plans and flew back with me to Chicago the next day, and he even made sure I got on my connecting fight to North Carolina. His kindness inspires me to this day.

The second saving grace was the fact that my dad's only sibling lived in Los Angeles. When my Aunt Rayma opened the door at 1:00 a.m., we embraced in sorrow and in comfort, and I plaintively said, "I can't believe

I have lost my dad." She replied, "We have all lost a dad. I was his big sister, but he was my dad."

That comment—"We have all lost a dad"—stayed with me in the days that followed. I couldn't stop wondering, *why did it ring so true?*

A week later it finally hit me. When my aunt said, "he was my dad," she was really saying that he had helped guide her through life. And it wasn't just my aunt. At his memorial, so many people shared stories about my dad that reminded me of Danny Kahneman and the leader amplification effect. They described how my dad's occasional but sharp criticism lingered with them, but also how his passion and frequent words of encouragement nourished them. My dad had inspired not only me and my aunt but the many people who came into his orbit.

I ended up writing my speech for his memorial service around my aunt's comment. I called it "My Dad, the Advisor."

THE GENESIS OF *Inspire* occurred two months after my dad passed away. I was conducting a leadership workshop for members of the Federal Bureau of Investigation (FBI) in the context of high-stakes decision-making. At one point, an agent began describing how his former manager was an amazing decision-maker. I was immediately struck by two aspects of his story. The first was physical. There was an immediate transformation in his body language as he recounted his manager's decision-making acumen: he sat up tall in his chair, his eyes lit up as if in awe, and his voice crackled with energy. The second was substantive: he concluded his remarks by saying, "His decision-making continues to inspire me to this day."

His story was so impactful that I paused my lesson plan and went off script. I turned to the sixty agents and asked if anyone else could identify a leader that inspired them. All of them could. I was surprised by the ease with which these agents could identify an inspiring figure in their life. What was even more revelatory to me was how many agents wanted to share their story of the person who inspired them. They seemed compelled to do so.

That simple moment was transformative for me. That workshop led me to rethink my entire approach to understanding leadership and human nature. I began to ask people all over the world to tell me about a leader that inspired them, and their answers became the foundation of my teaching and research. Just as I asked you to do in the introduction, I invite everyone to describe the feeling of being inspired and to precisely pinpoint the source of that feeling.

I created the *My Inspiring Leaders Reflection* to help people mentally connect with those who have transformed their lives.

Please think about an Inspiring Leader from your life. This person—through their behavior, words, or presence—inspired you and made a difference in your life.

Your inspiring figure can come from anywhere. They could be deeply personal, like a parent or spouse, a sibling or close relative. They could come from your childhood: a teacher, a coach, or a counselor. Perhaps they are from history: a religious figure, a politician, an athlete, or an artist. Or they could be contemporary, a boss, a colleague at work, a minister, a rabbi, or a fellow member of a congregation. Although these inspiring individuals are often in positions of leadership, they need not be senior to you; indeed, a child can inspire a parent, a student can inspire a teacher, a mentee can inspire a mentor. Anyone we look up to, no matter how small, has the chance to inspire us.

Once you have identified your Inspiring Leader, I want you to tap into that *feeling* of inspiration. What characterizes that experience of being inspired? People frequently describe it as a positive energy characterized by warmth and light, awe and admiration, a wellspring of hope and possibility.

Now, I want you to pinpoint the attribute or attributes that

made this person so inspiring to you. What was it *about* this person
that inspired you? Try to identify the precise characteristic they
possessed that filled you with the feeling of inspiration.

Your Inspiring Leader may exemplify a characteristic that
you also possess, but they harness it more effectively. They may
awaken or empower a part of you that you didn't know you held or
desired. Or they might embody a characteristic you don't aspire to
own, but you appreciate this unique capacity of theirs.

———

A SECOND MOMENTOUS discussion occurred a year later when I was again
teaching the FBI. This time, an agent didn't want to talk about an inspiring leader. Instead, he wanted to talk about a different type of leader, one
that also changed how he felt inside. Instead of producing a wellspring
of hope and possibility, this agent described a seething cauldron of rage
and resentment. I realized that the archetype he was describing was the
complete opposite of an inspiring leader: it was an infuriating leader.
And it wasn't just him: all the agents immediately could identify a leader
that made their blood boil.

This second serendipitous moment with the FBI was equally profound. I began asking people all over the world to also tell me about a
leader that infuriated them:

> Now think about another leader that also changed you inside. But
> instead of producing a wellspring of hope and possibility, this
> person created a seething cauldron of rage and resentment. Iden-
> tify the source of that infuriation. What was it about this person
> that made your blood boil? I want you to pinpoint the attribute or
> attributes that made them so *infuriating* to you. Try to identify the
> precise characteristic that filled you with infuriation.

Asking people around the globe to reflect on both an inspiring
leader *and* an infuriating leader led me to the three insights I mentioned

in the introduction. Inspiring and infuriating leaders are mirror images of each other and exist on a *continuum*. That continuum is made of up three *dimensions*. And those three dimensions are *universal*. The exact same characteristics emerge in every country across the globe. I have collected data in Australia, China, El Salvador, Thailand, Saudi Arabia, Israel, Mexico, Germany, etc., and there is not a single inspiring or infuriating attribute that is culturally unique. The continuum and its dimensions are universal.

These three factors—visionary, exemplar, mentor—signify how we inspire others through our words, our actions, and our interactions. Inspiring leaders are *visionary*: they see the big picture and offer an optimistic, meaningful vision of the future. Inspiring leaders are *exemplars* of desired behavior; they are calm and courageous protectors, authentically passionate, super competent but also humble. Inspiring leaders are great *mentors*; they empower, encourage, and are empathic toward others, but they also challenge others to be the best version of themselves.

I call these three universal factors the VEM Diagram of Inspiring Leaders. Just like a Venn diagram, the VEM Diagram of Inspiring Leaders has a set of overlapping circles—*V* for visionary, *E* for exemplar of desired behavior, and *M* for mentor—with *inspiring* at the center.

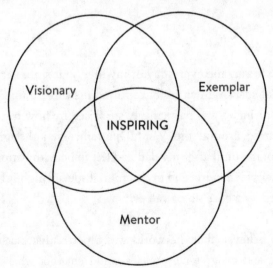

The universality of the VEM Diagram lies in the fact that each of the three dimensions of inspiring leadership fulfill a fundamental human need. *Visionary* fulfills the human need for meaning and understanding. *Exemplar* fulfills the human need for protection, passion, and the striving for perfection. *Mentor* fulfills the human need to feel supported but also valued and celebrated.

The fact that inspiring and infuriating leaders represent mirror images of each other and exist at the opposite ends of a continuum is pedagogically and practically important. Pedagogically, research has demonstrated that people learn more deeply through comparative analysis than through analyzing single examples. The scientific term for the benefits of comparative analysis is analogical encoding, which is a fancy way of saying that comparisons allow people to more easily identify and more deeply internalize principles and insights. Reflecting on *both* an inspiring and an infuriating leader helps us truly understand and appreciate this universal continuum.

Practically, the fact that infuriating and inspiring leaders exist on a continuum offers a warning: it means we can easily slide down to the infuriating end of the continuum. But the continuum also delivers a promise by offering a path back to the inspiring side. As we will learn, with the right practice, commitments, and habits, we can be more inspiring more of the time.

MY DAD INSPIRED me every day of my life. So it's not surprising that my memorial speech unwittingly captured the three universal features of being inspiring. I was particularly surprised by how my speech had been structured around the VEM Diagram, even though the ideas wouldn't emerge until after my dad had left to be with better angels.

My dad was *visionary*, and my memorial speech highlighted how he was animated by a core set of values:

My dad believed that the world was a perfectible place where effective and progressive policies could emerge, where justice could prevail, and where discrimination and corruption could be diminished.

My dad was an *exemplar* of desired behavior. In my speech, I noted how my dad was authentic, passionate, and humble.

I have always wondered how a man who said so many inappropriate things and challenged so many people could have been chair of a department for so long and with such great effect. Perhaps it was because as professor and chair he was the anti-politician—he was who he was at all times and everyone knew that. Or perhaps it was because, even in a position of authority, he was often nondefensive and could listen to his critics' perspectives with an open mind. Or maybe it was his evident passion and humor that smoothed over the edges and endeared him to others.

My dad was an amazing *mentor*. He loved helping people find their way in the world by both encouraging *and* challenging them.

As an advisor and mentor, both at home and in the university, he was supportive and encouraging, cheering people towards pursuing their dreams, wanting what was best for each person he came in contact with. But he was also challenging, holding high expectations, wanting everyone to strive for excellence and to refuse mediocrity.

———

BEFORE DESCRIBING THE VEM Diagram of Inspiring Leaders in more detail, I want to share one final FBI moment that highlights the essence of *Inspire*. Two years later, during another teaching session, one of the agents asked if she should reach out to her inspiring leader and let him know the impact he had on her life. She was hesitant, however, because she had lost touch with this person and felt guilty about the many years of silence. I encouraged her to contact her inspiring mentor and not be held back by feelings of guilt. I told her I would do the same and reach out to one of the inspiring figures, one of my doctoral advisors, Joel Cooper, who had elevated my life, even though I had not communicated with him in a few years.

I wrote Joel and let him know the profound impact he had on my life, an impact I will describe in more detail in Inspiring Mentors (Chapter 5). Here is a piece of what I wrote:

> Dear Joel, I haven't expressed it enough, but you had such a positive influence on me so early on in my career. I want to mention three specific ways you impacted me in a positive way . . . I just wanted to say thanks for all the care you have put into my concerns over the years. I wouldn't be where I am today without you.

When I received a reply two days later, I knew my email had positively struck a chord, especially given Joel wasn't the most effusive person in the world:

> What a touching e-mail! That's the nicest present I've ever received. You never know if you have ever reached anyone or have had any influence whatsoever on anyone's life.

His over-the-top reaction made me realize that letting someone know their positive impact on us can be one of the greatest gifts we can give the inspiring people in our lives. As we will discuss in the next chapter, all of us have a fundamental need to have a sense of meaning and purpose. And there is nothing more meaningful than knowing that we had a positive impact on someone's life.

My first FBI moment led me to investigate what it means to be inspiring. My second FBI moment led me to understand that leaders change us inside, but they often infuriate instead of inspiring us. My third FBI moment led me to realize we can, in turn, inspire our inspirers.

By reaching out to them, we can reciprocate their positive impact and fulfill their need for meaning. Our gratitude can make them even more inspiring.

Collectively, my experience with the FBI helped me discover both the virtuous cycle of inspiration, and the vicious cycle of infuriation. Let's explore these more deeply together.

CHAPTER 3

Inspiring Visions

YOUR LIFE GETS worse when you have kids. You barely sleep. You rarely shower. You seldom eat. You never have sex . . . well, almost never. Your house is a mess. Your body is a mess. Your mind is a mess.

Yet our species hasn't died out. Why?

As a first-time parent, I experienced each of these deprivations. But I also experienced a transformation that envelops many new parents. It was a feeling deeper than I ever felt before. My twin brother, Michael, described it as a love fiercer than he'd ever thought possible.

My life suddenly had a larger *purpose*. My life had a newfound sense of *meaning*.

The link between new parenthood and finding meaning tells us something profound about human nature. We are all biologically conditioned to crave meaning. That's true regardless of whether we are parents or not. The emotional architecture of the human mind is geared toward finding a sense of purpose. We are, at our core, meaning makers.

Nietzsche perfectly captured the importance of meaning when he said that people who have "a why to live can bear almost any how." We crave a *why*. But not just any why. We crave an optimistic *why*, one full of hope and possibility. That's what Tammie Jo Shults gave her passengers when her plane was rapidly descending: "We are not going down. We are going to Philly." When we have an optimistic and meaningful why, we can endure the slings and arrows of even the most outrageous of fortunes.

The deeply rooted thirst for meaning also represents our desire to be inspired. And it explains why being visionary is one of the three foundations of inspiring others.

INSPIRING TITLES

WHEN WE DON'T have a vision, we feel lost. Consider this simple yet profound experiment conducted half a century ago by one of my dissertation advisors, Marcia Johnson. Marcia had her participants read the following passage and tell her what it was about:

> The procedure is actually quite simple. First you arrange things into different groups. Of course, one pile may be sufficient depending on how much there is to do. If you have to go somewhere else due to lack of facilities that is the next step, otherwise you are pretty well set. It is important not to overdo things. That is, it is better to do too few things at once than too many. A mistake can be expensive as well. After the procedure is completed, one arranges the materials into different groups again. Then they can be put into their appropriate places.

I have given this scenario to thousands of people all over the world, from students to CEOs, and fewer than 5 percent of them can figure out what this paragraph is all about.

But this description only represents one of the conditions in Marcia's experiment. In the other condition, she gave participants a title: "Doing the Laundry." Notice how everything changes once we have the title: each sentence takes on meaning, each sentence connects to and coordinates with the other sentences. Without the title, we are baffled and bewildered. With a title, everything starts making sense.

Of course, it's not very surprising that the passage is easier to understand when we have the title. What is more interesting is what happened later. Marcia gave everyone a memory test. The people who got the title did pretty well. Sure, they didn't remember the passage word for word, but they remembered a fair number of details. But without the title, people could remember little about what they had read.

This simple experiment conveys a powerful point about the value of a vision. A vision, like a title, imbues every utterance with meaning and every action with a sense of purpose. Without a vision, people can't process information and they can't coordinate action. Without the vision, we are lost. But with a vision, we are found.

Having a sense of understanding is so pivotal to the human condition, it has healing powers. Simply learning details about an upcoming medical procedure reduces anxiety, which predicts faster recovery times. Knowing the *why* and *how* of a medical procedure literally helps the body heal faster.

Without a vision, the world becomes confusing. And when the world becomes confusing, we seek meaning anywhere we can find it.

ILLUSORY VISIONS

OBDULIA DELGADO WAS the first one to see it. "I was so stunned I couldn't move. People were honking. It was a dream. I don't even know how I got home."

While driving in the spring of 2005, Obdulia was praying to the Virgin Mary for success on an upcoming culinary exam. And then suddenly, there she was, the Virgin Mary herself, clear as day, glistening on the concrete wall of an underpass on the Kennedy Expressway in Chicago.

Obdulia's sighting created a national sensation. Many saw what Obdulia saw, the Holy Mother's cloaked face encased in a virginal white outline. As one high school student recounted, "If you look, you see her face popping out and the veil and her hands. That's the image that's portrayed in the Bible."

My former doctoral student Jennifer Whitson was fascinated by this Lady of the Underpass. She wasn't stirred with religious fervor, however, but from scientific curiosity. She walked into my office and said, "I know what I want to study: I want to know why people think they see the Virgin Mary in a water stain."

Whitson was really asking two questions: *When* does the human mind see randomness as representing something significant? *Why* do some people see something when there's nothing there?

Coincidentally, I had studied a related topic—what psychologists call *causal reasoning*—ten years earlier when I was in grad school. This research found that people search for and create explanations more often when bad outcomes happen than when they experience good fortune. We accept the good without further explanation, but we frantically try to understand *why* the bad happened in a desperate attempt to undo the damage or prevent it from reoccurring in the future.

What was even more interesting is people also seek explanations for *unexpected* events. In fact, the effect of unexpectedness was often larger than the effect of negativity. Unexpected events lack a title; they challenge our sense of meaning and our sense of control. When the world stops making sense, people construct causal explanations to try and understand what the heck just happened.

Building off the research on causal reasoning, Whitson proposed that not having a sense of meaning and control is so aversive that the mind will do anything it can to regain it. But she went further, she proposed that even seeing illusory or false patterns will help people find that missing sense of meaning. She and I defined *pattern perception* as *the identification of a coherent and meaningful interrelationship among a set of stimuli*. To define *illusory pattern perception*, we simply added a single word: the identification of a coherent and meaningful interrelationship among a set of *unrelated* stimuli. Armed with this definition, we realized that many different phenomena all represent, in their own way, the exact same phenomenon: illusory pattern perception.

Superstitions are a form of illusory pattern perception. Step on a crack and you'll break your mother's back. This superstition proposes a coherent and meaningful interrelationship among a crack and a back.

Conspiracies are a form of illusory pattern perception. For example, the idea that US government officials masterminded the 9/11 attacks or secretly created the COVID-19 virus. These conspiracies propose a coherent and meaningful interrelationship among government officials and tragic events.

Seeing figures in water stains is a form of illusory pattern perception. Seeing correlations in random data is a form of illusory pattern perception.

Each of these seemingly disparate phenomena offer the same psychological medicine: a sense of meaning and coherence. Before Obdulia saw the Virgin Mary, she was feeling uncertain and worried about her upcoming culinary exam. At that moment, seeing the Virgin Mary let her feel a divine connection heralding a positive and purposeful future.

Whitson argued that it is uncertainty that often drives us to seek a sense of control. It's why the tribes of the Trobriand Islands who fish in the uncertain deep sea engage in more elaborate rituals than their fellow shallow-water fishermen. It's why parachute jumpers see nonexistent figures in visual static just before they jump but not when they are still on the ground. And it's why new MBA students are more likely to believe in conspiracies than second-year students. Building off these real-world observations, Whitson and I set out to demonstrate that lacking a sense of understanding *causes* people to see patterns, even ones that don't really exist.

Across our experiments, we manipulated a sense of uncertainty and confusion in several different ways. In some studies, we had people engage in a task that was impossible to solve. Other times we had people recall a time in which they lacked a sense of control. And in some cases, we activated emotions associated with uncertainty like fear and worry. In the comparison conditions, people could solve the task, they recalled a time in which they had control, or they experienced emotions associated with a sense of certainty, like anger or disgust. Notice that anger and disgust are both negative emotions; using these emotions in our experiments helped us establish that it is a sense of uncertainty, and not just negativity, that drives the need to see patterns.

After varying a sense of uncertainty or certainty, Whitson and I asked our participants if they saw a pattern in a wide variety of ways. In some experiments, we showed them visual static and asked if they saw an image in it or not.

After experiencing the unsolvable task, people were more likely to see patterns in these images of visual static. After experiencing worry or fear (vs. disgust or anger), people were more likely to see a conspiracy among their coworkers. After recalling a time in which they lacked a sense of control, people had a stronger desire to knock on wood or stomp one's feet in a ritualized order before an important meeting. And when we placed investors in a volatile and uncertain market, they erroneously saw nonexistent market patterns that biased their investments. Even uncertainty at the societal level can drive people to see patterns that don't exist. For example, superstitions increase during periods of economic uncertainty.

When we are feeling lost, we are also attracted to strong leaders even if they are infuriating. Aaron Kay of Duke University and I found that uncertainty, both uncertain emotions and when facing volatile financial markets, increased support for more autocratic forms of government. When people are experiencing high levels of uncertainty, they are even more likely to believe in a very specific deity, a controlling God who actively determines what happens on earth; for example, we found that people were more likely to believe in a controlling God just before an election, when uncertainty is higher, than after the election had been decided.

Across all our experiments, we have found that whenever we are feeling uncertain, unmoored, dislocated, or anxious, we are desperately in need of a meaningful and clear vision. And as we discovered in March of 2020, there is nothing like a global pandemic to produce these feelings of uncertainty, worry, and dislocation.

THE UNIVERSAL MIDLIFE CRISIS

GIVEN THE HUMAN quest for control, it is not surprising that the COVID-19 pandemic attracted a wide range of conspiracy theories. Some suggested COVID was created by the wealthy to consolidate their power, while others claimed it was the result of 5G phone towers. And many dismissed the pandemic as a hoax altogether. People also desperately searched high and low for preventions or treatments, from kitchen items like garlic, hot peppers, and fennel tea to potentially poisonous medications.

One of the most fascinating trends during the COVID-19 pandemic was the number of people who quit their jobs. It became such a wide-scale phenomenon that it got its own name, the Great Resignation. In just six months in 2021, more than thirty million US workers left their jobs, both white-collar and blue-collar. That's the equivalent of the entire population of Texas declaring, "I quit!"

Laura Kray of UC Berkeley and I saw something bigger in the Great

Resignation. The pandemic not only forced us to reconsider where we work, but it also led many of us to wonder *why* we work. Laura and I proposed that COVID led to mass resignations because it had created what we called a *universal midlife crisis*.

Think about what the traditional midlife crisis represents. It is the emotional upheaval that occurs when we suddenly recognize our time on earth is rapidly diminishing. Death is the ultimate state of uncertainty, the definitive loss of control. The realization that death is approaching leads to a crisis of identity (who am I?) and of trajectory (where am I going?).

With more than six million deaths worldwide, COVID made us all profoundly aware of our own mortality. My research has shown that reminders of death make us concerned with our legacy, increasing our desire to be remembered as inspiring and not infuriating. For example, when Kimberly Wade-Benzoni of Duke and I had people think about the burden of an existential crisis like global warming or a pandemic, they were more likely to want to have a positive and lasting impact on the world, to have their life mean something even after it was over.

Like the midlife crisis, the pandemic led us to feel an acute desire to conceive a more purposeful identity and to forge a more meaningful trajectory. It's why the Great Resignation wasn't all about money.

The beginning of life and the end of life are deeply rooted in the same instinctual drive for meaning. The birth of a child *gives* our lives a new sense of purpose while awareness of death motivates the *need* for meaning, leading us to seek and connect with a larger purpose that transcends the confines of our time on earth. It's why being visionary is so inspiring: it fulfills the human need for meaning.

HOW TO BE VISIONARY: OFFER A GLORIOUS FUTURE

And may it be said of us, both in dark passages and in bright days, in the words of Tennyson that my brothers quoted and loved, and that have special meaning for me now:

I am a part of all that I have met . . .
Though much is taken, much abides . . .
. . . that which we are, we are,
One equal temper of heroic hearts
. . . strong in will
To strive, to seek, to find, and not to yield.

For me, a few hours ago, this campaign came to an end. For all those whose cares have been our concern, the work goes on, the cause endures, the hope still lives, and the dream shall never die.

This is how Ted Kennedy concluded his 1980 speech at the Democratic National Convention. There are two things to note about this passage: First, it is optimistic, pointing to a brighter future. Second, it highlights the values of faith, courage, and connection. This speech was very important to me after I graduated college, when I felt lost and uncertain about where I was headed in life. Both the optimism and the values of Kennedy's speech offered me solace during those darker days of my life.

A sense of optimism is embedded in the sense of purpose that a new parent feels. The innocent eyes of a baby radiate hope and possibility, the promise of a better tomorrow. It's why being visionary involves seeing a bright and optimistic future.

Optimism is essential because it inspires energy. In my research with Thomas Mussweiler of London Business School, we found that having people think about what they hope to achieve in a negotiation leads them to secure better outcomes. The energy from optimism keeps us going during our lowest moments, like Kennedy's speech helped me after college. Optimistic visions are also more likely to be shared and remembered. When Jonah Berger of the University of Pennsylvania analyzed the most emailed articles in the *New York Times*, he found that optimistic and inspiring articles were the most likely to be forwarded to others.

It's not surprising, then, that the political rhetoric most remembered throughout American history has focused on a brighter tomorrow, the sunrise side of the mountain, even when we are in our darkest hours. Franklin Delano Roosevelt's quote from his first inaugural address "the only thing we have to fear is fear itself" spoke to the value of courage and fortitude as the country faced the Great Depression. John F. Kennedy's inaugural address highlighted the value of sacrifice and group commitment when he implored Americans to "ask not what your country can do for you—ask what you can do for your country." And Abraham Lincoln's second inaugural address spoke to the value of compassion and forgiveness as the Civil War was coming to an end: "With malice toward none, with charity for all . . . to bind up the nation's wounds . . . and cherish a just and lasting peace among ourselves and with all nations."

To be inspiring, we need to offer an optimistic and values-based vision. We also need to make sure our vision is easy to understand.

THE INCEPTION RULE: KEEP IT SIMPLE

COBB: Have you done it [inception] before?

EAMES: We tried it. Got the idea in place, but it didn't take.

COBB: You didn't plant it deep enough?

EAMES: It's not just about the depth. You need the simplest version of the idea for it to grow naturally in the subject's mind.

In the movie *Inception*, Leonardo DiCaprio's character, Cobb, is tasked with planting an idea into another person's mind while they are dreaming. The problem is that he's only stolen information from people's dreams. So he seeks the guidance of Eames, who has tried inception before. But Eames explains that it's not how many levels you descend into a person's dream—the dreams within a dream. What matters is how simple the idea is.

I call this the *Inception* rule. We always want to create and share the simplest version of an idea. It's why Denzel Washington's character in the movie *Philadelphia* asks his witnesses, "All right, look, I want you to explain this to me like I'm a six-year-old, okay?" In research, we call this parsimony, which involves identifying the simplest explanation, requiring the fewest number of assumptions, to accurately describe a phenomenon.

Research shows that simplicity really is the key to inception. Simple ideas get embedded in our minds because they are easier to process. Cognitive psychologists call this the principle of *fluency*. Fluency is the psychological experience of easily and effortlessly understanding a piece of information. It's why the title "Doing the Laundry" makes the passage easier to read, i.e., it makes it more fluent.

Fluency also makes an idea more meaningful because it infuses it with validity. When an idea is easy to process, it seems more true and more probable. Simplicity increases fluency and fluency increases truth value. If we want to get people to both believe and buy into an idea, we need to make it simple.

Drew Carton of the University of Pennsylvania has shown that one way to simplify a vision is to focus only on a few values. When we overstuff our visions with an overflowing number of values, others feel like they are drowning in ideas. But when we pick a few values—Drew found four or fewer was optimal—we create a vision that offers fluency and a sense of control.

Simple visions are so valuable because they make decision-making easier. Consider the company Zoom, which became a virtual lifeline for many of us during the COVID pandemic. Zoom's vision is "deliver happiness." Very simple. Not only is "deliver happiness" easy to understand, but it served as a decision-making guide when the company faced a period of unprecedented chaos unleashed by COVID. This vision allowed everyone in the company to make complex, time-urgent decisions quickly because every decision simply had to answer this question: *Will it deliver happiness?* This vision was particularly helpful when making tech design and customer service decisions. In designing their product, "deliver happiness" led to a focus on increasing positive engagement and reducing frustration. As a result, Zoom was designed to be both highly functional and easy to use. In practice, this meant carefully selecting which features to include: too many features and customers would get overwhelmed, but too few could lead to a different set of annoyances. "Deliver happiness" also shaped the design of customer service: the company recognized that the long wait times for customer support delivered extreme unhappiness. So they made speed a top priority when clients had a problem and invested in having numerous skilled customer service agents.

MAKE IT VIVID

FLUENCY AND A sense of meaning don't just come from simplicity. Fluency also comes from the vivid details that can bring our simple vision to life. Consider this scenario: What is the probability that a large flood in Los Angeles will kill one thousand people in the next year? Now consider this one: What is the probability that a large flood caused by an earthquake kills one thousand people in Los Angeles in the next year?

Every year, I give this scenario created by Danny Kahneman to my students. Half the class gets the first scenario, and the other half gets the second scenario. On average, the earthquake-causing flood is given a probability that is *100 percent higher* than the simple flood alone. But my students have it wrong. The first scenario, by definition, has a higher probability than the second one. What's going on here?

The addition of the earthquake detail makes that scenario more fluent. It's hard to conjure up a specific cause of the flood in the first scenario. But it's easy to mentally simulate an earthquake causing a flood, especially in LA. As a result, the second scenario just *feels* more probable.

Notice that as we add more details to any scenario, we mathematically reduce its objective probability. Details make any scenario a more specific case of a larger set, where the detailed scenario is a subset of the more general one. In this example, an earthquake is only one potential cause of a flood killing one thousand people in LA: intense rain, tidal waves, and breaking damns could also cause floods. But details make a scenario seem more probable because they make it easier to visualize. Because details make a scenario more fluent, they increase the subjective probability of a scenario even though they decrease its objective probability.

The key to vividness is not just random details but relevant ones that stick in the brain. Consider another experiment run by Drew Carton: He created three-person teams who were tasked with designing a new toy. Drew varied the vision statement—which emphasized the quality of the product and the happiness of the consumer—given to the toy makers.

One vision lacked vivid imagery: "Our vision is that our toys—all of them made to perfection by our employees—will be enjoyed by all of our customers."

The other vision used strong imagery: "Our vision is that our toys—all of them crafted flawlessly by our workers—will make wide-eyed kids laugh and proud parents smile."

Drew then had experts, a group of seven- to twelve-year-olds, rate how much they wanted to play with the toy. The teams exposed to the vivid imagery vision produced more engaging toys. What was particularly interesting is that the vivid imagery vision led to better toys because these teams were more effective at coordinating their behavior. Vivid imagery takes "doing the laundry" to the next level.

Drew also showed that keeping it simple *and* vivid is the key to being truly visionary. When he analyzed the vision statements from 332 hospitals that provided acute short-term care, he found the hospitals who emphasized only a few values and used vivid imagery had the lowest readmission rates.

Bringing your vision to life by using vivid imagery can even help you get elected as the president of the United States. When Vita Akstinaitė of ISM University in Lithuania and I analyzed every convention speech of the Democratic and Republican nominees for president of the US since World War II, we found that the nomination speeches of the eventual winners were more vivid and visual. The future winners used more than twice as many metaphors and image-laden words compared to the soon-to-be losers. Importantly, the positive impact of vividness occurred over and above economic factors (e.g., unemployment rates and inflation) and above political factors (e.g., incumbency). Winning words visualize the world and make the speaker seem more visionary and inspiring.

Any factor that makes information easier to process and more fluent—even rhymes—helps make a scenario seem more probable or an idea seem more valid. Consider the infamous murder trial of OJ Simpson. When OJ was accused of murdering his ex-wife and her friend, a key piece of evidence was a bloody glove found on his ex-wife's property. During the trial, the prosecuting team asked OJ to put on the glove. What originally looked like a brilliant courtroom maneuver turned into a prosecutorial disaster. OJ struggled so much to put the glove on that his face grimaced. The glove was too tight!

Now, there are a lot of reasons why the glove, even if it was used by OJ during the murders, was too small that day. Since the glove was found outside, the elements could have shrunk it. OJ was wearing latex when he tried the glove on, which may have made it difficult to pull on. And OJ strategically stopped taking arthritis medications to make his hands swell up. Regardless of the reason, it was a vivid repudiation of the prosecutor's argument. Vivid simulations are memorable whether they succeed or fail. OJ's glove struggles likely raised a reasonable doubt in at least some jurors' minds.

That reasonable doubt was made even more fluent by OJ's lawyer Johnnie Cochran, who turned it into a catchy rhyme during his closing arguments: "If it doesn't fit, you must acquit." And that's exactly what the jury did, unanimously voting to acquit OJ Simpson of murder.

Johnnie Cochran didn't mention the glove only in his rhyme. He referenced the glove more than a dozen times in his closing statement. It turns out that repetition is also a key to inspiring visions.

REPEAT, REPEAT, REPEAT

IS THIS A true or false statement? Eighteen newborn opossums can be placed in a teaspoon. How about this one? Three hundred thousand pencils can be made from the average cedar tree.

Whether we think these comments are true or false depends on many factors, but one of the biggest is the number of times we've read them. The more times we've seen a statement, the more times we are likely to think that it is true. The effect of repetition is so powerful that it leads to something called the illusion of truth. Repetition increases fluency, and fluency increases the truth value of a statement. We even believe a demonstrably false statement to be true when we have seen that statement repeated enough times. The link from repetition to truth is why Johnnie Cochran mentioned the glove, and the fact it didn't fit, so many times in his closing statement.

Repetition is not only critical for getting our ideas recognized but also getting ourselves noticed. My student Blaine Horton and I tested whether repeating one's personal or product name gives us a boost in competitive markets. To test our theory, we analyzed the repetition of personal names in 2,452 TED talks, the repetition of product names in 17,007 app descriptions on Apple's mobile gaming store, and the repetition of start-up names in 14,766 venture descriptions on a digital platform used by angel investors. Name repetition had a remarkable effect across these varied contexts: it increased the viewership of TED talks, the ratings of app store games, and the number of investors start-ups received.

To demonstrate that saying your name directly *causes* attraction, Blaine created a clever experiment. He put together a mock jury for a venture competition and created a description of a fashion start-up, along with another start-up for furniture. The only element he varied was whether the founder mentioned their name or not.

[I'm Haden Thompson]. I'm the founder of Fashion.com. We take advantage of innovations in the fashion industry to provide customized designs tailored to each customer. By linking quality fabrics to an international network of trained designers, our company combines the customized touch of high-end tailors with discounts you would see at your favorite retail store.

Half the jurors saw the "I'm Haden Thompson" and half didn't. Although the difference between the two versions is tiny, its impact was large. When the name Haden was included, Fashion.com increased its probability of funding by nearly 20 percent! Simply repeating your name can be the key to future success.

Like having a vision, repetition is not just a key to understanding, but also for taking appropriate action. When I run exercises in the classroom, I have learned that I need to repeat instructions at least three times or my students will be confused about what to do. Marketers talk about the rule of seven, that consumers need to hear a message seven times before they will buy a new product. It's why a CEO once told me he used the throw-up rule. "The throw-up rule, what's that?" I asked. He said he knows when he has repeated the vision enough when his employees get so sick of hearing it, they throw up a little in their mouth when he shares it again!

FEAR DOESN'T HEAR

REPETITION IS ALWAYS useful. But it is particularly necessary when we are in a crisis or scared. It turns out that *fear doesn't hear*.

Consider what happened when anxiety immediately enveloped my wife, Jenn, and me after our OB-GYN Sophia Drosinos said, "There may be an issue with your baby's weight," as she was reviewing the third-trimester ultrasound of our second child. Seeking a solution, Jenn naturally turned to her diet: "How much more should I be eating? Are there any foods that will help our baby boy grow more quickly?"

Dr. Drosinos reassured us that Jenn's diet wasn't the issue. She explained that it was probably an error, and we would redo the ultrasound to make sure. And if there was a problem, it most likely was due to pressure on the umbilical cord, which would require adjusting the baby's positioning. She reassured us again, "Don't worry, your baby's weight is most likely in the normal range."

After a few minutes, Jenn asked, "So how should I change my diet?" Dr. Drosinos reiterated that the issue, if there was one, had nothing to do with her diet or caloric intake. A couple of hours after our doctor's appointment, I got a call from Jenn. She was at a vitamin store asking what protein shakes she should buy to help build the baby's weight!

This example highlights how anxiety alters our attention. When we get anxious, our attention narrows and we can't see the bigger picture. We also get stuck in a cognitive rut, fixated on a particular idea or a recurring thought. And our attention focuses on the self. That's what happened to Jenn: her attention narrowed, she got stuck on the idea of changing her diet, and she focused on what she could do.

Because of her fear, Jenn couldn't hear. The solution was repetition. She needed to hear the reassurance multiple times, in this case three times, before it finally stuck. But the idea that repetition is particularly necessary during times of anxiety isn't unique to expecting mothers. It is a general problem. In fact, the role of repetition and fluency is so foundational to being visionary that it is necessary to get elected president of the United States.

INSPIRING SLOGANS

REGARDLESS OF YOUR feelings toward Donald Trump—and he inspires strong feelings from both his supporters and his detractors—his 2016 presidential slogan, *Make America Great Again*, had many of the elements of an inspiring vision. It was both simple and optimistic, elegantly capturing the idea that the once-great America could be great again, but only with the right leadership. It was easy to repeat again and again and again. *Make America Great Again* was not only easy to understand but it was even reducible to the catchy acronym MAGA. Trump even took the power of repetition to the power of capitalism by emblazoning MAGA on hats and shirts and anything else he could sell.

Sometimes optimism isn't captured only in a slogan but in a picture. I believed that Barack Obama's campaign slogan from 2008 was the word *Hope*. It turns out his official slogan was *Change We Can Believe In*. But I also wasn't wrong. What I was remembering was a poster created by street artist Shepard Fairey, who had taken an Associated Press media photograph and transformed it using a high-contrast stencil technique, while adding the word *HOPE*. This grassroots poster quickly turned into an official image of the campaign. And we can see why, as it perfectly captures the vision Obama was offering: a hope for a better tomorrow. This simple poster was more vivid, and more effective, than his actual campaign slogan.

Let's contrast the victories of Trump and Obama with Bob Dole's unsuccessful run for president as the challenger to then-president Bill Clinton in 1996. His slogan—*A Better Man for a Better America*—was quite clever: it was not only optimistic, but it elegantly contrasted his moral integrity against the purported perversity of Bill Clinton. The problem was that Bob Dole almost never repeated the line, and when he did use it, he would mangle it *and* dismiss it, "*A Better Plan, a Man for a Better America*—whatever that slogan is they're working on." His butchering of his campaign slogan made it less fluent! Bob Dole would have been more likely to win if he had repeated and repeated his simple optimistic vision that effectively contrasted his strengths with his opponent's weaknesses.

———

"Dy-no-mite!"
"I'll be back."
"I've a feeling we're not in Kansas anymore."
"Did I do that?"
"Bazinga!"

"I'll have what she's having."
"Say hello to my little friend."

The above quotes are famous catchphrases from television and movies. Catchphrases are like tiny visions that evoke sentiment and connect people within a relationship or group. They function a lot like jargon, which I have defined in my research with Zachariah Brown of Hong Kong University as *special words or expressions that are used by a particular group and are difficult for others to understand*. Because catchphrases are often understood and appreciated by people who share a history, they help create a deeper connection and sense of meaning.

"My bags are packed for you." That's the phrase my wife, Jenn, and I use whenever the other one is going through a difficult time. It is our ride-or-die sentiment, emphasizing that we are always there for the other person. Its origin in a speech by the coach Jim Valvano connects us through our mutual passion for college basketball. Jenn frequently told me her bags were packed for me when I was struggling to finish this book!

A catchphrase can come from anywhere as long as it's meaningful to the people we use it with. An executive at one of my workshops turned "doing the laundry" into her own catchphrase. She wrote it on a Post-it and put it on her computer screen the day after my presentation. A few weeks later, one employee asked her, "Are you *ever* going to do your laundry?" She laughed and explained its meaning. They then started using it as an inside joke whenever they found themselves deviating from their shared vision. "Doing the laundry" served as their reminder to always be sharing the team's vision.

GETTING INTO A VISIONARY STATE OF MIND

BEING VISIONARY IS one of the three universal facets of inspiring others because it fulfills a fundamental human need. As humans, we crave meaning. We crave a simple, vivid, optimistic, values-based *why* that is repeated and repeated.

So, how can we get into a visionary state of mind? It starts with our values and ends with taking a time machine back to the future.

Identifying and reflecting on our values is a key to getting into a visionary state of mind. Here's an exercise I give all the MBA students in their first week at Columbia:

Please list up to five values that are important to you. Please challenge your first assumptions and dive deeper into the meaning of your personal values. If you need additional inspiration, here is an exhaustive word bank of values (see endnotes for the link). Now place your values into a hierarchy, where the most important value is listed first, and the other values support and flow into this top value. This is your Values Hierarchy.

All students get a laminated values card with their name and values hierarchy on one side and a word cloud of all student values embedded in their class year on the other side.

Adam Galinsky's Values	Visionary Exemplar Mentor
Generosity Positive Energy (Humor/Passion) Courage Creativity Kaizen	INSPIRE

Why do we give the students their values hierarchy card? Because reflecting on our values is a key to remaining on the inspiring side of the continuum, especially in the more stressful moments of our lives.

Consider the stress of losing one's job. It is one of the five most stressful events we can experience in life. Not only does job loss cause financial strain, but it also threatens two fundamental needs: the need for meaning and the need for status (to be respected and valued by others). It's not surprising that unemployment can lead to reduced motivation, depression, anxiety, and even an increased risk of suicide.

I know this pain well. I was fired three months after starting my first postcollege job as a research assistant at Mass General Hospital. My termination filled me with shame. It took me months to get the motivation and courage to even apply to a comparable job. It was during this period that I found solace in Ted Kennedy's speech that I quoted earlier.

It turns out that instead of immersing myself in Ted Kennedy's inspiring words, I would have found a new job more quickly if I had simply reflected on my own values. That's what Julian Pfrombeck and I found in an experiment we conducted with a Swiss governmental employment agency. Swiss citizens are required to register with the employment agency in order to receive unemployment benefits. We randomly assigned newly unemployed individuals to engage in the following values reflection:

Please take a moment (10–15 minutes) to reflect upon your selected values. Please describe why these values are important to you, and how you have demonstrated these values in your life.

Here are two examples of the values reflections our participants wrote:

Sixty-two-year-old female: My family with my husband and children comes first for me. I can always rely on them. We have a deep bond of trust and are in close contact. Having a lively private life in addition to work is enormously important to me. There I find relaxation, recreation and input. With humor, many situations can be loosened up and relaxed. People with a sense of humor are more open and sociable. People without a sense of humor often react doggedly; they are less flexible and less open to new things. Creativity is also very important to me. I paint myself and love various handicrafts. In doing so, I can take time out all to myself. It's like meditation. Time becomes unimportant, I alone determine the pace. It is nice that I have a result afterwards.

Forty-seven-year-old male: Sports and fitness give me the strength in my life to keep myself physically and mentally fit. It's like letting go of something when I'm under pressure. Afterwards I feel much better and confident. My faith in God and Jesus also helps me a lot to live a harmonious life. Friends are also very important, in my opinion not too many, but just the right ones, where you can do things together or exchange ideas. I also enjoy and value my time with my mother, who is over 80 years old. My father unfortunately died 9 years ago and therefore my mother needs my support, which I am more than happy to provide.

This values reflection task seems simple, right? But it has incredibly powerful effects. The group that reflected on their values was three times more likely to find a job than those in a baseline condition. And because our values intervention reduced the number of days that an individual received unemployment benefits, it also saved the government tens of thousands of dollars. The effect was so powerful that we gave the baseline participants the values reflection task two months into our project to make sure they received the same benefits as our experimental group!

The good news is that the values reflection task doesn't just help the unemployed. It helps anyone regardless of their struggle. Geoff Cohen of Stanford University found it boosted the GPAs of at-risk middle school students. For example, it doubled the number of Black students who received a passing grade. The effects even persisted years later, after the students entered high school. Here is a values reflection from one of Geoff's middle school students:

> Dance is important to me, because it is my passion, my life. My second home is the dance studio, my second family is my dance team. My family and friends are so important to me, even more than dance. My family, I can't live without them. My friends, I am my real self around them (and my sister). I can be silly, goofy, and weird and they don't care, they accept me for who I am. . . . And for being creative, I LOVE being creative in dance. When I'm dancing or making a dance it takes me to another place.

In the unemployment study that Julian and I conducted, the values reflection was a single dose. In Geoff Cohen's experiments, the values reflection exercise was presented an average of eight times over a two-year period (or four times a year). This is an important point because research shows that reflection exercises are more powerful when they are repeated, but not too frequently. Reflecting on values too frequently turns it into a rote exercise that zaps it of its emotional energy. For example, a six-week experiment found that doing a gratitude reflection once a week increased well-being but engaging in the same reflection three times a week tended to *decrease* well-being.

To get into a visionary state of mind, we need to reflect on our values. We also need to reflect on our past and the winding road that led to our present.

> Think about a close friend of yours. How did the two of you meet?

That's a question Laura Kray of UC Berkeley and I asked in one of our studies. But what we asked next is where things get interesting. For half of our participants, we had them "describe any other details about the way you met that determined how things ultimately turned out." We called this the *factual condition*. But in a different experimental group, participants were asked to "describe all the possible ways that you might not have met this person and how things could have turned out differently." In this condition, people thought about all the *counterfactual* worlds that might have been.

After engaging in the counterfactual versus the factual reflection, our participants expressed their agreement with the following statements about their friendship: "My friendship defines who I am." "Being friends has added meaning to my life." "My decision to become friends was one of the most significant choices of my life."

Notice that in both conditions everyone thought about a close friend in their lives, and we only varied whether we framed their friendship as traveling on a straight path or one with many connecting roads not taken. This framing made all the difference. When our participants reflected on the roads not taken, they viewed their close friendship as even more meaningful, even more important, and an even more significant part of their lives. Reflecting on possible but unfollowed paths imbues our current path with greater meaning.

Counterfactual reflections don't just enhance the positive events of our lives. They even help us recover from our traumatic experiences. Laura and I found that even when people experienced a negative turning point in their life (e.g., losing a loved one, getting fired), reflecting on it counterfactually (i.e., "Describe how your life would be in a world where the turning point had never occurred") versus factually (i.e., "Describe how the turning point occurred") transformed how people experienced both the event and their lives. Counterfactual reflection not only gave their life more meaning, but it also led people to see the turning point as more fated and meant to be; it made the experience seem woven into the fabric of their destiny. Even though the turning point was painful, considering roads not taken helped people find the hidden benefits in the unique path they were on. Counterfactual reflection is so powerful in creating meaning that it even produced a greater sense of meaning than asking people to think about the importance and significance of their turning point!

What's going on here? By thinking of all the ways our lives might have turned out differently, it makes the way our life *did* turn out seem more remarkable. Our minds naturally turn what might have been into *what was meant to be*.

One of the biggest turning points of my life was moving to Columbia University and New York City because it was where I met my wife, Jenn. I had been at Northwestern University for more than a decade and had turned down multiple opportunities to move to other cities. The fact that I stayed in Chicago for so many years makes it a very strong counterfactual road not taken. Whenever I think about the alternative world of staying at Northwestern and not meeting Jenn, I can physically feel the wonder of our marriage and my connection to her deepen.

As leaders, we can leverage the power of counterfactual reflection on the roads not taken to inspire greater commitment. In a project led by Hal Hershfield of UCLA, Laura and I had full-time employees imagine their company's origins either factually (i.e., "Describe all the ways that your company came into being") or counterfactually (i.e., "Describe all the ways that your company might not have come into being"). Reflecting on their company's origins counterfactually led employees to feel more attached to their organizations. In another study, we even found that counterfactually reflecting on a country's origins led its citizens to feel more patriotic.

Reimagining our past and present can help us get into a visionary state of mind. So can letting our imagination leap into the future.

My former doctoral student Brian Lucas of Cornell University conducted a fascinating experiment that helped people get into a visionary state of mind. He and Drew Carton asked government officials from the United Kingdom to craft a vision for their governmental agency. In one condition, they specifically asked the government officials to use vivid imagery in their vision. That should increase how engaging the vision is, right? But let's look at another condition in their experiment, where they asked participants to mentally time travel to the future:

Imagine you enter a time machine and emerge in the future just after you have achieved your vision. What does this future look like? Take a picture with your camera. Think of how to make your vision embody what you saw in the picture you took.

Drew and Brian found that the government officials used even more vivid imagery in the future time-travel condition than when they were told to specifically use vivid imagery. They replicated the exact same effect with senior executives from all over the world (including China, Honduras, India, the Netherlands, Philippines, Singapore, Ukraine, and the United States).

Why is mentally traveling to the future so effective in putting people into a visionary state of mind? Psychologically imagining oneself in the future helps people mentally touch the shape of buildings, smell the scents, hear the cacophony of sounds, and take in the expressions on people's faces. By activating the experiential part of the brain, mentally leaping into the future transforms it into a tactile experience.

Mental time travel, back to the past and forward to the future, offers a robust pathway for getting into a visionary state of mind. It's why reflecting counterfactually on our past produces more meaning than directly reflecting on the meaning of our lives. And it's why leaping into the future produces more vivid imagery than directly telling people to produce vivid imagery. When we mentally travel, meaning and vividness naturally and authentically occur.

Being visionary is one of the three facets of being inspiring. Inspiring visions satisfy the human need for a sense of meaning and control by offering a simple, vivid, optimistic, values-based *why* that is repeated and widely shared. We can prime our visionary pump by reflecting on our core values, imagining the roads not taken, and leaping psychologically into the future.

Once we have our vision, we are on the path to be truly inspiring. But first we need to bring our vision to life through our own behavior.

CHAPTER 4

Inspiring Exemplars

"TELL ME ABOUT a passion of yours."

This is a great way to start a conversation. It's also an easy way to learn why passion is so foundational to inspiring others.

I have asked people all over the world to tell me about a passion of theirs. But I'm less interested in *what* they say and more interested in *how* they say it. In a method pioneered by my late colleague Kathy Phillips, I randomly pair up the members of an audience and ask each of them to describe a passion of theirs for two minutes. This passion can come from anywhere in life: a hobby, their family, their job, etc. One person shares their passion while the other one listens, and then they switch roles.

After their conversations, I ask the audience to tell me what they noticed about their partner when they started to describe their passion. Their responses follow a familiar pattern. They first mention their partner's eyes, how they lit up and sparkled. Then they describe their partner's smile, how big and beaming it was. And then someone will reference their partner's speech, how quickly they spoke or with a slightly higher pitch. Multiple people will notice the animated movement of their partner's gestures. Someone usually mentions that their partner began to lean in, as if telling them a secret.

My research with Jon Jachimowicz of Harvard University confirms these transformational effects: passion shines through the many windows of the body—it can be seen in our eyes, in our mouth, in our voice, in our arms, and in our body.

This exercise reveals two additional insights. The first occurs when I ask my audience what happened to them as they listened to their partner's passion They immediately recognize how their partner's energy and behaviors were infectious. "*My* eyes got wide, *I* started to smile, *I* leaned in." They can almost feel their partner's passion start to percolate inside of them.

Second, the passion exercise demonstrates how deeply connected passion and authenticity are. Authentic passion is almost impossible to fake. You would have to force your eyes to light up, put on a smile, talk at just the right pace, and move your hands just so—and you'd have to do all these behaviors at the exact same time. But when our passion is authentic, these behaviors happen spontaneously and simultaneously.

Authenticity isn't just tied to passion. It is also about finding our own style in the world. Consider how Carla Harris helped take UPS from a privately held company to a publicly traded one in 1999. That initial public offering turned into the largest IPO in history; its $5.5 billion post-IPO valuation was nearly double the previous record, making UPS worth more than General Motors and five times its largest competitor, Federal Express. Carla not only helped the executives get rich, but also the sixty-six thousand shareholders who were hourly UPS workers.

How did she do it?

A successful IPO all starts with a road show, where executives work with a deal team to pitch their company to potential investors. Sounds pretty straightforward. You let investors peek under the hood and show them the numbers. But that's not how it really works. It requires presenting an inspiring vision. As Carla stated, "It wasn't just about the company's performance, but it was about . . . [telling] the story in a compelling way . . . and [creating] the 'I must have this stock now.'"

Based on her reputation, you might think Carla is a natural

storyteller. But her early road show presentations weren't successful; they fell flat. What was going wrong? She hadn't found her own voice, her own unique style.

This is how she described it to me when I interviewed her. "My presentations were criticized because I was emulating the styles of my colleagues. Each of their styles worked for them. But I had to find my own style, the one that worked for me. I couldn't resonate with others until I resonated with myself." Carla Harris became an IPO legend only after she was able to identify and tap into her authentic style.

Like Carla, I had to find my own authentic voice in front of the classroom. When I first started teaching leadership at Northwestern, I was given a mentor, Brian Uzzi. Now Brian is an amazing teacher, winning award after award for his ability to hold the attention of his audience. But Brian also has a very specific way of teaching. He's both serious and theatrical. Because I had never taught before, I copied Brian's style, mimicking his posture, vocal tone, and mannerisms. Even though my imitation was perfect, my performance wasn't. Because I felt like a fraud, my lectures didn't resonate with me, and, as a result, they also didn't resonate with my students. Over time, I began to experiment with different styles, searching for what clicked with me and with the class. Eventually, I found a style that captured my passion for the material, one where I described the underlying research, while mixing in a little humor and personal stories. Not only did my love of teaching soar, but more importantly, so did the learning of my students.

Carla's and my stories reveal a critical insight: it's really hard to inspire others when we ourselves aren't inspired. Remember the passion exercise: our passion is infectious, percolating inside others. To inspire others, we need to make sure we feel inspired.

Passion and authenticity are part of the second universal dimension of inspiring others: being an exemplar of desired behavior. Exemplars are universal not only because they fulfill the fundamental human need for passion and vitality, but because they also satisfy the need for safety, security, and protection.

A COURAGEOUS PROTECTOR

The Greek heroine Laskarina Bouboulis, known as Bouboulina, and the American hero George Washington couldn't be more different. Yet Washington's depiction in the famous *Washington Crossing the Delaware* painting is strikingly similar to Bouboulina's depiction in the painting *Bouboulina Attacking Nafplion*. Their boat is the lead boat. They are standing up in the boat. They are taking on the most risk. Like Tammie Jo Shults, they are calm and courageous protectors even in the face of adversity. These paintings are so iconic because they tap into the fundamental need to feel safe and protected. We are drawn to leaders who present themselves as our protectors because they satisfy this deep-seated desire.

My dad was my protector. When he passed away, we spread his ashes in one of his favorite places: Topsail Beach, North Carolina. As I bobbed up and down in the ocean waves with my brother and sister following our simple ceremony, I mentioned that my most cherished childhood memory was being held by him in the ocean. Being in his arms, as the waves broke all around, made me feel both adventurous and safe at the same time. It turns out that experience was also a favorite memory of my siblings! That ocean time in our dad's arms fulfilled our deep desire for protection in a topsy-turvy world.

It's not just humans who desire courageous protectors. Our evolutionary ancestors craved them also.

———

WHY DID THE monkey cross the road? To lead his troop to the other side.

To fully appreciate how deeply ingrained being a courageous protector is embedded in our evolutionary DNA, let's travel with an alpha ape leading his troop across a road. In a video I often show, a solitary ape tentatively emerges from the shrouded woods, careful to remain hidden while scanning his surroundings. He notices a potential threat: a group of humans walking down an otherwise clear jungle road about fifty meters away. He ventures a little farther out, ever watchful of the people and vigilant for any threatening movements toward him.

Sensing safety, he takes an even bigger risk: he walks out and stands unprotected in the middle of road, never averting his gaze from the humans. When the group of people offer no threatening movements, he signals to his group that they should leave their forest protection and begin crossing the road.

One by one, the apes pass the leader as he remains centered on the road, watching over them, protecting them from any unexpected danger. At first blush, it looks like the leader lingers on the road even after the last ape has crossed. But then suddenly three more pop out from the shrubs. The leader waits for these slower members of the group to pass safely across the road. As they walk, he makes one final gesture, swinging his body back and forth, telling the three slowpokes to hurry up.

Only after all the members of the group have crossed the road does the leader complete his own journey. As he enters the forest, he begins to race forward to again take the lead, and to take on the most risk.

The leader was the first one out of the forest and the last one back in. He ensured it was safe before allowing the others to cross the road. He stood over them as they crossed, offering constant protection. He even waited for the weakest members of the group to fully cross.

The simple act of one ape leading his troop across a road reveals how hardwired being a calm and courageous protector is in our evolutionary DNA. Being calm and courageous in a crisis is so powerful that it can even turn a small country's president into a world leader.

THE EYE OF THE HURRICANE

"DOES THIS MEAN Clarke can now build a shed out back?" asked the show host. "No, no, it does not. Because he already has a shed and the last thing we need is another shed . . . he has two," answered Jacinda Ardern, prime minister of New Zealand.

There was nothing remarkable or noteworthy about this conversation between a newscaster and a politician on May 24, 2020. They were discussing the mundane issue of whether the prime minister's fiancé would be allowed to build a third shed in their backyard. There was also nothing noteworthy about the setup: the host was in the TV studio while the prime minister was at another location.

What happened next, however, was remarkable. Before the prime minister could offer more insights on the exciting topic of backyard sheds, the ground at her location began to tremble. The lights began to sway back and forth, and the cameras shuddered, moving in and out of focus. Everything shifted in the room. Everything, that is, except the prime minister.

Ardern's smile barely faltered as she politely warned the host, "We're just having a bit of an earthquake here, right? Quite a decent shake here. If you see things moving behind me [the building] moves a little more than most."

The prime minister was right: it was a quite decent shake. A 5.8-magnitude earthquake, to be precise. To give you some context, a 5.8-magnitude earthquake centered in Virginia in 2011 led to $300 million in damages and was felt in more than a dozen different states, and even in Canada.

When the interviewer asked, "And you're feeling safe and well to continue the interview?" the prime minister reassured the host, the crew, and the audience at home, "We're fine, Ryan! I'm not under any hanging lights, it looks like I'm in a structurally sound place."

Prime Minister Ardern's calm reaction led to a frenzy of public praise, with one person commenting on YouTube: "Her reaction to the earthquake is more stable than my entire life." Another YouTube comment elevated her from mere politician to inspiring leader: "This woman has nerves of steel. She isn't a politician, she is a leader." Being calm in a crisis is deeply resonating.

A little over one year later, on October 21, 2021, Ardern found herself onstage giving a national press conference. As she was about to answer a reporter's question, Ardern paused and lifted her head as if recognizing a familiar sensation. In that moment, a 5.9-magnitude earthquake shook the building so violently that viewers at home could actually hear the structure of the building move. But the prime minister, already equipped with seismic experience, simply responded with a knowing smile, "Sorry, a slight distraction. Would you mind repeating that question?"

I often refer to the calmness of inspiring leaders as the eye of the hurricane. The eye is the hurricane's center, with the rest of the storm rotating around it. But the eye is also the calmest section of any hurricane, with clear skies above it and light winds around it. During a crisis, being the eye of the hurricane is deeply reassuring to others, a beacon of calm amid the surrounding chaos. Tammie Jo Shults was the eye of the hurricane when she calmly declared that her rapidly descending Southwest plane was not going down but going to Philly.

Emotions are generally contagious. We feed off the passion of others and get soothed by their calmness. But the leader amplification effect makes emotional and psychological states truly infectious. When we are leading others, our calmness becomes their calmness, our passion becomes their passion, our courage gives them courage. But our anxiety and cowardice also become their anxiety and cowardice. It is why being an exemplar of desired behavior is a universal dimension of inspiring others. The amplified and infectious nature of leadership makes our behavior more impactful.

Inspiring leaders are authentically passionate. They are calm and courageous protectors. They are also creative problem solvers.

INSPIRING CREATIVITY

MY DAD WAS the most creative person I know. I constantly marveled at his ingenious solutions to any problem he faced.

My favorite example of his ability to find ingenious solutions was the way he bought plane tickets on a warm summer evening in 1992. Northwest Airlines had announced a 50-percent-off summer sale, and the timing could not have been more perfect. My sister was getting married that summer, so my dad was set to buy a bunch of tickets, twenty-two in all. Because this was before the age of the internet, you had to purchase tickets over the phone. But there was a problem: the deal expired at midnight, and every time my dad called the reservation line, he received a busy signal. Back then, you weren't put on hold when no agents were available. Instead, you had to hang up and dial again until you reached a live person. At 11:45 p.m., my dad started to panic. He was pacing back and forth, dialing, hanging up, and dialing again. He was holding the Northwest pamphlet in his agitated hand, when he suddenly noticed another 800 number in tiny print on the back. It was the phone number for Spanish speakers. He immediately called the number and it miraculously rang. When the agent answered and said, "*Hola, buenas noches. ¿Cómo puedo ayudar?*" my dad responded, "*¿Habla inglés?*" The ticket agent laughed and said, "Yes, but no one has ever asked me that before." My dad asked if the agent could take the reservations of a non–Spanish speaker. He could. And my dad got all twenty-two tickets just in the nick of time!

There is a hidden key to this story. To understand why, imagine I've given you ten minutes to generate as many original ideas for things to eat or drink at a Thanksgiving dinner as you can.

Okay, ten minutes are up. Now I want you to work on the same task for another ten minutes. But before you do, I want you to predict the number of ideas you can come up with.

If you are like most people, you probably think you will come up with far fewer ideas in the second ten minutes than the first. And you would be right, but only sort of. When my former doctoral student Brian Lucas of Cornell University ran this study, people came up with about twenty ideas in the first ten minutes. They also predicted that they would only generate eight or nine ideas in the second stage; however, they ended up producing around fifteen ideas. But there was an even more interesting result: the ideas generated in the second stage were significantly more original than ideas generated initially. People vastly underestimated the value of *persistence* for creativity. In another study, Brian found that people predicted that the creativity of ideas would decline over time and eventually fall off a creativity cliff. But in reality, the cliff never came and creativity continued to increase with persistence.

Persistence was the hidden key to my dad's ingenious solution. He had his creative insight because he didn't give up. He kept calling and calling for hours, and his mind kept searching and searching for solutions. It turns out that persistence is one of the biggest yet least valued drivers of creative insights.

James Dyson and Thomas Edison both understood that innovation requires persistence. Dyson was dismayed at how traditional vacuum cleaners would inevitably lose suction as they filled with debris. Starting with an initial cardboard design, Dyson went through 5,127 prototypes before producing the final version of his famous design. Similarly,

Thomas Edison tested two thousand different materials before identifying carbonized bamboo as the perfect filament for a light bulb. When one of his assistants lamented the stunning series of filament failures, he replied, "Oh, we have come a long way and we have learned a lot. We now know that there are two thousand elements which we cannot use to make a good light bulb." And when a reporter asked, "How did it feel to fail 1,000 times?" Edison replied, "I didn't fail 1,000 times. The light bulb was an invention with 1,000 steps."

I discovered the creative value of persistence—and channeled my dad—while overlooking the Las Vegas strip in December of 2019. I was standing on a pedestrian overpass, and I was stumped. I had no idea how I was going to get my wife's family out to the Nevada desert.

My wife, Jenn, really wanted her extended family to visit Ugo Rondinone's *Seven Magic Mountains* art installation ten miles south of Las Vegas. So I made a reservation for a minivan and went to pick it up. When I showed up, there was a problem: the rental company didn't have any minivans. In fact, they didn't have any cars at all. So I made another car reservation from another company, but when I arrived, I was again told that my reservation was worthless; they said there were literally no available rental cars in Vegas. I was stuck.

I pledged I would not go back to the hotel until I found a solution. As I watched cars pass by on the Vegas strip, I had an epiphany: a limo! When I called a limo company, it quickly became clear that this was the ideal option. We could fit everyone in a single vehicle, we would get driven out to the desert in style, and the cost was only marginally more than renting a car for the day. The driver also turned out to be a true mensch: he helped carry my three-year-old son around and brought us to a cozy hot chocolate place on the way home.

EXEMPLARY COMBINATIONS

INSPIRING EXEMPLARS ARE passionate and courageous, they are creative, and they persist and persevere. But these attributes don't just exist in isolation. It is their combination that is particularly inspiring. To be visionary, we need to see the big picture *and* imbue it with optimism and meaning *and* make it simple and vivid, *and* repeat it again and again. Similarly, we are our most inspiring when we can combine the inspiring exemplar attributes, just as we saw with persistence and creativity.

To understand how the combination of exemplar attributes really matters, let's examine the popular concept of grit, which captures the tenacious ability to pursue and achieve long-term goals. Popularized by Angela Duckworth, grit has been found to increase dedication to practice and greater task effort. Based on these promising findings, numerous schools have redesigned their curriculum to make students "grittier." But the scientific literature linking grit to long-term outcomes was inconclusive at best. Meta-analyses, which are large-scale integrations of an entire scientific literature, have found little evidence that grit predicts various indicators of success. As a result, grit has been called "overrated" and "overhyped."

Jon Jachimowicz of Harvard and I solved the scientific conundrum of grit by recognizing that it really involves two inspiring exemplar attributes. Although grit is often used synonymously with perseverance, we found that its key to predicting success is the combination of persistence *and* passion. Working with a technology company, we measured the persistence and passion of 422 employees and linked their responses to their performance evaluations. We found that perseverance positively predicted performance *but* only when an employee was also high on passion. To be successful, an employee needed to possess both passion *and* perseverance.

Inspiring exemplars are super. But they are also human.

SUPER BUT HUMAN

LINDA ROTTENBERG IS pretty super. She is the cofounder and CEO of Endeavor, a nonprofit company that fosters entrepreneurship in emerging economies in over thirty countries around the world. *U.S. News &*

World Report identified her as one of "America's Best Leaders," and *TIME* named her one of their one hundred "Innovators for the 21st Century."

"Too much Superman, not enough Clark Kent." That's what her husband, Bruce Feiler, a *New York Times* columnist, said about a speech she wrote. Linda realized that she was only playing the part of the steely and commanding CEO, which was the version of leadership that danced in her head. It turns out her husband was not only insightful but also prescient. Linda would not become an inspiring leader until she stopped being super and started being more human.

Just as Endeavor was on the precipice of achieving a global scale, Linda's husband was diagnosed with a rare form of cancer. She was filled with panic, but she was too scared to share her fears with her team. She finally heeded her husband's advice, "because I had no choice—I couldn't hide my emotions from my colleagues and employees, so I let it all out." Here's what happened next:

> Rather than freak teammates out and distance me from them, my vulnerability drew us closer . . . much to my surprise, they respected me more for it. And it changed me as a leader. By showing my true self, by revealing that I needed other people, by communicating through every meeting, email, and, yes, the occasional tear that I wasn't invincible, I allowed people—especially employees—to relate to me as they never had before. By indicating that I needed help, I received it in ways I never would have otherwise.

When I interviewed her, Linda told me, "They saw me as *super* before, but they didn't really connect with me until they also saw me as *human.*"

Sharing our vulnerabilities does more than humanize us. It also sends an inspiring message: Having doubts is *normal*. Having fears is *typical*. *None of us* is perfect. *We all* experience insecurities.

Sharing vulnerable stories not only normalizes life's difficulties, but it often includes pathways that can help others better handle their own challenges. When we describe our past failures, we can also detail how we overcame them.

Here's a story I tell my grad students when they face the typical obstacles encountered in a doctoral program: I almost got kicked out of my PhD program.

When I was at Princeton University, you got an evaluation letter at the beginning of your second year with one of three designations translated as: 1) you're doing great, 2) you're in trouble, or 3) you're out of here. The "doing great" designation signaled that you were on the right track to passing the master's hurdle and getting promoted to the dissertation stage. The "you're out of here" let the student know there was little hope they would remain in the program after this academic year, and they should start preparing for their next chapter in life. The "you're in trouble" let them know they were on the wrong track but there was still time to shift course and right the ship.

Even though I had near-perfect grades in my classes, I was put into the second category—I was told I was in trouble. What the hell was going on? In a PhD program, grades don't really matter. Sure, you don't want Cs or to fail a class, but getting straight As isn't necessarily a bonus. Your job is to start doing original research, and that is where I was coming up short. I had ideas but didn't have the implementation skills to put them into practice. I was lost because the very skill that got me into grad school—getting great grades—no longer mattered. In fact, spending too much time on class was detrimental because it took me away from research.

So, what did I do? I started working with Joel Cooper, whose inspiring mentorship I will detail in the next chapter. And I teamed up with his postdoctoral fellow Jeff Stone, who had amazing implementation skills. By the end of my second year, I had produced original research that was good enough to publish. Joel and Jeff saved me from the dust heap of discarded doctoral students.

I share this story with grad students when they hit the very predict-able obstacles when pursuing a PhD. I also share the story of failing as a teacher until I found my authentic style. Students see me as a finished product, and they infer I have *always* been a good researcher and an engaging teacher. What they don't see, unless I share it with them, are the stumbles along the way and how I overcame them, often with a lot of help from others. My vulnerability gives them confidence that they too can overcome their own struggles.

But students shouldn't listen to just me and my stories. They should also hear stories from other faculty too. There is wisdom in seeing the many different paths that people have taken to overcome their trials and tribulations because you never know which one will work for you.

When Loran Nordgren arrived at Northwestern University, I was assigned to be his teaching mentor. Loran was coming from the Netherlands, and he had never taught in an American classroom, let alone to demanding MBA students. Like I did with Brian Uzzi, Loran sat in on my leadership class every morning. But I encouraged Loran to also sit in on the other three faculty teaching the same course in the afternoons. For the decision-making lecture, he watched Vicki Medvec weave stories from her expansive consulting experience. For social net-works, he observed Brian Uzzi mesmerize students with his unique style. And for teams, he saw Kathy Phillips speak from the heart and share personal stories while also detailing her seminal scientific research on the topic.

That experience was transformative. If Loran had only seen me teach, he would have instinctively copied my style, just like I did with Brian. Seeing four different faculty each successfully engage their students, but with very different approaches, helped Loran discover his own unique style. When Loran taught leadership the next semester, he shattered the record for the best teaching evaluations by a first-time instructor.

GETTING INTO AN EXEMPLAR STATE OF MIND

BEING AN EXEMPLAR is one of the three universal facets of inspiring leadership because it fulfills our needs for protection, for energy and passion, and for the possibility of perfection.

So how can we feel more super, more calm, more courageous, and more authentic more of the time? How can we get into an exemplar state of mind?

Here is what one of my doctoral students, Gillian Ku, did to get herself ready for an important job interview at London Business School. Before giving a talk on her research in front of all the faculty, Gillian was given about thirty minutes alone to help her mentally get ready. She decided to write a little essay while sitting there in London. The essay she wrote wasn't a random one, but it had a particular prompt, one that I had created for some experiments I had just started conducting.

> Please recall a particular incident in which you had power over
> another individual or individuals. By power, we mean a situation
> in which you controlled the ability of another person or persons
> to get something they wanted, or were in a position to evaluate
> those individuals. On the next page, please describe this situation
> in which you had power—what happened, how you felt, etc.

As Gillian recalled her experience of being in charge and in control, she could feel confidence start to course through her veins. She knocked her presentation out of the park and got the job. Twenty years later, she is currently the chair of her department at London Business School!

Recalling a time when she had power made Gillian *feel super*. She then went out and *acted super*.

Along with Deb Gruenfeld and Joe Magee, I created this power recall exercise at the turn of the century. Since then, it has been used in hundreds of experiments around the world. Recalling an experience when we had power, when we were in control and had agency, puts us in an exemplar state of mind. It calms us down and gives us courage. It makes us feel authentic and more like our true selves. And it jump-starts our creativity. It even imbues our voices with a little bit of gravitas.

Petra Schmid ran a clever experiment to demonstrate how recalling an experience with power moves us into the eye of the hurricane. In her experiment, Petra used what is called the Trier Social Stress Test. True to its name, the test puts people under social stress by having people make a presentation about oneself to a jury who will evaluate the performance. It's scary even thinking about it!

But before her participants were put under social stress, Petra asked some of them to think about a time in which they had power. Then, while her participants gave their speeches, Petra measured their stress levels.

Petra found that simply recalling an experience with power dramatically lowered people's physiological arousal, even in the face of severe stress. Recalling an experience with power also led people to appear less nervous and to give better speeches. They felt super, and they came across as super.

The same year that Petra published her research, Joris Lammers and I published a paper showing that power reflections can even help us write more persuasive job applications. When our participants arrived, we asked them to do what we called "a warm-up task" to help them become familiar with writing about themselves. Half of our participants recalled a time in which they had power, and the other half recalled a time when they lacked power.

Next, we gave our participants a job ad taken from a national newspaper for a "Sales analyst at Corporate Clients & Solutions." Each person wrote a cover letter for this position, put the letter in a sealed envelope, and turned it in.

We then had a group of evaluators, blind to the experiment, read the cover letters and indicate how likely they would be to offer the job to the candidate. These evaluators loved the job candidates, but only when they had thought about an experience with power. Recalling a time when they had power made our interviewees significantly more likely to be offered the job.

We also content coded the cover letters using linguistic software to determine which components made the power primed applications more successful. The cover letters of high- and low-power applicants didn't differ in the total number of words or sentences they wrote. They also didn't differ in their use of tense (past, present, future), big words, or first person. They even didn't differ in their expression of positive or negative emotions.

However, their cover letters did differ in one critical respect: self-confidence. Like Gillian, recalling a time when they had power made our applicants feel super, and they then expressed that sense of super-ness in their written applications.

Job interviews and public speaking are especially stressful because they are high-stakes situations. My research with Sonia Kang of the University of Toronto shows that feeling powerful is especially helpful when the stakes are high. Feeling powerful acts like a psychological beta blocker, lowering the pressure we feel within even as the pressure rages outside us.

Recalling experiences with power even changes how we sound. In a study led by Sei Jin Ko, then of Northwestern University, we ran an experiment with four stages. First, participants read a simple passage, which allowed us to measure their baseline vocal acoustics. We then had participants recall an experience in which they had power or lacked power. Third, we recorded participants delivering their opening state-ment for an upcoming negotiation. Fourth, we played the recordings of their opening negotiation pitch to listeners at a different university.

Recalling an experience with power changed the acoustic properties of our participants. When they made their opening negotiation statements, they did so with a steadier and more dynamic voice. Although their pitch variability decreased (suggesting a steady voice), their volume variability increased (suggesting a dynamic voice). Our listeners could pick up on these differences: they perceived those who had recalled an experience with power (even though they were blind to this fact) as sounding more inspiring. And it's not just our participants: Margaret Thatcher, the former British prime minister, was trained to project greater authority by varying her volume more but her pitch less.

Recalling an experience with power affects every aspect of being an inspiring exemplar. Petra showed it makes us physiologically *calmer*. Sei Jin revealed it makes our voices more *dynamic*. Yona Kifer of Stars Behavioral Health Group and I found that it makes people feel more *authentic*. Joris demonstrated it makes us more *compelling*. My research with Joe Magee discovered that it makes us more *creative*. And Pam Smith of the University of California, San Diego, showed that it helps us be more visionary by seeing *the big picture*. Reflecting on our personal experiences with power helps us turn our visions into VISIONS.

There are other ways that people have tried to feel and become more super. Many of you have likely heard about power posing, the idea that standing tall and expanding our body posture will make us feel more powerful and be more successful. It sounds amazing. All we need to do is strike a pose and we will rock our interviews and presentations.

The problem is that power posing doesn't have a strong empirical foundation. When a team of researchers reviewed every study conducted on power posing, they found that it didn't improve performance. Not only were the distributions of effects "indistinguishable from what would be expected if the average effect size were zero," but they also found that the ability of each study to detect an effect was only 5 percent.

In contrast, when my colleagues and I conducted a similar set of analyses on all the experiments conducted using the power recall essays, we found strong evidence that it made people become more super. Furthermore, the set of power recall studies had a strong ability to detect an effect at 80 percent.

Why is recalling an experience with power more effective in making us super and improving our outcomes than striking a power pose? The answer lies in one of the characteristics of inspiring exemplars: *authenticity*. When we recall our own experiences with power, we are tapping into our authentic lived experience.

This isn't to claim that power posing can never be effective. Many people swear by it. Although the scientific data clearly show that recalling an experience with power has stronger, deeper, and more long-lasting effects than power posing, each person needs to find the dose of power that works for them.

To feel more super, my wife, Jenn, likes doing Lion's Breath, where she makes a lionlike gesture before an important event. Roy McAvoy, Kevin Costner's character in the movie *Tin Cup*, says "dollar bills" just before he swings his golf club. Ted Lasso says "barbecue sauce" before taking important actions. I used to get so nervous before high-stakes presentations that I could barely breathe and even had trouble using my fingers. But then I borrowed a quote from one of my favorite TV shows, *Sports Night*: "I'm suddenly filled with this sense of 'I know what the hell I'm doing.'" Mentally saying that quote helped put me in the eye of the hurricane when I was feeling the swirling winds of nervousness all around me. We can all create our own ritual that helps us meet any moment.

Recalling an experience with power helps us become an inspiring exemplar, and to be more visionary. However, the power recall doesn't help us become more human. To tap into our humanness, we need to get into a mentor state of mind. Let's learn what it means to be an inspiring mentor.

CHAPTER 5

Inspiring Mentors

WHEN YOU PUT force and pressure on an object, in what direction does it go? If you said that the object goes in the direction of the force, you are well-versed in Newton's first law of physics.

Now let's change one word in that sentence. When you put force and pressure on a *person*, in what direction do they go?

Notice how simply swapping the word *person* for *object* changes everything. If I put force and pressure on another person, they often push back, reacting against the force. And even if they go in the direction of the force physically, they may oppose it psychologically, mentally planting seeds of resentment.

By replacing the word *object* for *person*, I changed it from a physics problem to a leadership problem. This one-word transformation offers a straightforward yet radical insight that sits at the center of *Inspire*.

People aren't objects.

Objects go in the direction of force, but with people, force creates a counterforce. And even when force doesn't immediately create a counterforce, it may lie dormant until it gets released in sound and fury.

So, why do people infuriatingly use force so often? Because at first blush, it looks like it works to get things done. But the effectiveness of force, even when it looks effective, is often short-lived.

INSPIRING LEADERS TREAT people like people and not as objects. How do we do that?

We can start by giving others a *choice*. To understand the power of choice, let's consider the everyday yet stressful situation of buying a car. Let's say you are looking to purchase a new Toyota RAV4 and the salesperson offers you one in your favorite color for $34,875 with a three-year warranty. How would you feel about the price, the salesperson, and the experience?

Now imagine the salesperson had offered you the same car but for $35,875 with a five-year warranty. Does that change your reaction?

Okay, let's consider a third scenario. The salesperson offers you a *choice* of both options: "I can offer you RAV4 Premium in your favorite color for either $34,875 with a three-year warranty or $35,875 with a five-year warranty." Now how do you feel? At one level you should feel the same as the choice offers the same options as the individual ones. But receiving a choice changes everything.

Why is offering a choice so inspiring? Because the dealer is asking for *your* preferences. From the dealer's perspective, the two offers are equal in value, where each additional year of warranty is worth about $500. But the dealer is letting you decide how much each year of warranty is worth *to you*. Offering a choice gives others a sense of autonomy. When we offer a choice, we are treating others as people and not as objects.

My research with Geoffrey Leonardelli of the University of Toronto shows just how powerful offering a choice is. In our studies, receiving a choice made our participants feel that the choice was a genuine and sincere attempt to truly understand and accommodate their own interests. It turned potentially contentious situations into cooperative ones by making the receiver feel seen and understood. What is particularly interesting is that offering a choice also changed how the receiver viewed the person making the offer. Without choice, our participants viewed the offerer with suspicion and were wary of any offer they received. But when they received a choice, they saw the offerer as not only more flexible but also more trustworthy.

Offering a choice is not only effective as a leader, but it is also a key to being an inspiring parent. When my niece Fiona was four, she began to resist getting dressed and rejected any outfit her mother selected. My sister-in-law Suki then started to offer her daughter a choice for each type of clothing—i.e., a choice between these two shirts and then a choice between these two pants, etc. It worked beautifully: Fiona began to dress quickly and without resistance. Offering options helps parents to move their kids through daily life because choice offers a sense of autonomy instead of force and pressure. Choice offers what childhood experts call *high autonomy support*.

In contrast to the feelings of freedom that come from receiving choice, being micromanaged is infuriating. I frequently hear this refrain: "My leader drove me crazy because they micromanaged everything I did." We hate it when our bosses are constantly looking over our shoulders. When we micromanage, we are signaling we don't trust or believe in the other person. It feels demeaning and disrespectful.

Rather than interjecting ourselves in our employees' activities, we can do the reverse. We can delegate important assignments or invite others into influential meetings. Delegating advanced tasks feels so inspiring because it says, "I trust you" and "I believe in you." Because it feels like a developmental leap in responsibility, it activates our inner conscientiousness. Inviting someone to join a high-level meeting activates the wonder of a child entering new spaces. When we offer responsibility and invite involvement, we inspire people to live up to our faith in them. We inspire people to meet the moment.

There is a quote by Confucius that perfectly captures the power of involving others. "Tell me and I will forget, show me and I may remember, involve me and I will understand." Involvement fundamentally changes how we approach a task. It moves us from the sidelines onto the field. We go from disengaged observers to active participants.

That's how Renee LaRoche-Morris felt when she was given a seat at the table during a critical meeting. Long before she became the chief financial officer of the Depository Trust and Clearing Corporation (DTCC), Renee was working at a consulting firm. Going into an important meeting, she was told to sit against the wall and only observe the discussion among thirty senior leaders of a bank and their important clients. One of the clients motioned Renee to come join the table, but she resisted; she wasn't supposed to be part of the discussion. But the man wouldn't give up, and eventually Renee relented. As she sat down, her boss looked horrified, his eyes infuriatingly saying, "What are you doing, why are you at the table?" That disapproving boss wouldn't stay her boss for long. Soon after that meeting, the client reached out to ask Renee to help him on a deal. And a short time after that, that client asked her to come work for him. A simple invitation to sit at the table created one of Renee's longest and most important professional relationships.

Sherry Wu of the University of California at Los Angeles has conducted numerous field studies showing that involvement is truly inspiring. In her experiments, she goes into organizations and randomly assigns work groups, from factory workers to administrative staff, to either a baseline group or a high-involvement group. In the baseline condition, the leader runs their twenty-minute weekly meeting as they always have. But in her high-involvement condition, the supervisor steps aside and the workers lead the discussion of goals, challenges, and new ideas. This little bit of participation—just twenty minutes a week—is transformative. Not only does high involvement boost productivity, but it also increases satisfaction and reduces quitting. And Sherry finds that these effects occur because active participation fulfills the fundamental need for control. Samantha Shapses, the dean of students at Columbia Business School, follows this model: a different member of her staff leads her team's weekly meeting on a rotational basis. And this is how I run my doctoral seminars: every week a different student leads the class discussion. Consistent with Sherry's research, Samantha finds it creates a more engaged team, and I find it produces more active learners.

Involving others and offering them choices provides people with a sense of autonomy and control. At the same time, giving people too much autonomy can make them feel unmoored and adrift. That's why involving others and offering them choices are so powerful: they give people a sense of autonomy within a sense of structure.

Eileen Chou of the University of Virginia and I put the simultaneous need for structure and autonomy to a test. Across numerous studies, we hired workers to do tasks for us. But we varied the type of contract each worker received. One group of workers didn't receive any contract: we simply told them the hourly wage. This was our *no-contract group*. Another group of workers got a *detailed contract* that was very precise:

> *Purpose*: You are assessing materials being developed for a group that meets on Tuesdays and Thursdays.
>
> *Time commitment*: You will work for exactly 6 minutes in one study or about 300 seconds in another study.
>
> *Payment timing*: You will receive your payment within 48 hours.
>
> *Expected effort*: During the entirety of the employment (defined as when you start working to when you submit your work), you shall devote your full energy and attention to the assigned tasks.
>
> *Monitoring*: We might check up to 25 percent of your responses in today's session. Try to spend all of the time concentrating on today's task.

A final group of employees also received a contract, but it was more *general* in nature:

> *Purpose*: You are assessing materials being developed for a bi-weekly group.

Time commitment: You will work for about 6 minutes.

Payment timing: You will receive your payment within 2 days.

Expected effort: During your employment, you shall devote your-self to completing the tasks in more general terms.

Monitoring: We might check some of your responses. Try to spend good effort working on today's task.

Notice the two contracts convey similar information and their only difference is their degree of specificity (e.g., forty-eight hours versus two days). But these seemingly minor differences had a big impact. In study after study, workers who received the general contract persisted longer and performed better than our workers receiving the detailed contracts or no contract at all. General-contract workers spent almost twice as long working compared to detailed-contract and no-contract workers. In one study, we gave our workers insight problems to solve, such as this one:

A man who lived in a small town in the United States married 20 different women of the same town. All are still living and he never divorced any of them. In this town polygamy is unlawful; yet he has broken no law. How is this possible?

Workers who got the general contract answered nearly 30 percent more problems correctly than those in the detailed-contract group. (Answer: *He was the marriage official.*) In another study, general-contract workers generated more original and unique ideas than detailed-contract workers.

What was driving this effect? A sense of *autonomy*. Although the differences are subtle, we found that workers receiving the general contract were more likely to agree with statements like "I felt a sense of choice and freedom in how I completed the task." The detailed contracts reduced participants' sense of autonomy, which in turn lowered their motivation, decreased their effort, and undermined their performance.

The general contract wasn't just better than the detailed contract, it was also better than no contract at all. The absence of any contract left our workers feeling rudderless. They needed structure *with* autonomy to feel inspired.

A study by Glen Nix of the University of Rochester highlights just how important a sense of control and autonomy is for humans. Glen conducted a simple but clever study involving a sorting task. In the autonomous condition, participants could structure the sorting task any way they wanted. For each of these participants, the experimenter carefully coded every step they took. In the controlled condition, the experimenter gave participants step-by-step instructions. But here's the clever part: each participant in the controlled condition followed the exact same steps as the previous participant in the autonomous condition.

Participant 1 (autonomous condition): Completed the task any way they liked.

Participant 2 (controlled condition): Completed the task following the exact same steps as Participant 1.

Participant 3 (autonomous condition): Completed the task any way they liked.

Participant 4 (controlled condition): Completed the task following the exact same steps as Participant 3.

Etc.

This design brilliantly matched the steps taken across participants and only varied whether they had autonomy in selecting the steps or were instructed to follow them. Glen found that autonomy created a burst of energy and motivation.

ENCOURAGE OTHERS

IN INSPIRING VISIONS (Chapter 3), I mentioned my wife, Jenn, and I use a phrase—"My bags are packed for you"—whenever one of us is going through a difficult or stressful time. That phrase comes from a speech that basketball coach Jim Valvano gave:

> My father calls me upstairs in his bedroom, which I've never been in my father's bedroom . . . there's a suitcase [but] my father's never left New York. My father thinks everything north of the George Washington Bridge is Canada, right? He's got the suitcase, "What's that for?" He said, "I'm gonna be there when you win national championship, my bags are packed." I said, "Pop, it's hard to win." "You'll do it." We lost the first round. Next year same thing, we lost the second round. He said, "You're gaining." I move to North Carolina, we made the tournament, I called him, it became a phrase. My father said, "My bags are packed for you." . . . The gift my father gave me. I think it's the strongest, most powerful gift I've ever received . . . The gift my father gave me, every day of my life, was he believed in me. My father believed in me . . . he'd look me in the eye and say, "You're going to make it, I know you are, my bags are packed, you're going to make it."

His father was right, his son did make it. In 1983, Valvano's team, the North Carolina State Wolfpack, did the impossible: they won the national championship in college basketball after playing nine consecutive do-or-die games, seven in which they were tied or behind in the final minute. It was such a remarkable achievement that sportswriters selected it as the *top* US college basketball moment of the twentieth century. Valvano credited his father's steadfast encouragement as the driving force behind his team's astonishing achievement.

Like Jim Valvano, we all need a strong *encourager* in our corner. Most of us can think back to a person in our lives who truly believed in us. A person who saw potential in us before we noticed it in ourselves. A person who saw more possibilities for us than we could even conceive.

I have asked people all over the world to identify someone who encouraged them, to think of a person that truly believed in them. Like the broader category of inspiring leaders, our encouragers come from every aspect of our lives. Sometimes it is a parent, like Jim Valvano's father. Other times it is a teacher. Or it could be a current or former boss. We have long memories for our encouragers, the people who believed we could successfully take on a new challenge even when we had our own doubts.

Inspiring leaders elevate us by encouraging us. They also elevate us by making sure we get the credit we deserve.

ELEVATE OTHERS BY GIVING THEM CREDIT

JONAH ROCKOFF WAS running on a treadmill while watching President Barack Obama's State of the Union Address in 2012 when he stumbled. Then an untenured professor of economics at Columbia, he suddenly realized that President Obama was referencing his research documenting the value of good teachers. Jonah was so shocked to hear his study showcased in front of thirty-eight million viewers that he lost his balance and flew off the treadmill. By the time he got back on his feet, his phone was already blowing up with texts of congratulations.

Jonah's State of the Union stumble is an extreme example of a fundamental truth: as humans, we crave for our efforts and contributions to be acknowledged and recognized by others. It's why the need for status has been classified as a fundamental need. And it's why leaders that share credit for successes and take the blame for blunders and disappointments are so inspiring. In contrast, leaders who steal credit but "generously" share blame and failure are uniquely infuriating.

Not getting credit for our efforts or having our ideas stolen is a blood-boiling experience. When the president of Harvard Claudine Gay was accused of plagiarism for not properly citing the words and ideas of prior scholars, there was a fierce debate over how egregious Gay's actions were. One person who saw no ambiguity was Carol Swain, a professor who had been at both Princeton and Vanderbilt universities during her career. Swain wrote that "Ms. Gay's damage to me is aggravated because her early work was in the area where my research is considered seminal. Her scholarship . . . builds on terrain where I plowed the ground. When scholars aren't cited adequately or their work is ignored, it harms them because academic stature is determined by how often other researchers cite your work." Swain declared she was "incensed" by Gay's "pilfering" of her work. Every word of her op-ed in the *Wall Street Journal* was dripping with infuriation.

Notice that President Gay was a high-profile leader. That amplified the effect of her claiming credit for Dr. Swain's ideas. Typically, the duplicitous mooch is a peer, a direct competitor trying to climb over us for a promotion or a raise. But when a *leader* takes credit for our efforts, that infuriation is amplified. And when a leader does it publicly, that infuriation is amplified even higher.

The good news is that the joy of recognition is also amplified when a leader is the one doing the recognizing, especially when that admiration is expressed publicly. After Tammie Jo Shults safely landed her damaged Southwest plane, she was quick to credit her copilot Darren Ellisor for recognizing that Philadelphia would be the ideal place to make an emergency landing. Similarly, Jonah was on cloud nine after the president mentioned his research during the State of the Union.

Sharing credit with others doesn't just elevate others, it also elevates ourselves. My research with Maren Hoff of Columbia University shows that when we give credit to others, not only does their status grow, *but so does our own*. In our series of experiments, participants read about two strategy consultants:

> Jamie and Hayden worked together on a project for an important client in the luxury industry. The client was seeking help in creating and implementing a new online rental service. They created a detailed business model that proposed a path to profitability while also providing a go-to-market strategy involving targeted marketing. Jamie created a minimalist design for the presentation while Hayden optimized the flow. After Jamie's presentation, the client

mentioned how impressed they were with both the minimalist design and the flow of the presentation.

We varied how Jamie responded to the compliment. In the *credit-claiming condition*, Jamie said, "Thank you so much! It's been weeks of hard work for me, and I am proud of the result. I'm happy I put together a compelling presentation."

In the *credit-sharing condition*, Jamie said, "Thank you so much! It's been weeks of hard work for me, and I am proud of the result. I want to acknowledge Hayden, who helped me put together a compelling presentation."

In our first experiment, our participants rated how much they respected and admired both Jamie and Hayden. Not surprisingly, Hayden was given higher status when their contributions were explicitly acknowledged. But more interesting is that *Jamie* was also more respected and admired when they shared credit with Hayden. Sharing credit expanded the status pie, increasing the standing of both the person receiving credit and the person sharing credit.

Credit sharing helps us maintain our status for years to come. The story of one of the longest-running dynasties in China tells us why. In Imperial China, Liu Bang defeated Xiang Yu to establish the Han dynasty. After his rival had died, Liu Bang (now going by his emperor name of Gaozu) asked, "Why is it that I won possession of the world and Xiang Yu lost?" His advisors noted that Gaozu always gave his generals credit for and the rewards of victory, whereas Xiang Yu was forever stingy with praise and selfish with the spoils of success.

Sharing credit doesn't just expand the status pie, it also expands the generosity pie. In another set of experiments, Maren and I had our participants put themselves into the shoes of Hayden, and they responded to a subsequent request by Jamie asking for help on a different presentation. Hayden was almost twice as likely to help Jamie again when Jamie had shared credit on the earlier presentation.

What is particularly fascinating is what happened when a different consultant asked for help. When our participants had received credit from Jamie, they were also more likely to help a totally different person. Sharing credit expands the generosity pie, leading people to pay it forward and offer more favors to more people in the future.

My research with Maren shows how being generous with credit sharing is a utility-maximizing approach to life. It elevates others, fulfilling the fundamental human need for status and filling them with pride. But it also elevates us, moving us even higher up the status ladder. And it plants the seeds for future favors, both for us and others. Sharing credit makes the world a more inspiring place to be.

DIFFERENT PEOPLE HAVE DIFFERENT
NEEDS AT DIFFERENT TIMES

ONE OF MY former students, Chloe, was the manager of a talented and valued employee, Charlotte. Chloe wanted to reward Charlotte for her efforts, so she offered Charlotte a promotion with more responsibility and more pay.

Charlotte quit.

Chloe was shocked and befuddled. She thought she was rewarding her employee, but Charlotte acted as though she had just been punished.

Chloe approached Charlotte and expressed a desire to understand what she had done wrong. It turned out Charlotte didn't want more responsibility and pay, as it would only bring her more anxiety. Charlotte thought her current amount of responsibility was just right.

Chloe then asked Charlotte a simple but profound question: "What do you want?" Charlotte replied that what she really wanted was more flexibility. So they worked out a deal: Charlotte kept her original position and pay but was given a slightly shorter working week with more flexible hours.

This example highlights one of the biggest mistakes we make in trying to mentor or motivate others. We assume that *they are just like us*. My former student Chloe was a goal-oriented go-getter—that's why she got an MBA, after all—and there was nothing more valuable to her than a promotion and a raise. But her employee wasn't her clone. Charlotte had different interests and needs.

To understand what motivates others, we can directly ask them what they want. That's what Chloe did: she asked Charlotte what kind of reward she was looking for.

There are times, however, when directly asking someone about their motivations is not possible or pragmatic. So sometimes we can ask for advice from those who know the person well. Chloe could have asked Charlotte's closest colleague to recommend ways to recognize Charlotte's hard work. Other times, we may need to infer or intuit what another person wants; here, Chloe might have observed Charlotte to see what contexts ignited her passions.

Identifying the motivation of others isn't a one-shot solution. It's a dynamic and ongoing process. I crafted a phrase to capture this principle: *Different people have different needs at different times.*

This phrase encompasses a key insight about inspiring others. Just because you understood your colleague's or your spouse's or your friend's needs yesterday, it doesn't mean you will automatically be good at identifying them today. And even if you understand them today, the person's preferences may grow and change over time. That is why we need to really listen to others and carefully observe their behavior: it helps us recognize their evolution and changing desires.

BE A TERRY-CLOTH LEADER, NOT A WIRE-MESH ONE

IN DECEMBER OF 2012, my collaborator Dana Carney yelled at me, "Unless you become more tender, you will never ever get a girlfriend!"

She was responding to a story I shared about a playful comment I had made to a recent girlfriend. When my now ex-girlfriend and I were lying together on the couch, I said, "Our bodies fit really well together."

She looked up with a beatific smile and doe eyes and said, "They do." I then playfully teased, "It's too bad our souls don't." Although I had intended it to be a mischievous but purely humorous comment, she wasn't pleased to say the least. Our relationship never recovered.

What Dana was telling me was that my jokes often burrowed into the insecurities of others. She also explained that my own ability to handle stressful situations could make me blind to the struggles of others. She was encouraging me to be more empathetic and nurturing in my interactions, to accommodate the doubts and concerns that others harbored.

Dana explained that I needed to be a terry-cloth boyfriend and not a wire-mesh one. Let me explain. In the 1950s, Harry Harlow conducted a series of revolutionary studies. He took motherless monkeys and offered them two "mothers" who both provided food through a bottle. But one mother was constructed out of wire mesh, while the other out of terry cloth. What Harlow found is that the monkeys always chose to feed from the terry-cloth mother. In a second experiment, only the wire-mesh mother had food. Although the monkeys would feed on the wire-mesh one, they would quickly return to the terry-cloth mother. And when the monkeys got scared, they always darted to their terry-cloth mother for comfort and safety.

These observations may seem obvious, but at the time they were revolutionary, proving that parents not only satisfy our basic biological need for food and hydration, but they also satisfy the fundamental need for comfort. Dana was saying that if I truly wanted the type of meaningful relationship that I claimed I wanted, I needed to be less wire-mesh and more terry-cloth in my romantic interactions.

Three weeks after Dana yelled at me, I met my now-wife, Jenn. I always credit Dana's words for putting me in a terry-cloth state of mind and leading me to deal more empathically with the natural insecurities that occur at the beginning of any relationship.

As humans, we crave terry-cloth connections. We want others to feel our pain. We want to be seen. That's how Greta Gerwig, the writer and director of *Barbie*, described Ryan Gosling's performance in her movie:

At first, I felt the need to apologize to him, to say, "I'm sorry we're having a deep philosophical conversation about Ken." But as time went on, I realized I didn't need to caveat anything. He thought it was important. He knew it was important . . . Ryan never for one moment doubted the value of the interior lives of girls. By bringing his immense talent, his passion, his dedication, his total commitment to Ken and to Barbie, he is saying, "[This] matters" . . . I have never felt more seen than by his performance.

When someone we admire sees and understands our dreams and visions of the world, they inspire us to achieve them.

To appreciate the difference between wire-mesh and terry-cloth leaders, consider this study Joe Magee of NYU and I ran with a group of executives. We asked our executives to write out how they would lay off one of their employees. For half of the executives, this was the only instruction we gave them. Here is one of the responses from this group of executives; as you can see, it is very wire-mesh:

> I would call the person in with human resources or another manager present. I would get right to the point and not beat around the bush. I would say, "I'm sorry to inform you, but we have decided to lay you off. This is strictly a business situation, we can't financially afford you right now and we wish you the best."

The other executives were given a dose of perspective-taking: these participants were exposed to descriptions of taking another's perspectives and acknowledging other viewpoints. Our perspective-taking intervention turned these executives into terry-cloth leaders:

> I would deliver the message in person, in a private room with a door, away from his/her current workspace. The message would be something like this: "We truly appreciate all that you have done for the company and respect that this is not easy for you and your

family. Unfortunately, we are in this painful situation and we have to eliminate your job. I understand that this is not easy, but I am glad to see that we can offer a little bit of severance as well as career counseling to help you find another opportunity. If you feel like it, you can go home now and come back next week to get your things—but you are welcome to stay for the day as well. Further, know that we are here to support you through your next steps. Let's schedule some time for you to come in a couple of weeks from now and talk about what you want to do next. I would personally like to be a reference for you to help you with your future work prospects."

After activating their perspective-taking, this executive thought about the context and considered the traumatic shock that the news would carry. As a result, they decided to meet alone and in person. They offered options for how the employee might handle the situation. And they provided support to help the person get back on their feet.

After changing the boardroom behavior of executives, Benjamin Blatt of George Washington University and I wondered whether giving doctors a dose of perspective-taking would change their bedside manner and turn them into terry-cloth doctors.

For two years, we conducted an experiment with the entire cohort of medical students at George Washington and Howard Universities during an exam designed to measure their basic clinical skills. Each medical student saw six standardized patients presenting a variety of symptoms, from acute upper abdominal pain to anxiety and pediatric vomiting.

Half of the medical students were given a dose of perspective-taking before meeting their patients:

When you see your patient, imagine what the patient is experiencing as if you were that person, looking at the world through the patient's eyes and walking through the world in the patient's shoes.

What effect did our perspective-taking intervention have? It vastly improved the experience of their patients. The patients who saw perspective-taking doctors rated them as more caring and more trustworthy. This latter finding is particularly important because patient trust is critical for treatment compliance. If a patient trusts their doctor, they are more likely to follow their advice and more likely to get better.

There is one more noteworthy finding from these experiments. Although Black patients often feel dismissed and disrespected by doctors, the perspective-taking intervention increased satisfaction for both White *and* Black patients. Giving these soon-to-be doctors a dose of perspective-taking was the perfect medicine for their patients regardless of their race or ethnicity.

Perspective-taking is necessary to truly understand others, but perspective-taking without empathy isn't just quintessentially wire-mesh, but it's also dangerous. Indeed, perspective-taking without empathy is associated with the foundational elements of antisocial personality disorder, aka sociopaths. Sociopaths are so scary because they use perspective-taking to manipulate, but their lack of empathy often means their cruelty knows no limits. I call perspective-taking without empathy the *bully effect*. Bullies are experts at getting inside the heads of others and recognizing their deepest insecurities and their core weaknesses. And because bullies don't feel any compassion for the people they target, they exploit those insecurities. When it isn't accompanied by empathy, perspective-taking can be infuriating in its callousness.

MY TERRY-CLOTH MENTOR (WITH JUST THE RIGHT AMOUNT OF WIRE MESH)

BEING IN A PhD program is a bit like being a motherless monkey.

My first year as a doctoral student at Princeton was a disaster. I was paired with a professor who had a brilliant mind but had trouble helping me translate my discursive ideas into actionable studies. We met weekly but basically spun our wheels in intellectual mud. This professor was also wire-mesh in his approach as he didn't have much patience for my struggles. At the end of the year, I was the only graduate student with nothing to show for myself; I hadn't conducted a single study. I came very close to dropping out of graduate school. And as I mentioned in the last chapter, the psychology department came very close to kicking me out.

Joel Cooper saved me. One of the classes I took in my first year was Joel's class on attitude formation and change. One day I got inspired by an idea and wrote a two-page memo detailing it. Joel was extremely encouraging of the idea and met with me to discuss and develop it. As I contemplated the end of my research career, Joel's encouragement was my glimmer of hope. Without his enthusiasm for my idea, I would have given up. When I tentatively reached out to Joel about switching advisors, he enthusiastically agreed to officially take me under his wing.

Joel did more than just encourage me. He really listened to and *empathized* with me. Joel's terry-cloth approach was most apparent when he and I worked to turn my idea into an experiment exploring the roots of attitude change. Our experiment required participants to prepare and give a tape-recorded speech on one side of a particular issue. To make their essays psychologically impactful, they would be told that a university committee was going to listen to the speeches to help the committee make their decision on the topic.

But here's the thing: there was no committee. That is, the experiment involved deception. We wanted our participants to think their speech was going to have a real impact. The deception was designed to create the feeling that their words mattered and had consequences.

The experiment was all set and ready for me to run, but the week before we launched it, I started having nightmares. I started waking up in a cold sweat. On the third night of sleeplessness, I realized it was the thought of deceiving people that was fueling my anxiety. My body and mind just wouldn't let me do it.

It was incredibly difficult for me to go to Joel's office and let him know I was suffering at the thought of misleading the participants and creating discomfort in them. Joel listened empathetically. He said he wanted to think about my concerns and see if he could come up with a way to solve them.

A day later, Joel brought me into his office and proposed an idea. He would hire an administrator in the department to run the study so I wouldn't have to. *But* he wanted me to debrief every participant, to tell them what the study was really about. Joel wanted me to reveal the deception and explain why it was necessary, and then to listen to and answer any concerns the participants had. I was still anxious at the thought of revealing the deception, but I felt it was a fair compromise.

When I began debriefing the participants, I quickly realized the study wasn't a traumatic experience for them. Sure, some of the participants were a bit annoyed about the deception, but they all understood its importance. And many of them were fascinated by the topic and had lots of follow-up questions. In the end, I found debriefing the participants to be intellectually and emotionally gratifying.

I later reflected on how ingenious Joel's plan had been. He supported and affirmed my palpable concerns. But he also kept me involved. And that involvement allowed me to take a small first step toward feeling more comfortable with the process. Joel guided me to overcome my fears without invalidating them. The gift that Joel gave me is he took my concerns seriously while also designing a path for me to move forward.

The experiment Joel and I designed and conducted produced interesting results and I wrote it up for my master's thesis. When I orally defended my thesis in April of 1996, it was so well received by my three-person committee that the faculty encouraged me to turn it into a scientific manuscript and submit it for publication. I was so elated to get this positive feedback that I celebrated all weekend.

But then I got stuck. The task of turning my thesis into a potentially publishable research article just seemed too daunting. One month went by. Then two months. Three months passed and I hadn't written anything. I began to avoid Joel in the halls because I felt so ashamed of my procrastination.

Then on August 1, 1996, I found the following note in my mailbox.

To me, Joel's letter epitomizes tough love. It represents the perfect integration of the terry-cloth and wire-mesh approaches to mentorship. Joel asked if I was stuck and empathically offered to help me get unstuck.

8/1/96

Adam,

I was thinking about the shatterance study. Are you making progress getting a draft prepared?

I have a proposition for you:

The obvious road is for you to prepare the draft, let's say in a week. If you're stuck, speak to me or Jeff and perhaps we can get you unstuck.

If you cannot get to the paper in a week, or wish you did not have to do it, then Jeff or I can do it. If we go that route, whoever prepares the draft will become first author.

Let me know. Better still, let me see the draft.

Best,

Joel

He gave me a choice (although one option was clearly superior to the other one). And he provided a clear deadline. The letter's tone is also notable: he expressed his frustration, but he did so dispassionately.

The note was so perfect that it got me unstuck and moved me forward. I completed a draft of the article by the next week. Joel's note empowered me by challenging me. It helped me meet the moment and advance to the next phase of my career.

That's what inspiring mentors do: They meet people where they are but lead them to where they can go. They find the right balance between being supportive while also challenging people to push themselves toward a better tomorrow.

GETTING INTO A MENTOR STATE OF MIND

BEING A MENTOR is one of the three universal facets of inspiring leadership because it fulfills the fundamental human need for belonging and status. As humans, we crave someone who supports and guides us while also valuing and celebrating us. It's like learning how to ride a bike: we want someone who holds and steers the bike, but also knows when to let go, while cheering us on along the way.

So, how can we get into a mentor state of mind?

It starts with *where* we seek new ideas. We can get into a mentor state of mind when we recognize that many new insights and perspectives come from those who have less power and authority than we have. Ting Zhang of Harvard and I introduced the concept of *downward learning* to capture the tendency to see those below us in a hierarchy as valuable sources of knowledge.

In one of our initial studies, we found that when a mentor scored high on downward learning—they agreed with statements like the following, "I learn a lot by interacting with those who have LESS power than I do"— they invested more time in answering their mentees' questions. Focusing on what they could learn from those below them led our mentors to see mentoring as an opportunity to learn new knowledge and new skills.

To explore downward learning in the field, we collaborated with an online programming boot camp that uses one-on-one mentorship to help individuals acquire coding skills needed for technical jobs. The mentors in our study were seasoned coders (e.g., researchers, computer scientists) who engaged in weekly one-on-one interactions with their mentees over a period of several months. Importantly, the matches between mentors and mentees were randomly assigned, i.e., they were based solely on whether there was a match in their schedules. Near the end of their program, students completed a series of practice interviews involving coding problems that were designed to assess their hireability and technical competence. To maintain objectivity, the mock interviews were performed by a third-party who had never met the students.

What did we find? The students who were identified as having stronger technical skills and as more hireable were the ones who had mentors who scored high on downward learning. By seeing less powerful people as worthy sources of information and insights, these mentors became inspiring encouragers who empowered their students to become better coders.

To demonstrate that downward learning *creates* more inspiring mentors, we also conducted an experiment. Our experiment had two groups of individuals: mentors and mentees. We asked our mentors, who were successful professionals, to deliver career-related advice to individuals searching for work, who served as our mentees.

Right before they engaged in their mentoring session, we had our mentors participate in a reflection task. This reflection task allowed us to vary their learning direction. Mentors in the *downward-learning condition* read: "Please think about a time in which you learned from someone with less power than you." In contrast, mentors in the *upward-learning condition* read: "Please think about a time in which you learned from someone with more power than you." Mentors then wrote three to five sentences that described what they learned from this person.

Mentors next offered advice to their mentees. Importantly, the mentees were completely unaware of the experimental conditions. Afterward, mentees rated how encouraging their mentors were (e.g., "I believe this person would value and encourage my unique skills and talents") and how empathic they were (e.g., "I believe I could bring up problems and tough issues with this person"). They also rated the quality of the advice they received.

The results were remarkable. First, simply having our mentors engage in five minutes of downward learning led them to be more engaged and to offer more thorough advice. Their mentees, in turn, found them to be more inspiring: they rated downward-learning mentors as better encouragers and more empathic supporters. Our downward-learning intervention turned our professionals into terry-cloth and inspiring mentors.

Another interesting finding from this study is that the effect of downward learning was especially valuable for more powerful mentors. As we discussed with the Leader Amplification Effect (Chapter 1), power tends to decrease perspective-taking, which is why our downward-learning intervention was so impactful for those higher in the hierarchy. The powerful normally don't look downward for insights, and that impairs their ability to mentor others. By helping them widen their knowledge aperture, our downward-learning intervention helped powerful mentors see mentoring in a new light, as a source of untapped insights. It was this mental shift that allowed these powerful individuals to become more engaged mentors.

LET'S END OUR inspiring mentor conversation with a paradox. Research shows that we are more naturally inclined to connect with people who are similar to us. But to truly understand another person we need to recognize how they are different from us. Solving the Chloe/Charlotte example required recognizing that other people aren't just like us.

My late colleague Kathy Phillips studied the power of appreciating differences. She turned her research into a useful exercise, which she described in one of her talks:

> Most of the time when you are trying to make a connection with someone new, you look for what you have in common with them, you look for similarities . . . you believe it will help you overcome any differences. I am going to argue to you that you are wrong and challenge you to try something very different. The next time you are interacting with someone new . . . look for and talk about what makes me unique and different from you and what makes you unique and different from me. Tell me about your life, your story, the experience you went through that I can perhaps learn from. I don't want to know exactly how we are alike. In fact, if I do that, I haven't learned anything.

Kathy's research found that focusing on what makes us similar feels safer, but it also limits our learning and prevents us from truly understanding another person's perspective.

My former doctoral student Andrew Todd, now at the University of California, Davis, and I put the benefits of focusing on differences versus similarities to an experimental test. We had half of our participants focus on *differences* by asking them to list the differences between various pairs of pictures. Another set of participants was instructed to list the *similarities* between the images.

We then had our participants go through a maze together. We sat two people at opposite ends of a table and had one person direct the other person through the maze as quickly as possible, using only four directions: left, right, forward, and backward. But there was a catch: *the follower was blindfolded.* To effectively give directions to the person blindfolded on the opposite side of the table, the leader needed to look at the maze from the *other* side of the table. To effectively mentor people through the maze, our directions need to be tailored to *their* perspective. That means turning our world upside down and inside out, where our right is their left and our up is their down.

The group of participants who we had focus on the *differences* in the pictures were better able to look at the world from the other side of the table. Difference-focused leaders helped their partners speed through the maze much faster than the participants focused on similarities. Although focusing on similarities feels good, recognizing differences helps get us into a mentor frame of mind.

INSPIRING LEADERS ARE visionary, exemplars of desired behavior, and engaged mentors. These universal features of inspiring leaders are rooted in the fundamental needs of human nature. Being visionary is so inspiring because it meets our needs for meaning and understanding. Exemplars meet our need for safety through calm courage, our need for energy through passion, and our desire for perfection by being super. And mentors meet our need to be accepted and respected.

The link to fundamental needs also informs how we end up on the infuriating end of the continuum. When our own needs aren't met— when we lack meaning or feel a loss of control, when we don't feel secure, and when we don't feel respected—we get trapped in a vicious cycle of infuriation. Let's explore this vicious cycle next.

CHAPTER 6

The Vicious Cycle of Infuriation

E VERYONE HERE IS great, except for Kate.* She's a tyrant who will terrorize your life and fill you with hate."

"Wait, *what?*"

I had just arrived at Northwestern University to start a postdoctoral fellowship and a graduate student was giving me the lay of the land. Naturally, I was very curious to know who Kate was. I imagined she was one of the most important people in the school. But that wasn't the case: Kate was just a low-level administrator. However, as I would soon find out, Kate wielded tremendous power.

Kate oversaw the reimbursement process, and she used the power of the purse to force everyone to navigate through a labyrinth of rules and rigid procedures. If a request was asked without the correct language, a tirade would follow. She literally put red tape on the ground around her desk and forbade others from crossing it.

After observing Kate in action, I immediately thought of the Soup Nazi, the infamous character from the TV show *Seinfeld*. In the show, there was a storefront in NYC that offered a variety of succulent soups.

---

* Kate is a pseudonym.

THE VICIOUS CYCLE OF INFURIATION   101

But there was a catch: the chef required each customer to ask for, collect, and pay for their soup using a ritualized set of behaviors. And if you didn't strictly follow the precise gestures, he would declare, "No soup for you!" Kate wasn't quite as abrupt, but the effect was similar. If you violated her precise protocol, your reimbursement would languish in a bureaucratic black hole.

Eventually I found the key to Kate's heart—snow globes! Kate couldn't travel, for both economic and medical reasons. So she traveled vicariously through snow globes from around the world. Faculty and grad students could get in her good graces, at least temporarily, if we returned from our travels with a snow globe in hand. Once I offered snow globes from my trips, all my reimbursements were magically expedited.

I first interacted with Kate just as I was beginning to study the psychological effects of power. But it wasn't until a decade later that I had my first insight into what drove Kate's infuriating behavior. That year, Joe Magee of New York University and I published what would become my most cited scientific paper. In that paper, we made a critical distinction between power and status. Although power and status are often used interchangeably, both colloquially and scientifically, we suggested that they were two very different elements of social hierarchy. We specified that *power* is based on how much control we have over valued resources, whereas *status* represents the respect and admiration we have in the eyes of others.

A few years later, Alison Fragale of the University of North Carolina used this distinction to explain why people hate gatekeepers—from bouncers to custom agents to reimbursement clerks like Kate. These positions don't carry a lot of status, but they are quite powerful because they control valued resources. Alison suggested that high-power/low-status positions are inherently disliked by others.

Reading Alison's paper gave me a eureka moment. I realized that positions defined by high power but low status are not inherently objectionable. Instead, it's that these positions lead their inhabitants to become infuriating in their behavior.

I now truly understood Kate for the first time. It wasn't that her role lacked power, it was that her role *lacked status*. It was the low status of her position, combined with the power that she did possess, that led her to demean and terrorize others.

This all makes sense when we realize, as we discussed in Inspiring Mentors (Chapter 5), that status is a fundamental need. Research shows how great it is when you have status. You see respect radiating from people's eyes. People laugh harder at your jokes and applaud your ideas more loudly. They open doors for you, literally and figuratively. The world's an awesome place to be when you have high status.

Now consider what it's like to lack status. Instead of awe, you see contempt in the eyes of others. People mock your jokes and scoff at your ideas. They close doors in your face, denying you opportunities. It's lousy living in the world when you lack status.

My hypothesis was that having power while lacking status is a toxic combination that leads people to engage in infuriating behaviors. Low status leaves people seething with resentment, but having power frees them to act on that resentment by mistreating others. Low status is a powder keg of resentment, and power lights the fuse.

I now appreciated why bringing Kate a snow globe was so critical for turning her from an adversary into an ally. The snow globe took her preferences and desires seriously. It signaled that she was worthy of time and attention. It made her feel seen. The snow globe gave her the very respect that her position was lacking.

INFURIATING LITTLE TYRANTS

I WAS NOW ready to test my hypothesis. Along with Nate Fast of the University of Southern California and Nir Halevy of Stanford University, we examined whether randomly assigning a person to a position that had power but lacked status would turn that person into a little tyrant that demeaned others.

In our experiment we brought people into the lab and informed them that they would be interacting with, but not meeting, a fellow student who worked for the same consulting firm, "Grow Inc."

We assigned half of our participants to be idea producers. The idea producer generated and worked on important ideas. We told them that others had a great deal of admiration and respect for the role. This condition served as our *high-status role*.

In contrast, the other half of our participants were randomly assigned to be workers, which we designed to be a *low-status role*. The worker had to do menial tasks, such as checking for typos. We stated that others tended to look down on this role.

We also gave half of our participants power over their partner. Those in the *high-power role* read:

One other element of your role is that you get to dictate what "hoops" your coworker must jump through in order to qualify for a $50 bonus drawing which will happen after the study. Thus, you control the amount of effort he/she must exert in order to win the $50. He/she has no such control over you.

These people had power over their partner, and there was nothing their partner could do about it.

In contrast, the other half of the participants were in a *less-powerful position*. Although these participants could decide what their partner had to do, these counterparts could *retaliate* against them:

However, your coworker has control over your fate because he/she can remove your name from the raffle if he/she doesn't like the hoops you have selected for him/her to jump through.

We next gave participants a list of ten activities and asked them to select the behaviors their partner had to do to be eligible for the $50 prize.

We selected the ten activities based on an initial study we conducted. We had fifty-eight people read statements and instructed them to indicate the extent to which it would be demeaning, humiliating, and degrading to perform each activity. Here are the five behaviors that were rated as the *least demeaning*:

- Write a short essay on your experiences yesterday.
- Tell the experimenter a funny joke.
- Clap your hands 50 times.
- Do 5 push-ups.
- Jump up and down 10 times on one leg.

These are the five behaviors that were rated as the *most demeaning*:

- Say "I am filthy" 5 times.
- Say "I am not worthy" 5 times.
- Bark like a dog 3 times.
- Tell the experimenter 3 negative traits that you have.
- Count backwards from 500 in increments of 7.

Notice what we did here. We varied how much power each participant had *in relation* to their partners. We then gave every participant the opportunity to demean their partner. Importantly, we didn't tell our participants that some of the behaviors were more demeaning than others; we simply randomly interspersed these behaviors and asked them to select the behaviors that their partner would be required to do.

So, what did we find?

When people were randomly assigned to have power (they controlled their counterparts' behavior without fear of retaliation) but lacked status (they were lowly workers), they assigned more demeaning behaviors *than any other group*. What was particularly interesting was comparing the workers versus the idea producers in the high-power condition. Both groups had the unfettered ability to assign demeaning behaviors to another person. But the lowly workers were almost *twice as likely* to do so as the high-status idea producers. The low-status workers used their power to take out their resentment on others. By placing people in a disrespected position but giving them power over others, we had turned them into infuriating little tyrants.

In follow-up research led by my former student Eric Anicich, now at University of Southern California, we established that roles that lack status but possess power are the starting point for a vicious cycle of infuriating behaviors. Demeaning behavior begets demeaning behavior. When we are demeaned, we demean right back.

But here is where things get even more interesting. These infuriating behaviors create another vicious cycle, this one around conflict. We found that whenever one person had high power but low status in a relationship at work, people reported that this relationship was marked by higher levels of conflict. High-power, low-status positions are a breeding ground for discord.

We also conducted experiments to show that being in a position that has power but lacks status *creates* a vicious cycle of conflict. In these experiments, we varied both power (people were randomly assigned to be in charge or in subordinate roles) and status (we said their roles were either respected or disrespected by their coworkers). After being assigned to their roles, we asked participants to respond to their colleague's request for help:

Recently you patiently spent several hours teaching this person how to use a new software program even though it should take no longer than one hour of training to acquire all the knowledge that is required. This person just approached you and asked if you could go through the software with them again. How would you tell this person that you do not have the time to go through everything again? Please respond as if you are speaking directly to the person (e.g., use "you" language).

We had each participant write out their response. We then shared these responses with a second group of participants who read one of the original notes as if it were written to them. These coders rated how *demeaning* the note was and how much *conflict* they would feel with the colleague who wrote it. Importantly, these new participants were *unaware* of the power and status of the letter writers. We included this experimental feature to demonstrate that the feelings of being demeaned and the anticipated conflict were due solely to the content of the message, rather than negative reactions about their colleague's role (as Alison Fragale had shown in her research).

Here are two examples of notes that were rated as *not very demeaning*:

> *Non-Demeaning Example 1*: I apologize but I'm actually quite busy with other tasks at the moment, but if you are willing to stay after work for a little while I would be happy to assist you!
>
> *Non-Demeaning Example 2*: I'm sorry, but I have some important stuff that I have to get done. You should spend a little time messing around with the software and see if you can feel comfortable. If you have any problems, you can always feel free to contact me with any questions.

In contrast, here are two examples of notes that were judged to be *very demeaning*. Not surprisingly, both were written by someone in a high-power/low-status role:

> *Demeaning Example 1*: I have already spent several hours of my own time teaching you a very basic program that should have only taken you about 1 hour to learn. If you did not pay attention to me during that time then so be it. You are not going to last long here if you do not learn fast.
>
> *Demeaning Example 2*: You should already know how to use the software by now. I've even spent more than enough time teaching you how to use it recently. If you still can't use it effectively by the end of the week, then I'll be forced to find a replacement for you.

We also replicated the study, but this time used a layoff context. Here is a layoff notice written by a person randomly assigned to the *high-power/high-status role*. Notice how compassionate it is:

I'm truly sorry to have to inform you that the company has decided to end your employment with us. Please don't take this as a reflection of your performance—it is simply a matter of finances and management, and you can expect an enthusiastic endorsement from myself as your supervisor as you begin your search for a new position. Please let me know if there's anything I can do for you, I would be happy to help you in this process.

Now, here's one written by a person who was randomly put into a *high-power/low-status role*. Notice how cruel and dismissive it is:

You're fired. You have until the end of the day to move out your things before the cleaning crew comes in. Good luck with your future endeavors.

Being randomly assigned to a high-power/low-status role led to calloused communication dripping with derision. And these notes filled their recipient with resentment, fueling a vicious cycle of conflict. By randomly assigning people to different roles, these experiments established that having power without status is the *source* of demeaning treatment and the *instigator* of conflict. When we have power but also feel disrespected by others, we often find ourselves on the infuriating end of the continuum. It's hard to be inspiring when you're seething with resentment.

While we were in the middle of running these experiments, I was contacted by a federal agency that wanted advice on how best to transition from private offices to an open-office, hoteling plan where multiple workers would be utilizing the same desk space at different times. I jumped at the chance to help because I knew this would be an ideal setting to explore not only the power-without-status effect, but also how *changes* in status affect behavior. In the old office layout, having a private office was a status symbol, a sign you were respected. But now some of these employees would be losing this symbol of status.

How did the new office play affect the employees? We found that federal employees who had more power in their roles were especially sensitive to changes in their status. Powerful employees who suffered a loss of status reported the highest levels of conflict. In contrast, those who gained status—like Kate did whenever she received a snow globe—reported lower levels of conflict.

Our carefully designed experiments, our large-scale surveys, and my adventures with Kate all tell the same story. One of the biggest threats to being inspiring, and a potent source of infuriation, is feeling disrespected in the eyes of others. Feeling disrespected pushes us toward the infuriating end of the continuum.

As we will see next, even when we only feel *unsure* about our status, we still become infuriating.

INFURIATING INSECURITY

Please think of a time in which you felt insecure at work. That is, a situation in which you felt uncertain or doubted your ability to meet an important goal. Please recall and describe this sense of insecurity.

One of my doctoral students Maren Hoff and I have asked hundreds of people about their experiences with insecurity. Although the responses are rich and diverse, they also make up a universal tapestry of insecurity. The table below highlights the many ways insecurity can ensnare us.

Sometimes insecurity squirrels inside of us because *we feel we lack the experience, knowledge, or skills needed in a situation*. This lack of experience often occurs when we are in a new or novel situation. That was me when I was a new parent. Each new task was filled with a foreboding

SOURCE OF INSECURITY	EXAMPLE EXCERPT
Lack of experience/ knowledge/skills	"I had to come up with a solution to a problem that I was not trained for/didn't have knowledge of. My coworker had quit the day before and that was usually her job. I had no idea what to do."
Past failure	"I doubted myself at work when I made a mathematical mistake that was quite embarrassing. I was wrong and had to explain myself in front of my coworkers."
Others more advantaged	"I felt insecure at work when I was really wanting to be promoted. The reason I was insecure was because, in my opinion, other coworkers were more talented and better than me."
Infuriating boss	"I can recall when I had an abusive supervisor. We were separated for a while but then there was an attempt to put us back in close proximity and I could not perform."
High-stakes/pressure situation	"I was working on a really important project with a looming deadline. I was overwhelmed by how much [the] project mattered for both me and my firm and I felt like I needed more time. I was having trouble and felt so anxious."

sense of incompetence, from the first diaper change to the first bottle to the first bath.

Sometimes, our insecurity stems from past failures that make us feel like we don't have what it takes to get ahead. That was me after I got fired from my first postcollege job.

We also feel insecure from *negative social comparisons*, when we think others have more talent or resources than we do. That was me with my twin brother, Michael. Because he was 50 percent heavier than I was when we were born, he got to go home from the hospital while I spent weeks in an incubator. He got into the gifted and talented program in third grade, and I didn't. When we were twelve, I ran a 10k race in forty-six minutes, but Michael ran it even faster. He even had his first kiss before me. I felt like he had all the advantages, and I could never measure up.

A universal source of insecurity is *pressure*. Pressure comes in many forms. Time pressure from a pressing deadline, high-stakes pressure from an important and consequential task, crisis pressure when unforeseen events create immediate demands. Each of these types of pressure are fertile ground for our insecurities to flourish. When we feel a situation demands more than we can offer, it feels like we are barely treading water.

Inexperience, past failures, being disadvantaged, and feeling pressure all create that exact same state of insecurity, a sense of self-doubt in one's capacity to meet the fundamental goal of maintaining or improving one's status.

How do these feelings of insecurity affect our behavior?

When I reflected on my experience as a new parent, I realized that during those moments when I was feeling particularly insecure, I tended to focus on *my* contributions to childcare while minimizing the Herculean efforts of my wife. I was hungry for credit and validation, and too often stingy with sharing it.

Maren speculated that I wasn't alone, that feeling insecure generally makes us selfish. As we saw in Inspiring Mentors (Chapter 5), sharing versus stealing credit is a universal differentiator along the inspiring-infuriating continuum. Inspiring leaders share credit for positive accomplishments while infuriating leaders steal and hoard all the credit.

Maren and I predicted that status insecurity would turn people into credit hoarders, unwilling to acknowledge the contributions of others, i.e., insecurity would push us toward the infuriating end of the continuum. We have conducted numerous experiments to test whether status insecurity turns people into credit hoarders. In one of our experiments, we asked half of our participants to recall a time in which they felt *insecure* at work, just like you did above, while the other half recalled a time in which they felt *secure* at work. We then gave them the following scenario:

> Imagine you are taking on a new role at work, which comes with new opportunities for success but also risks for failure. Your mentor helped you get the role, and your team has been supportive throughout the process. You are feeling both excited and nervous. You want to share the news about your new role with friends, colleagues, and family on your social media. Please draft your post.

Note that participants were only asked to share the news about their new role; they could freely choose the content and length of their posts. What we were interested in is whether they *spontaneously* chose to acknowledge the contributions of their team or mentor.

Most of our participants focused only on themselves in their social media posts. Here's an example. "I just took a new position at work. I can't wait for all the challenges and successes I will soon see!"

Some of our participants acknowledged the role of others in their social media posts. "I'm amped to start a new opportunity in a new role! I am very excited yet a bit nervous and anxious to begin. I want to thank my mentor and team for helping me get to this point!"

Although the majority focused only on themselves, that was only true when they were feeling insecure. When people recalled a time when they felt insecure, only 39 percent acknowledged others in their social media post. In contrast, when people were randomly assigned to recall a time when they felt secure at work, the majority (53 percent) shared credit by acknowledging the contributions of others. Insecurity turned people into credit hoarders.

To demonstrate that the link between insecurity and credit hoarding is not unique to social media posts, Maren and I created a venture capital competition context where every contestant had to pitch their venture with a compelling presentation.

In each experiment, we varied whether our contestants felt insecure or not. In one of our experiments, we tried to capture the insecurity caused by *past failures*: "Giving a convincing pitch is critical to your startup as your presentation skills have been criticized in the past and you almost did not get invited this year."

In another experiment, we captured insecurity by having people focus on how they were *disadvantaged* relative to their competitors. "Giving a convincing pitch is critical to your startup as you constantly feel that the other contestants are better set up for success than you (e.g., more resources, better connections, more established, etc.)."

After varying their levels of insecurity, we gave our participants the following information about their presentation, which included help they received from a colleague named Blake:

While you were working on your presentation, you received help from Blake, who is competing in the hospitality sector of the competition. Blake suggested that you tailor your presentation to elegantly use the principles of graphic design as a way of highlighting your venture. You ended up using user experience design elements throughout your slides to emphasize the appeal of your venture. To highlight Tuned's interactive gaming features even better, you also included motion design elements.

Participants next found out that they *won* their sector: "You gave a strong presentation and won the competition in the education sector. This means that you advance to compete across all sectors for the grand prize. When receiving the prize for the education sector, you are supposed to submit a speech of your final thoughts."

Like our social media post study, their speeches could include any content and be of any length. Thus, we could measure whether each person *spontaneously* chose to explicitly acknowledge the help of Blake to their success. Here is an example of a speech that *shared credit* by acknowledging Blake:

I am very happy to be moving on to the next step of the competition. I hope to continue improving my company "Tuned" regardless of the outcome. I would also like to thank Blake for his suggestions and help earlier in this competition. I hope he can make it to the next step as well. I look forward to my next presentation and improving from here.

In contrast, the following person was *stingy with credit* and did not acknowledge Blake:

I'm so happy and proud for Tuned to be competing for the grand prize. In a world where you need to make your product stand out, Tuned offers the course material and education to better equip yourself for this task. Much like our product, we look to make ourselves stand out in the final competition!

Notice that we made sure to keep the context and the outcomes identical; in all conditions, people prepared well, Blake helped them on their presentation, and they won their sector. The only element that we varied was whether we made our participants feel insecure.

What did we find? Across our experiments, participants in our baseline conditions were almost *twice as likely* to acknowledge Blake than participants in the insecure conditions. Insecurity consistently robbed people of their generosity.

Maren and I also tested our theory in the real world—well, at least the world of reality television. We analyzed the final pitches from the first twenty-nine seasons of the US reality competition show *Survivor*. This is how we described the show in our research: "*Survivor* is filmed on an isolated location, where contestants compete in challenges that test their physical and mental abilities to win the title of "Sole Survivor" and a $1,000,000 prize. Because contestants are progressively eliminated from the competition by their fellow competitors, there is also a social element to winning, in addition to feats of endurance. To become the Sole Survivor, you need to gain allies and form coalitions. On the final day, two or three players hold a final pitch in front of a jury consisting of former contestants from that season. In the pitch, the players make their case for why they should win the competition."

We were interested in whether the contestants took sole credit for their achievements or whether they acknowledged the efforts of other players.

To determine both the insecurity and credit sharing of the *Survivor* contestants, we used text analysis software and ChatGPT artificial intelligence. Replicating our experimental studies, we found that when *Survivor* contestants expressed more *insecurity* in their speeches, they were also *less likely to share credit* in their final pitches.

Here is a final *Survivor* speech that scored particularly *high* on acknowledging others:

> I came into this game, you know, wanting to do two things. I wanted to play a loyal game, and I wanted to fight physically, strategically, and mentally to the end. And, you know, I'm really proud of how I played. And I know I wouldn't be sitting here without, you know, help from all of you. So, thanks. I wanted to say thanks.

In contrast, here's a speech scoring *low* on acknowledging others:

I came to this game with one goal, and that goal was to win a million dollars to better my life and my son's. I played the game to win, I played it hard. I know I didn't do everything that I should have done and should have done more in some other incidents, but it came from my soul. Everything I did was to win these million dollars, and that's why I believe I should be the Sole Survivor tonight. I believe I've earned it. I worked hard for it. That's all.

In the real world and in the lab, in social media posts, victory speeches, and even pitches on reality TV, insecurity led people to focus on their own accomplishments and neglect the efforts of others. This may not seem like that big a deal but remember that not receiving proper credit for one's efforts is one of the most infuriating experiences in our lives. By making people socially stingy, insecurity instigates a vicious cycle of infuriation.

WHY DOES INSECURITY turn people into credit hoarders? Maren and I found that it's because the insecure come to see status as zero-sum, where any increase in the status of one person comes at the direct expense of another person. The insecure worry that sharing credit will boost the status of others at their own expense. The insecure hoard credit to protect their own status, even if it means infuriating those around them.

But here's where things get interesting. The insecure fear that giving credit to others will hurt their own status. But as we discussed in Inspiring Mentors (Chapter 5), the insecure have it *backward*! Sharing credit with others doesn't just move us toward the inspiring end of the continuum, it also moves us up the status ladder. Sharing status expands the status pie.

Maren and I used our venture capital context to give our theory its most extreme test. We examined what happens when someone credits their direct competitor for helping them. Surely then credit sharing would be a losing proposition, right? Not at all—we found that sharing credit still increased one's own status. The status advantages of credit sharing occur even when we acknowledge the contributions of our direct competitors! These results completely undermine the zero-sum status assumptions of the insecure. Although the insecure hoard credit to increase their own status and standing, it only reduces their status instead. Thus, credit hoarding isn't just infuriating, it is also counterproductive and self-defeating.

INFURIATING EMOTIONS

INSECURITY IS A psychologically painful state that leads to the infuriating and counterproductive behavior of credit hoarding. Insecurity is inherently intertwined with anxiety, which helps explain why the insecure are so selfish and so infuriating. In research conducted with my former student Andy Todd, now at UC Davis, I have found that anxiety is a key source of infuriation because it impairs a psychological foundation of inspiring leaders that we have discussed throughout *Inspire*: perspective-taking.

In one study, we induced anxiety in some of our participants by asking them to "describe a time in the past in which you felt very anxious." We asked them to really feel that anxiety and focus in on what caused it. In contrast, our other participants wrote about how they spend their typical evening.

Next, we gave them the following photograph and asked them, "In the photo below, which side of the table is the book on?"

This question might seem obvious and straightforward, but how you answer it reveals a lot about whose perspective you're taking. If you're like many people, your answer was the right side. But notice the

book is on the right side of the table only from *your* perspective. From the perspective of the person looking at the book, it's on her left.

After thinking about their typical evening, more than half of the participants (55 percent) offered the perspective-taking answer of the left side. But after mentally reexperiencing an anxiety-producing situation, only 28 percent engaged in perspective-taking. Anxiety trapped people on their side of the table, pushing them toward the infuriating end of the continuum.

Little tyrants like Kate don't create anxiety, but they do provoke anger. And anger, like anxiety, also impairs perspective-taking. Consider this study by Jeremy Yip of Georgetown. He made his participants feel angry by asking them about the angriest moment of their lives; his participants were seething with rage just thinking about this experience. The other participants described their typical day, similar to my anxiety experiment. Next, participants, who were all on the East Coast, wrote an email to schedule an important call with a client who was on the West Coast. Jeremy coded whether the email acknowledged the Pacific time zone or not. Non-angry participants were great perspective-takers, with almost 75 percent offering meeting times that acknowledged the West

Coast time zone. But when participants were seething with anger, the majority remained trapped on the East Coast.

Anxiety and anger are even more infuriating when leaders display anxiety or anger. Remember the leader amplification effect: The emotions of leaders get amplified, and in doing so, it infects and affects others. Our anxiety becomes their anxiety. Our anger overwhelms others.

Anxiety, anger, insecurity, and resentment all push us toward the infuriating end of the continuum. And when we are infuriating, we create anger and anxiety in others, which in turn increases their own propensity toward infuriation. By turning us into demeaning tyrants and credit hoarders, these forces create vicious cycles of infuriation.

INSPIRING SELF-REGULATION

LOW STATUS AND insecurity, and the emotions of anger and anxiety, push us toward the infuriating end of the continuum. They make us less visionary, trapping us in a narrow and seething perspective. Under their spell, we are less capable of being exemplars; instead of being calm and courageous protectors who authentically present both superness and humanness, we are anxious and cowardly and come across as political and conniving. And they turn us into wire-mesh mentors who are selfish and abusive.

How can we regain control of our emotions and grievances? How do we find our way back to the inspiring end of the continuum?

The first step is to make credit sharing an enduring habit, to be more generous more often. As we discussed with inspiring mentors, when we acknowledge the contributions of others, we leave others beaming rather than seething. The leader amplification effect turns our generous gestures into GENEROUS ones. Remember that all it took to transform Kate from a little tyrant into a teddy bear was a snow globe. The importance of being generous in both thought and deed is why generosity is my number one value.

Next, we need to find ways to get control of our strong emotions, like anger, anxiety, and insecurity. Getting a handle on these strong emotions is the key to stopping the vicious cycle of infuriation.

Let's start with feelings of insecurity. We have discussed how reflecting on our values can help us get into a visionary state of mind and reflecting on times when we felt secure, powerful, and in control can help get us into an exemplar frame of mind. Each of these techniques directly reduces feelings of insecurity.

We can also be an inspiring mentor to ourselves. Steven Rogelberg of the University of North Carolina at Charlotte conducted a fascinating study with senior executives. He asked them to write future-oriented letters to themselves as part of a program on personal development. He then coded their letters for whether they were being inspiring or infuriating mentors to themselves. Infuriating letters were castigating and denigrating, referring to themselves as losers and betting they were unable to grow and develop. The inspiring letters were encouraging (*you can do it*) but challenging (*don't forget your promise to spend more time really listening to others*). To measure whether self-talk predicted their actual leadership, Steven had the colleagues and subordinates of the executives rate them on their leadership effectiveness and creativity. So what did Steven find? Inspiring self-talk was associated with more effective leadership, while infuriating self-talk was associated with lower creativity. When we are an inspiring mentor to ourselves, we can break the vicious cycle of infuriation.

We can also tackle negative thoughts and emotions through meditation. It turns out that meditation soothes anxiety and anger, as well as helps calm our insecurities. My collaborator Andy Hafenbrack of the University of Washington has done some of the most seminal work on meditation. In one experiment, Andy had everyone engage in a twelve-minute period of silence and he simply varied how they spent that time. In the *meditation condition*, he guided his participants to focus their attention on their breath.

Gently maintain attention on your breathing. Stay with each breath for its full duration as it goes in and for its full duration as it goes out. If your mind wanders, acknowledge that it has wandered without judgment. Reconnect to the present by gently shifting your attention back to your breath.

In the *control condition*, he told them to let their mind wander freely:

Think about anything that comes to mind from the past, present, or future. This is a time for your mind to wander freely. You don't have to think about one thing; you can think about as many different things as you want. Don't focus too hard on anything. Think freely.

Both groups sat in silence for twelve minutes, and the only difference was whether they focused their attention on their breath or let their mind wander.

After meditation, Andy entered his participants into a lottery with a jackpot of €120. He also gave them a chance to expand the jackpot and make it bigger. But there was a catch: the only way to make the jackpot bigger was to give at least some of your winnings to another person. Here's the choice he gave people:

You can keep all the money if you win or you can share some of your winnings with another participant where any money you send will be multiplied by 1.5. So, if a participant kept €70 for themselves and transferred €50, the other participant would get €75 (€50*1.5).

What did Andy find? In the control/mind-wandering condition, the participants weren't very generous: they shared only €23. But in the meditation condition, this amount nearly doubled, with those who had focused on their breathing sending over €40. Meditation dramatically increased generosity.

Meditation not only makes us more generous, but it also helps us make better decisions, handle negative feedback less reactively, and even makes us less likely to retaliate against others. Andy has found that meditation produces all these inspiring effects because it reduces the emotional roots of infuriation: anger, anxiety, and insecurity.

Reflecting on our values, recalling experiences with power, and focusing on our breath keep us calm and focused so we can see the bigger picture, be more courageous, and act more generously. Feeling calm and secure moves us from the infuriating to the inspiring end of the continuum.

Mediation is a type of practice. It turns out that practice more broadly is the real key to staying on the inspiring path, even in a life-or-death crisis.

CHAPTER 7

Inspiring Practice

WHEN ANTOINETTE TUFF looked up from her conversation, she noticed a man dressed in all black. At first, she didn't pay him much attention. But then he demanded her attention—"This is not a joke. This is for real"—and fired a bullet from his AK-47 assault rifle right in front of her. "I knew then that it was for real and that I could lose my life."

Antoinette immediately dialed 911 from her desk in the front office of the Ronald E. McNair Discovery Learning Academy elementary school. But her call was quickly interrupted by more shooting. The man was firing bullets at the police officers outside. And the police were firing right back.

Her first instinct was to run. She told the 911 dispatcher, "Yeah, I gotta go." But she didn't run. Instead, she turned to the gunman and spontaneously stated to the man that the dispatcher was "getting the police now to tell them to back off for you, okay?"

Over the next twelve minutes, Antoinette would serve as a calm conduit between the trembling kids inside the school and the armed cavalry outside of it. Through her words and actions, she inspired the mysterious gunman to give himself up before causing any injuries or harm.

ANTOINETTE TUFF: OK, he said to tell them to back off . . . He doesn't want the kids, he wants the police. And what else, sir? He said, he don't care if he die, he don't have nothing to live for. And he said he's not mentally stable.

911 DISPATCHER: OK. OK. Ask him, is he willing to give his name?

ANTOINETTE TUFF: He said no, he knows that if he gives his name, he's going away for a long time. . . . He's on probation. Tell them to stand down now. Tell them to stand down now he said.

911 DISPATCHER: OK. Tell him I'm going to give them the instructions.

ANTOINETTE TUFF: He said that he should just shoot himself.

Immediately, Antoinette began to *reassure* the man, shifting him away from his panicked state.

ANTOINETTE TUFF: You want me to tell her to let her come, sir? She sounds like she loves you a lot. [Referring to the man's relative who ANTOINETTE has on the phone]

911 DISPATCHER: You're on the phone with a relative?

ANTOINETTE TUFF: Yes. . . . He said he should have just went to the mental hospital instead of doing this because he's not on his medication. . . . I can help you. . . . Want me to talk to them and try—OK. Well, let me talk to them and let's see if we can work it out so that you don't have to go away with them for a long time. No, it does matter! I can let them know you are not trying to harm me or do anything with me if you want to. . . . but that doesn't make any difference. You didn't hit anybody.

In the next sentence, she offered to be his courageous protector. She also shared her own vulnerabilities. Notice how she changed the nature of their relationship by calling him "baby" instead of "sir."

ANTOINETTE TUFF: If I walk out there with him . . . they won't shoot him or anything like that. He wants to give himself up. Is that OK? They won't shoot him? . . . And he said he just want to go to the hospital.

911 DISPATCHER: Just hold on one moment. OK?

ANTOINETTE TUFF: OK. She said hold on . . . and she's gonna talk to the police officer and I'll go out there with you. . . . Well, don't feel bad, baby. My husband just left me after 33 years. . . . yes, you do, I mean I'm sitting here with you and talking—just talking to you about it. I got a son that's multiple disabled. Can I speak to her [the operator]? . . . Let me talk to her, let her know that I'm going to go with you. You want me to talk to her? No, you didn't, baby. It's all going to be well. And they just going to talk to the police.

Antoinette then amplified his voice, sharing with the community the remorse he felt for causing this traumatic situation.

911 DISPATCHER: . . . don't hang up the phone.

ANTOINETTE TUFF: OK. He wants me to go over to the intercom . . . So can you talk to the police and let them know that I'm going to walk out there with him and he wants to give himself up? . . . and you let me know what we need to do? He wants me to go on the intercom and let everybody know that he's sorry, OK?

911 DISPATCHER: OK.

Instead of bringing him outside, she created a calmer and less volatile situation by having him lie down and wait for the police to come inside to get him.

ANTOINETTE TUFF: OK. . . . he wants to know what you want him to do with the gun.

911 DISPATCHER: OK.

ANTOINETTE TUFF: Or you want to send a police officer in? He said, he'll be on the ground with his hands behind his back and I'll take the gun from him and put it over here on the other side by me.

ANTOINETTE TUFF: [Put] all that over here . . . so that way they won't see it. OK? Come over here and put it over here . . . Put it all up there, okay?

As he got ready to surrender, Antoinette didn't rush him; she let him take his time. During this time, she never stopped encouraging him, empathizing with him, and challenging him. She even offered her love. And she created an inspiring *vision* for him, leading him to view his surrender as a form of heroism.

911 DISPATCHER: He's put the weapons down?

ANTOINETTE TUFF: Yes. So hold on before you come. He's putting everything down. . . . So let him get everything to-gether. . . . OK. He wants to drink his bottle of water so let him drink it. Let him get it together.

ANTOINETTE TUFF: OK. We not gonna hate you, baby. It's a good thing that you're giving up. So we're not going to hate you.

911 DISPATCHER: Ma'am, you're doing a great job.

ANTOINETTE TUFF: He said he don't have no more weapons. . . . OK, he's on the ground now with his hands behind his back. Tell the officers don't come in with any gun—don't come on shooting or anything, so they can come on in and I'll buzz them in.

ANTOINETTE TUFF: Just sit right there, I'm going to buzz them in, OK, so you know when they coming. OK? . . . I'm going to sit right here so they'll see that you trying not to harm me. OK? OK. It's going to be all right, sweetie. I just want you to know that I love you, OK? And I'm proud of you. That's a good thing that you're just giving up and don't worry about it. We all go through something in life. No, you don't want that. No, you don't want that. You going to be OK. . . . I thought the same thing, you know, I tried to commit suicide last year after my husband left me? But look at me now. I'm still working and everything is OK.

Finally, the man was ready to end the standoff, and even share his name:

ANTOINETTE TUFF: Your name is Michael what? Michael Hill? . . . Oh, OK. So you came with the kids that play the drums for in the harbor? . . . Oh, so you was actually in there doing all of that with them? Oh, how awesome. . . . So that means I seen you before then. Oh, OK. You all play them drums and stuff real good. OK. He said that they can come on in now. He needs to go to the hospital. . . . He said, do you want him to go out there with his hands up or you want him to—

911 DISPATCHER: Stay right where he is.

ANTOINETTE TUFF: . . . You said Michael Hill, right? Guess what, Michael, my last name is Hill, too. You know, my mom was a Hill. . . . Tell them to come on. OK. He just got his phone. That's all he's got is his phone.

As Michael Hill was taken into custody, and all eight hundred elementary students and one hundred staff members were safe and uninjured, Antoinette concluded her fateful 911 call with a sigh of relief: "Let me tell you something, babe. I've never been so scared in all the days of my life. Oh, Jesus."

———

"IF YOU WANT to go deeper into the cave, you will need to dive to get there," Ekapol Chanthawong, the twenty-five-year-old soccer coach, told the twelve teenagers on the Wild Boars soccer team. But for now, he said, it was time to head home for their teammate's birthday celebration; perhaps they could go deeper into the six-mile Tham Luang caves tomorrow.

But Coach Ek soon realized they were already in too deep and too far. The sunny skies that had followed them into the cave earlier had transformed into a sudden storm so torrential that water began surging toward them.

With the water rising, Coach Ek had to act quickly. He tied a rope around himself while giving the other end to the boys and dove into the churning water to look for an exit. "If I pull twice, that means that I saw the exit," he said. "But if I don't pull two times, then pull me back." When Coach Ek didn't pull the rope, the boys started to panic and quickly pulled him back to the ledge. It was a good thing they did— the water's current was so strong that Coach Ek had been knocked into the surrounding rock and was on the brink of passing out.

As even more water began to charge toward them, the team had no choice but to seek shelter deeper into the cave. They found a relatively dry place for the night, but the next morning "the water was still there when we woke up. I turned around and the water was next to us. It was so quick, it was chasing us and chasing us." Coach Ek suggested they look even deeper for an exit. But eventually, they "reached a point where it was the farthest we could go. We couldn't find an escape, there was only darkness."

On day five in the cave, they heard what they thought was a sign of hope: a helicopter. Instead, Coach Ek realized that it was "a dark shadow coming towards us. Like a tidal wave. Once I saw it, I told everyone to run to higher ground." They escaped into chamber nine, one of the highest points in the cave. They were now surrounded by water on all sides.

How on earth did the boys survive for ten whole days trapped with no food, no water, and no way to call for help?

Coach Ek *inspired* them to survive.

It began with his *vision*. Coach Ek never used the word *trapped* or *stuck*; he knew those words would only amplify their panic. Instead, he consciously framed their time in the cave as temporary: "I told the boys that we just had to wait for a bit longer, then the water may go down and we could get out." He framed this temporary adversity as a good story to tell their families.

Coach Ek understood the importance of hope. "I had to stay positive, so that they wouldn't give up." He continually expressed *optimism* that they would escape. He frequently reassured them that he had a plan to keep them safe and to get them out. As one boy mentioned, "Coach Ek always said there was a way out. So, we worked on finding a way out every single day." He emphatically declared that no one was dying in the cave.

Coach Ek set one of the boys' alarms to 6:00 every morning because he understood what astronauts have long known: without a strict structure during isolation, people lose a sense of time, and very quickly the moorings of everyday reality. "If we hadn't known the time, it would have been more stressful. We would have spent the day without a plan."

To counteract the tensions fueled by fear and scarcity, Coach Ek emphasized their *shared goal*. Without a common purpose, their community would descend into conflict. "If there was nothing for the kids to do, they would start imagining the worst. And then the group would start to break apart for sure." Coach Ek also countered conflict with an emphasis on connection: "I would tell them no matter what happens we must never fight, we must always help each other out."

When the team found itself stuck on that ledge in chamber nine on day five, Coach Ek gave them a specific goal: to dig their way out through the ceiling. "The only thing left to do was climb up and dig our way out . . . Morning to evening, we would work on [digging] a way out." He knew that the collective digging would not only give them a sense of purpose but would make them feel like they were working as a team. One of the boys described it as "[Teamwork], like when we played football. You can't play football by yourself, right?" Another boy noted, "We were a team, we would win or lose together."

His optimism extended to their digging progress. "The kids would ask me how much farther I thought it was. So, I said five meters." As one boy noted of Coach Ek's pronouncements of progress, "Everyone believed it. All of us." Like Tammie Jo Shults, his optimistic conviction replaced panic with possibility.

Coach Ek painted a mental oasis of an orange field on the other side of the mud ceiling. The boys found comfort in imagining whether the owner of the orange field would scold them for eating the oranges. They pictured a store right outside the field where they could finally eat a meal, before hopping on their bikes and heading home. As one boy noted, "We had thoroughly planned it out."

Coach Ek was also a consistent *exemplar*. He understood the importance of being a calm and courageous protector. "I needed to do whatever I could to protect them, to make sure they're okay . . . I was a mess on the inside. It got to be too much while I was digging, so I would cry [but] secretly. I didn't want them to feel my weakness." Seeing his weakness and anxiety would have only amplified their panic. He appreciated that in this situation, his strength was their strength.

Coach Ek dug harder than anyone, to the point that "his hands were shredded [from the digging]." And his sacrifice for the boys wasn't new. "After playing, he always let all of us drink water first, and he'd drink last." Another noted, "Coach Ek always thinks of others before himself."

To help them truly believe that they could go longer without food than they ever thought possible, he recounted how, as a monk, he only ate one meal a day for nine years. This new framing on food and survival helped the boys accept their ever-present hunger.

Coach Ek was creative. Knowing that they couldn't drink the contaminated water from the muddy pools surrounding them, he looked for an alternative. He realized that they could drink the water dripping from the cave's stalactites since it was being filtered through the mountain's stones. This simple insight helped the boys find the necessary hydration to survive.

Finally, Coach Ek was an immeasurable *mentor*, encouraging and supporting the team every step of the way.

He helped the boys regulate their emotions. To lift their mood, he would sing with the team. But he also acknowledged and empathized with the pathos they were all feeling and understood the need to express it, telling his team, "Whoever wants to cry, cry. Let it all out."

He was always looking out for the weakest members of the team. When the youngest member of the group, Mark, wasn't feeling well, Coach Ek encouraged him, saying that he knew how tough he was despite his size. At the same time, he supported Mark by having one of the older boys give him his extra shirt for warmth.

To keep the boys calm, Coach Ek drew on his own training as a Buddhist monk. When he was six years old, his brother died. His mother couldn't recover from her grief and passed away shortly after. It wasn't long before his father got sick and left him as an orphan. Selflessness was imposed on him by a new reality: "I was ordained as a Buddhist novice so that I wouldn't burden my relatives."

Coach Ek understood he needed to mentally fortify the boys. "Being ordained as a Buddhist [for 10 years] helped strengthen my mind and body . . . if we get depressed our bodies will fall apart too. But if we are mentally strong, our bodies will restore themselves."

In the cave, he invited the boys to meditate with him and explained that when he got upset, he would meditate to calm his mind and overcome fear. "He wanted us to remain calm, so we didn't lose our heads," one boy noted. Importantly, Coach Ek also made sure his meditation was inclusive of every member of the team. One boy, Adul, worried that his Christian faith would prevent him from joining his teammates, but Coach Ek reassured him that he didn't need to be Buddhist to participate. He led them through meditation with these words.

Close your eyes

Focus on the tip of [your] nose

Inhale "Lord"

Exhale "Buddha"

Coach Ek knew that the meditation would not only calm and comfort the boys, but it would also help them conserve their energy. Even more importantly, it allowed the team to use the cave's rapidly diminishing oxygen more efficiently. Even when the cave's oxygen fell to 15 percent, which is below the level for sustaining life, the boys survived in the cave for three more days.

Despite the gravity of the situation, Coach Ek encouraged the boys to joke around, knowing it would help lift their spirits. When one boy asked what the others would do if a naked woman appeared, another boy joked, "I'd make her freaking dig."

As they headed into day ten, the batteries of the flashlights were finally running out. Coach Ek told the boys to turn off the flashlights and just be with one another. In that darkness, he heard something. The sound of air bubbles that seemed to float into a single word: "Hello."

The entire team raced down from the ledge, panicked that they might miss their opportunity for escape. As they nearly stumbled into the water, a headlight rose to the surface. A diver called out, "How many of you?" After five days of brutal diving, a pair of British cave divers had finally found the Wild Boars soccer team.

The divers were amazed that the boys were alive. But they were even more surprised by their demeanor. "I was slightly horrified how thin they looked . . . But it's incredible to me still that there was not one trembling lip, not a tear, not any sign of any concern."

As a global army of people struggled with a plan to safely extract the team from the cave, the divers were able to carry messages from each team member to their parents. Coach Ek sent this note to the boys' parents: "Dear all parents, we are fine. The rescue team is taking care of us very well. I promise that I will take best care of the boys. Thanks for all your support and I apologize to all parents."

After the daring effort of a team of international cave divers (which we will explore in Chapter 12: Inspiring Diversity and Inclusion), and eighteen unimaginable days trapped in the Tham Luang caves, all twelve members of the Wild Boars soccer team, and their coach, left the cave alive.

THE INSPIRING POWER OF PRACTICE

ANTOINETTE TUFF AND Coach Ek were each thrust into life-or-death situations. Despite facing unexpected and unprecedented events, they were both prepared to handle the unimaginable challenges before them. As a result, their adept handling of these high-stakes crises wasn't surprising but predictable.

Antoinette quickly became a media sensation and even received a laudatory call from then-President Barack Obama. Everyone kept asking her the same VEM questions: How were you able to stay so focused on peacefully ending the standoff? How were you able to remain so calm and courageous, so authentic and vulnerable? How were you able to be so caring, so supportive, and so encouraging? Her answer: practice.

> I owe that all to my pastor. He has actually trained us. We have had classes and he sits down and teach us how to deal with people and how to deal in desperate situations and how to pray. And we practice that at church. So, really, in all reality, all I was doing was carrying out what I'm taught every Sunday and Wednesday.

Because of her practice dealing with high-stakes scenarios, Tuff was able to take a step back and see the larger landscape. She understood Michael Hill was desperate and that her words were going to be the difference between life and death—for her, for him, for everyone in the school.

Cause remember now, he had already shot a bullet right there in front of my face, in the office, and it ricocheted. I'm sitting there literally watch him unfold mentally. You know, spraying bullets everywhere, loading up the magazines, you know loading bullets in his pockets everywhere. I'm actually seeing him self-destruct right there. So, I knew that the power of my words had to be powerful.

Coach Ek kept twelve teenagers, and himself, alive for ten days with no food, no warmth, and no means of escape. Here, again, we see the vital role of practice in helping him inspire those around him.

Coach Ek's training as a Buddhist monk had equipped him with the skills of self-regulation and mental fortitude necessary to handle extreme deprivation. His training allowed him to not only be an exemplar of discipline, but also to guide the boys to handle their shared adversity more effectively. As their coach, he had always put the boys' needs above his own. The simple habit of letting them drink first carried over to the cave. His spiritual offerings in the cave were both authentic and already embedded in his interactions with his team. For example, he noted, "It's standard when these boys are staying at my house. Before bed, I invite them to pray. This gives us good sleep and stops us thinking about other things."

Antoinette Tuff and Coach Ek had prepared themselves to be inspiring. Teams can also prepare to effectively face an unexpected crisis.

INSPIRING SIMULATIONS

ON MAY 2, 2011, a military helicopter settled into a hover above a courtyard so its passengers could fast rope down into the compound below. But the walls surrounding the compound created so much air pressure that the pilot lost control of the aircraft. A Black Hawk carrying twelve Navy SEALs was going down. Their mission—to capture Osama bin Laden—was suddenly in jeopardy.

On the northeast end of the compound, there was another hovering Black Hawk. Unsure of whether their fellow soldiers were engaging enemy fire or simply experiencing mechanical failure, they called an audible and landed outside of the compound.

President Barack Obama and his team of advisors waited in the Situation Room with bated breath for any communication. One official described those tense moments of silence as particularly excruciating: "Eternity is defined as the time between when you see something go awry and that first voice report."

Suddenly, the radio crackled. A voice emerged. It calmly stated that they were proceeding with the raid. Eighteen minutes after the first voice came over the radio, another voice declared, "For God and country—Geronimo, Geronimo, Geronimo. Geronimo E.K.I.A. [enemy killed in action]."

How did SEAL Team Six respond so calmly, recover so quickly, and complete their mission so effectively despite this unforeseen crisis?

Practice and experience.

This team of special forces had conducted so many operations in and around Afghanistan that almost nothing fazed them. As one Defense official noted, "This was one of almost two thousand missions that have been conducted over the last couple of years, night after night . . . [it was akin to] mowing the lawn. . . . Most of the missions take off and go left. This one took off and went right."

SEAL Team Six had also practiced this specific mission again and again. First, they built a replica of Osama bin Laden's suspected compound* in North Carolina, where they spent five days going through the mission day and night. They then flew to the Nevada desert for another week of rehearsals, complete with an elevated replica that approximated

---

* There was one critical distinction between the replica compound and the actual compound in Pakistan. In North Carolina, they used chain-link fencing to approximate the compound walls. But this fencing allowed the air from the hovering helicopters to move freely. In contrast, the thick walls in the actual compound trapped the air and created the aerodynamic problem that led the helicopter to crash.

the geographical location of the compound. Because they would be arriving under the cover of darkness, they practiced the helicopter ride and the fast-rope descent every night. One of the team members had never fast-roped down before, but he quickly mastered the process with continued practice. After two weeks of relentless simulations, they were ready to go.

But they weren't done practicing and simulating the mission. During the ninety-minute helicopter flight from Afghanistan to the compound, the members of SEAL Team Six sat silently, each one rehearsing the operation, from bow to stern, in their heads.

The deep and broad experiences of the special forces combined with their mission-specific training and repeated simulations prepared SEAL Team Six to redirect the mission when it went right instead of left.

INSPIRING REFLECTIONS

ANTOINETTE TUFF. COACH Ek. SEAL Team Six. Regardless of their specific crisis, their heroics were all steeped in the same principle: We can prepare ourselves, through experience and practice, to be inspiring.

Bill Simmons, the popular sports analyst and CEO of *The Ringer*, talks about the power of experience, or what he calls reps:

> Get enough reps with anything in life, and you're more likely to succeed. Trying not to sound nervous when I started to do TV and radio a few years ago, I'd [battle] a rush of adrenaline right before my segment started. I've learned to channel that energy now—I can speak in front of large crowds and everything. Why? Because I got my reps.

Practice and experience are the two foundations of expertise. But there is an additional element that is equally critical: reflection. Expertise comes from *reflected* experience and *reflected* practice. We develop deeper knowledge and understanding only when we cognitively integrate our experiences.

The military understands the importance of reflection. Not only do they extensively prepare for their missions, but they also build reflection into every mission.

Given the stressful, life-and-death nature of military assignments, these debriefs serve many functions. They allow the team to achieve clarity on the event chronology to ensure a factual understanding of what happened. They help the soldiers process their experiences to prevent stress from lingering and to increase proper adjustment. And these debriefs serve a cohesion and team-building function.

But equally important, they are designed to leverage an understanding of what happened to build more effective missions going forward. These lessons can then be integrated into daily habits and mission-specific preparation. Mission debriefs are a stepping-stone from experience to future practice.

During these debriefs, there is one thing left outside the room: rank. Hierarchy silences voices and the military needs every perspective to ensure a full understanding of the completed mission and to produce deeper learning for future practice. The easiest way to reduce rank differences is to leave their uniforms outside the room and have these discussions in civilian clothing.

I learned the combined power of reps and reflection when I went on the academic job market in 2000. I was beyond excited when I received one of the holy grails of interviews: UC Berkeley. Not only was Berkeley one of my dream schools, but my then-girlfriend had grown up in the area. Like my student Gillian Ku, who we discussed in Inspiring Exemplars (Chapter 4), I had to deliver a ninety-minute research presentation while constantly being bombarded with challenging questions. I answered several questions well. But I sometimes stammered, and I sometimes stumbled. My interview went well, but not perfectly. I came in second. I was crushed.

I couldn't stop ruminating on my interview. I kept rehearsing my answers to those questions in my head, practicing them again and again, making them tighter and tighter.

I ended up at the University of Utah, where I had wonderful and supportive colleagues. But in my first year at Utah, I was asked to give a job talk at Northwestern University and its Kellogg School of Management. This was an even better place for me than Berkeley—I had done my postdoctoral fellowship there and simply loved the research community. But there was some resistance to hiring me because the school had never hired one of their former postdocs before. I needed to hit a home run to have any shot at a job offer.

As I gave my talk, I realized something remarkable. Although I was being challenged with purposively difficult questions, I had already been asked *every* one of those questions before in one of my previous talks, some at Berkeley and some at other places. Although the faculty were throwing me nasty curveballs, my reps and reflections made them seem like softballs.

This example speaks to a scientific insight that I and others have discovered. Regret, when harnessed as reflection, is a stepping-stone to future practice and preparation. When we focus on what might have been, which are called *counterfactual thoughts*, it can look like dysfunctional rumination. But if-only thinking is often serving as reflected rehearsals. In Inspiring Visions (Chapter 3), we discussed how counterfactual thoughts help fulfill the fundamental human need for meaning. Although these thoughts are the roots of regret, they are also the foundation of preparation and future practice. My regret and rumination after Berkeley prepared me for the next talk I gave.

After this experience, I began studying some of the practical benefits of regret. Here is one of the scenarios I used in my research:

You are negotiating for a Persian rug and the seller asks you to make the first offer. You put in an offer that you think is not outlandish, but one that also gives you a good deal: $500. The seller immediately says, "Sold, the rug is yours!"

How do you feel? Well, at one level you should feel pretty good, because you didn't have to make a single concession. Given your first offer, you got the single best price you could get. But if you are like the participants in my experiments, many of you would feel *regret*. You might think that your first offer was way too high. I mean, why would the seller accept your first offer unless you made a mistake?

In another experiment, I had participants negotiate over a simulated sale of a house where the buyer made the first offer. But there was a catch—the seller was part of the experiment, and we told our experimental ally what to do. In the negotiation condition, we instructed our ally to make a counteroffer to the buyer's first offer, negotiate back and forth three times, and then accept the third offer they received. In the other condition, we told the experimental ally to immediately accept the buyer's first offer. Because the buyers in the immediate-accept condition did not make any concessions, they got objectively superior outcomes. These negotiators paid only $310k for the house. In contrast, in the negotiation condition, they paid $345k. By having their first offers immediately accepted, these negotiators saved nearly $35,000! But despite these superior outcomes, they left the bargaining table deeply unsatisfied.

After the negotiation was over, we asked our negotiators to reflect on their experience and share their thoughts. The buyers in the negotiation condition talked about how happy they were with their new home. In contrast, the buyers in the immediate-accept condition frequently mentioned the word *regret*. But here's what was really interesting. Embedded in their regretful ruminations were insights about what they could have done differently, and what they would do better next time. They were weaving their ruminations about the past into commitments for the future.

After reflecting on their house negotiation, our experiment wasn't over. We told our negotiators they were going to get a chance to engage in a second negotiation, this time over a job offer. We gave them as much time as they needed to prepare.

Here's where we see the constructive power of regret. The more a negotiator focused on how they could have done better in their house negotiation, the longer they prepared for their next negotiation! Their regret fueled them to prepare more thoroughly and more deeply. Their ruminating reflections had set them up for future success.

The experiences and practices of Antoinette Tuff, Coach Ek, and SEAL Team Six allowed them to remain calm, even in a crisis. Reflected experience and reflected practice helped turn anxiety into composure. Bill Simmons noted how his prior media experiences helped him learn how to channel his future adrenaline more effectively. My reflected experience at Berkeley helped me remain calmly focused in my next job interview.

Being calm not only helps us make better decisions, but it also matters because of the leader amplification effect. As we have discussed, emotions are generally contagious, but the leader amplification effect makes them truly infectious. Coach Ek understood that his strength was the boys' strength. The calm execution of SEAL Team Six reassured the president of the United States. Composure in times of stress is a key to having an inspiring impact. Being calm also helps us be visionary, to see the bigger picture. By widening our perspective, we can see creative solutions that would have otherwise remained hidden.

Antoinette Tuff and Coach Ek also speak to the value of daily generosity and inspiring habits. Antoinette practiced empathy every Wednesday and Sunday at church. Coach Ek practiced sacrifice with his team daily, and he built meditation into his life as an enduring habit.

INSPIRING COMMITMENTS

MANY OF YOU have probably heard of the legendary actions of Captain Chesley "Sully" Sullenberger, aka the Hero of the Hudson. He was the captain of a US Airways flight that lost both engines two minutes after takeoff. Four minutes after those birds took out his engines, Sully successfully landed his plane on the Hudson River. Sully's heroics were partly possible because he was a certified glider, i.e., someone who can fly an unpowered aircraft. But they were also the result of a conscientious commitment to caring for others that he embodied every day of his life.

> I heard from many of my colleagues . . . they began to tell me of what they had started to call Sully stories, of long-ago events, events that I had forgotten but they hadn't . . . Something I had done, something I had said, some situation we had faced and how I handled it had resonated with them. And sometimes I was simply told about the time we arrived at our destination late one night; there was an elderly passenger who needed a wheelchair, and the person who normally gets those was nowhere to be found. And so I went and got one and brought [the passenger] up into the terminal. My colleagues also told me they weren't very surprised by the outcome on Flight 1549 because of the way they had observed me living my life for years before . . . It turns out that my reputation had been built one interaction, one person, one day at a time.

So, how can we be more inspiring, more of the time? How can we be a Shults, a Tuff, an Ek, or a Sully?

It all starts with *reflection*. Once a month, we need to reflect on when we were inspiring but also when we were infuriating. When didn't I see the big picture or offer a sense of meaning? When was I cowardly or inauthentic? When did I fail to empower or comfort others?

We can also reflect on the inspiring and infuriating leaders that have populated our lives, as I had you do in the Introduction and in Universal Inspiration (Chapter 2). But we can go a step further and think of how we can *emulate* those inspiring leaders and the inspiration they have given us.

Now we can make a *commitment*, even if it's a small one, to a specific behavior we will do this month to be more visionary, a better exemplar, a more supportive mentor.

Finally, we need to set up a *habit* to carry that commitment forward. Remember Joseph Stagliano. He was able to send every one of his 1,200 employees a personalized birthday message—that's almost five emails per workday—by making it part of his daily coffee ritual.

My hope is that each of us can commit to making a daily act of inspiration. The good news is that these don't have to be grand gestures. We can start our inspiring practice with a genuine hello or an "I appreciate you" at the grocery store. When we commit to making small inspiring gestures daily, we become more capable of bigger gestures when the moment calls for them. Just like Tuff, Ek, and Sully.

The path from the infuriating side of the continuum to the inspiring side may seem impossible to traverse. But just remember, transformation seems impossible the day before but inevitable the day after. Through reflections, commitments, and practice, we can sow the seeds of a more inspiring tomorrow.

Practice and habits aren't the only way to put us on the inspiring end of the continuum. We can also design our worlds to increase the probability of inspiring rather than infuriating others. Let's learn how we can be inspiring architects.

PART II

Designing Inspiration

CHAPTER 8

Inspiring Architects

E VERY CASINO HAS one goal: to get you gambling . . . and to keep you
gambling. Casinos care less about the size of the bets and more about
the frequency of betting. Remember, if you play long enough, the house
always wins. Frequent bets are their currency, and "always be gambling"
is their mantra.

Let's take a walk through a casino and see if we can spot the many
ways the space is meticulously designed to keep you gambling.

As you enter the casino floor, you notice something is missing: there
are no clocks and no windows.

As you approach a blackjack table, you almost run into a waitress carrying a tray of drinks. She asks if you want a free drink. "Yes, please!" You
ask for a cocktail because these are way more expensive than regular drinks.

You're already starting to feel a buzz when suddenly, you're dis-
tracted by pulsating sounds and disco lights—someone just won big at a
slot machine near you. You then hear a loud roar from the roulette table.
When you turn back around, the people at the blackjack table are high-
fiving after the dealer busted. People are winning all around you. You
think, *I could be next!*

Those club-like lights and sounds seem to have given you a small jolt of energy. It's then that you notice how cold the temperature is in the casino. You're shivering, but awake.

At the blackjack table, you observe something surprising: the person sitting next to you has a lit cigarette in her mouth. You wonder if that's why people say casinos pump in oxygen—to clear the smoke.

You're finally feeling ready to try your luck, so you put $100 on the table and get back ten $10 chips. The chips feel a little like Monopoly money in your hand.

After a couple of hours of ups, but many downs, you're out of chips. You text your friend and joke that you didn't lose $100; instead, you just paid $25 a drink. Sure, those are expensive drinks but not the most you've ever spent on a cocktail.

When you open your wallet, you realize you're also out of cash. But that's okay because there are ATMs everywhere you look. You decide to take out another $200, and joke to yourself about getting eight more drinks. Thinking about those drinks has you running for the bathroom. But you need to run pretty far as the bathrooms are even deeper inside the casino.

After getting lost, you finally find your way back to the blackjack table. After a few more hands, you start feeling bored. The good news is that there are lots of other games to play. Since you're also feeling a little isolated, you decide to play craps, where almost everyone is on the same team, cheering the wins and commiserating the losses together.

You go to text your friend for advice on craps strategy but notice your phone is dead. You realize you have no idea what time it is or how long you've been gambling.

After a lively time at the craps table, you decide to cut your losses and cash out your remaining $60 in chips. But you can't find anyplace to do so. A waitress tells you the cashier is on the other side of the casino, the farthest point from the exit. While navigating the casino's maze, you start getting tempted by a new game you've never seen before, but you forge on. When you finally reach the cashier, you see a shockingly long line. You decide to try your hand at the new game until the line thins out.

When you finally reach the cashier, you're down to $20 in chips—

you've lost $280 on the night. When you ask the cashier for the time, you're shocked that it's past midnight; you've been in the casino for almost ten hours! It's time for bed, but to find your hotel room, you must first escape the casino floor. That's easier said than done because everywhere you turn, you find yourself right back in the middle, surrounded by more games. Miraculously, you finally escape and head to your room for some much-needed sleep.

OPENING AND CLOSING PSYCHOLOGICAL CHANNELS

CASINOS ARE ARCHITECTS of gambling. Every design decision they make is intended with one goal in mind: to keep you gambling. To do so, they open psychological channels that lead to more gambling, and close off any channel that might guide you away from the casino floor and more gambling.

Let's begin with the psychological channels that casinos *close off*. If you notice the time, you might stop gambling, so they remove all clocks and windows. Without these temporal markers, you feel suspended in time. It could be three o'clock in the afternoon, or three o'clock in the morning. You could have been on the casino floor for two hours, or for ten. Without an awareness of time, you keep gambling.

When you get bored, you stop gambling. Not a problem; casinos have a wide variety of games to keep you entertained, and they are constantly introducing new ones. They also have games, like craps, that make you feel like you are part of a community.

If you need to go outside to smoke, you aren't gambling. So, unlike most buildings in the world, you can smoke inside a casino, and keep on gambling. If you had to leave the casino floor to get more cash, you might stop gambling, so numerous ATMs offer a quick solution. And when you get thirsty, you don't even need to move a muscle—they bring drinks directly to you!

When you're sleeping, you aren't gambling. So casinos flood the floor with bright lights, flashing sounds, and cold temperatures, all designed to keep you awake. Although the idea that casinos pump in extra oxygen is most likely a myth, they are constantly recirculating the air to refresh it and keep your eyes wide open.

Casinos also *open* channels to make gambling psychologically easier. The drinks are free, which helps you rationalize putting more chips down on the table. And these drinks often have alcohol in them; as many of us know all too well, alcohol can lead to risky decisions. Free alcoholic drinks are designed to loosen you up, release your inhibitions, and silence that pesky conscience telling you to be careful.

The constant barrage of lights and sounds lets you know everyone's winning all around you, and you could be next! In fact, slot machines were originally designed with metal trays to intensify the sound of the coins rushing out. Now these machines are housed with "celebration toppers" armed with sparklers that emit lights and sounds.

The currency of casinos also helps grease the gambling lever: you don't bet with money but with chips. By using a type of foreign currency, casinos distance you from the underlying value and reduce the psychological weight of each bet. Because it feels a bit like play money, it's emotionally easier to put a $10 chip than a $10 bill on the table.

Even the physical architecture keeps you gambling. The casino floor is like a maze that traps you inside. The restrooms and the cashier are far away from the exit, forcing you to pass by other tempting options, both before and after you relieve yourself or cash out your chips.

And let's not forget that the hotel rooms are relatively cheap. Not to mention there are often world-class shows, concerts, and sporting events directly in the hotels. There is a reason to come, and a reason to stay. You're never far from the casino floor.

Our tour of the casino floor reveals how each of their design choices is intended to hermetically seal you into a self-contained universe of continuous gambling. Casinos may seem like a unique space, but they represent a much larger principle. Small design decisions can have large behavioral and psychological impacts. Let's see how we can design more inspiring worlds.

ARCHITECTURAL BLUEPRINTS

LEADERS ARE ARCHITECTS. Just as an architect designs a building to produce specific reactions within people and to facilitate certain interactions between people, leaders design policies and protocols to encourage a particular set of responses and behaviors.

The architectural metaphor also captures the idea that, as leaders, we are influencing and affecting people even when we're not present. Although an architect's job is complete once a building opens, their design decisions influence and shape the inhabitants of the space every day. Similarly, the policies, protocols, and processes we set as leaders influence people daily, encouraging some actions while discouraging others.

The leader-as-architect metaphor is not about physical design. It is about opening and closing off psychological channels that lead to desired behavior. The principle of opening and closing psychological channels is so simple and straightforward that sometimes all it requires is a map.

Consider this experiment conducted at Yale University back in the 1960s. At that time, very few Yale students had gotten the tetanus vaccine. Yale social psychologists used this context to explore the best method for increasing commitment. The first strategy they investigated was fear. In the high-fear condition, students read a pamphlet that contained both intense language (e.g., "convulsions") and graphic photographs (e.g., a tracheotomy wound, patients with urinary catheters or nasal tubes). The fear approach was very successful in scaring people: it made people anxious, tense, and even nauseated. But it was a total failure in motivating people to get the shot: fewer students went to get vaccinated in the fear than the no-fear condition. The fear approach scared people so much it seemed to paralyze them from action.

The other method the researchers examined focused on opening the right psychological channels. This pamphlet presented a map of the campus with the University Health Building clearly circled on it. It also detailed the times when the shots were available. Finally, it asked students to review their weekly schedule to find a convenient time to stop by. Although the pamphlet merely told people where and when to go, while asking for a small psychological commitment, it produced a 100 percent increase over the fear approach! Even though the pamphlet was simple, its impact was massive.

This study was top of mind when I was working with a 2004 presidential campaign in the state of Florida. The campaign's original endgame strategy was to hand out a Campaign Issues flyer at 6:00 a.m. on the day of the election. The flyer listed eight issues and compared the candidates' stances on each issue. But with over five hundred words crammed onto the page, it was completely unreadable!

My colleague Joe Magee of New York University and I suggested scrapping this approach entirely and focusing instead on opening the right psychological channels. We created a Where to Vote flyer. Our flyer was designed to open multiple psychological channels toward voting.

> *Timing*: Instead of dropping the flyers off on the morning of the election, we dropped them off the night before. This timing allowed people to integrate voting into their plans for the next day and let them simulate where and when they would vote before sleeping.
>
> *Vision*: The flyer opened with an inspiring vision: VOTING IS YOUR RIGHT.
>
> *Map*: There was a map of their precinct's location (based on their address).
>
> *Schedule*: A schedule provided the times when the polls would be open.
>
> *Access*: There was a phone number for people to call if they needed a ride.
>
> *Commitment*: The flyer helped them form a voting intention by asking them to indicate when they would let their voice be heard.

We implemented our Where to Vote flyer in a single county in Florida. Because we didn't conduct an experiment—i.e., everyone got the same flyer—we don't know how big a difference it made. But we are confident that the Where to Vote channels approach was more successful than the Campaign Issues approach would have been in increasing voter turnout.

CLOSING OFF THE WRONG CHANNELS

THE FIRST TIME was a tragedy. The second time was a coincidence. The third time was a pattern. Sometimes closing off the wrong channels is the difference between life and death.

After nearly a decade of construction, the Vessel at Hudson Yards in New York City opened to much fanfare in March of 2019. On its website you'll see two statements. The first extols the structure's grandeur:

> The extraordinary centerpiece of Hudson Yards is its spiral staircase, a soaring new landmark. This interactive artwork was imagined by Thomas Heatherwick and Heatherwick Studio as a focal point where people can enjoy new perspectives of the city and one another from different heights, angles and vantage points. Comprised of 154 intricately interconnecting flights of stairs— almost 2,500 individual steps and 80 landings—the vertical climb offers remarkable views of the city, the river and beyond.

The second statement simply says: "Vessel remains temporarily closed. Access to the ground-level base is free and open to the public."

Why was the Vessel closed? Because it was too easy to jump off it. Three people jumped to their deaths in the first year it was open, leading to a four-month closure. Two months after it reopened, a fourteen-year-old boy tragically jumped, and it is now closed indefinitely.

The Vessel was designed to be America's Eiffel Tower. It was created to be a public good, one that was free to the public. Its architect, Thomas Heatherwick, declared that this icon "must be free in the same way that it's free to walk in Central Park or free to walk on the High Line." It turns out it was *too* free.

These tragedies were made more heartbreaking by the fact that they were anticipated in advance. Four years before the Vessel even opened, Audrey Wachs, an urban planner, already foresaw tragedy in its design: "As one climbs up Vessel, the railings stay just above waist height all the way up to the structure's top but when you build high, folks will jump."

The barriers were too short, stopping at around chest height. The developer Stephen Ross and architect Heatherwick resisted increasing the size of the barrier because it would have obstructed the Vessel's key draw, its stunning views.

What changes did they make after the third suicide? Well, they didn't make any *design* changes as they refused to raise the height of the Vessel's barriers. They did, however, make the Vessel less free in one way: they started charging a $10 entrance fee. It was explained that this fee was necessary to cover the cost of tripling security and staff. They also installed National Suicide Prevention Lifeline signs. And they created a buddy system, where no one could enter the Vessel alone.

These solutions didn't work. A fourth suicide followed. If only the developer and designer had heeded the note left by a man who jumped off the Golden Gate Bridge: "Why do you make it so easy?"

Despite what the Vessel architects may have thought, physical barriers are remarkably effective at suicide prevention. Why? Because it turns out that many suicides are impulsive. We may think suicides are well-thought-out events, but interviews with survivors tell a different story. In one study, survivors of suicide attempts were asked, "How much time passed between the time you decided to complete suicide and when you actually attempted suicide?" One in four decided less than five minutes before they acted. Another study found that nearly half of the survivors they surveyed reported that less than ten minutes passed from their first thought to their actual attempt of suicide. It's why a Swiss study found that nets beneath bridges reduced suicide attempts by 77 percent. By making it more difficult to act, barriers decrease the number of people who tragically die by suicide.

The Vessel story heartbreakingly reveals how small changes in design can have profound effects. But it also speaks to the power of perspective-taking, of truly understanding what motivates different people in different contexts. In this case, it is understanding the impulsive nature of suicide attempts. But the principle is a general one: to open the right channels and close off the wrong channels, we need to understand how psychological motivations and physical cues intersect.

"PROFESSOR GALINSKY, CAN I talk to you about your exam format?"

That simple question helped me understand how small design decisions can unwittingly induce unethical behavior. This student wanted to talk about the closed-book take-home exam we used in the Negotiations course. We had created this format so students would be in a comfortable place when we tested them on their negotiation knowledge. But this student absolutely hated this format because she said it put her in an untenable bind where she felt compelled to cheat. What was going on?

Because my class was graded on a curve, all that mattered was how well she did *relative* to her classmates. She told me, "I want to be ethical and not look at my notes. But I am convinced that all my classmates are looking at their notes, putting me at a competitive disadvantage. I feel damned if I do and damned if I don't. I'm either a cheater or a sucker."

I realized that the combination of closed-book take-home exams *and* a grading curve is psychologically entrapping. My exam design had created an infuriating catch-22 between unethical behavior and competitive disadvantage.

I successfully advocated for a new rule where professors could either offer a closed-book *in-class* exam or an open-book *take-home* exam. But they were prohibited from using closed-book take-home exams. By closing off an easily accessible unethical channel, the rule lifted the students out of this infuriating bind.

Now consider the mundane problem of men missing the urinal and peeing on the floor. Amsterdam's Schiphol airport solved this problem by painting a fly right near the drain.* It turns out that giving men a target does a great job of improving their aim. The fly taps into an already existing psychological tendency: the desire to hit a target. Notice how much more effective this approach is than signs exhorting people to not pee on the floor. Or imagine the cost, both materially and psychologically, of punishing people who pee on the floor. This principle can even be applied as parents: it's better to give your toilet-training child a target than to yell at them.

Whether it's vaccinations, vessels, take-home exams, or urinals, psychological channels are often more effective and more efficient than more expensive and draconian alternatives. The key is to think like an architect. Thinking like an architect can even offer a blueprint to a more satisfying marriage.

INSPIRING SPOUSES AND SIBLINGS

MY WIFE, JENN, and I used to bicker every morning when we took our two preschool boys, Asher and Aden, to school. Not surprisingly, it takes Jenn longer to get ready in the morning than me. And she likes to wake up and get work done on the computer while sipping a cup of coffee. I would end up scrambling to get our boys ready for school while she was showering and getting dressed. When the boys and I wanted to leave for school, she often wasn't quite ready. I would be impatient, and she would feel rushed. I felt annoyed and she felt disrespected. Our walk to school would be fraught with tension, and Asher and Aden, feeding off that tension, would be sour and somber. The tension got so challenging that we sought out the help of a couples' counselor.

One morning, after more than a year of bickering, Jenn asked if I could take the boys to school by myself. It was a transformative experience. Jenn was able to have her ideal morning routine without feeling

---

* Schiphol airport later upgraded to a more exciting target: a soccer ball and a goal. When I was flying out of Amsterdam, I was so excited when I scored with my stream that I raised my hands and shouted, "Gooaaaalll!"

rushed. Instead of scrambling to get herself ready, she helped get the boys dressed. Since Jenn always picked them up from school, Asher and Aden seemed overjoyed at getting special time with Daddy. They were playful on the way to school in the delightful ways that five- and six-year-olds can be. We had serendipitously discovered a new morning routine.

By simply redesigning our morning protocol, our enduring conflict disappeared. This simple change was more effective than a year of couples' counseling!

A few weeks later, I discovered a second design change in our school routine that solved a conflict between Asher and Aden. When Jenn and I walked the boys to school together, I would drop off our younger son, Aden, while Jenn would drop off Asher. Now that I was dropping them off together, I would drop Aden off first because his classroom was on the second floor and Asher's classroom was on the third floor. But there was a problem. Aden likes to take his time putting away his things, and he loved having a goodbye ritual where he would run, leap, and spin in my arms. But Asher, like me, hates being late. Each day, he would get so annoyed at Aden for taking so long to say goodbye. He would bellow in anguish, "Hurry up, Aden!" And when we finally left Aden's classroom, Asher would angrily march upstairs.

As we walked to school one day, I suggested that I drop Asher off first and then bring Aden to his classroom on the way back down. This simple design change solved everything. Asher was now getting to his classroom without stress. Before, I would only get a cursory hug as he quickly disappeared into his classroom, but now he lovingly embraced me. And Aden got to take his time and have a long goodbye with no one rushing him. Even Aden's teacher noticed the difference. A few days after the change of drop-off order, she spontaneously mentioned that dropping Asher off first seemed to be a great success.

The school context is an ideal one for thinking about architectural design and psychological channels that set people up for success or failure. I know of a family whose first-grade son was labeled a trouble-maker because he had trouble sitting still. But when his parents moved him to a new school, he suddenly became a model student. What helped him to go from troublemaker to model student? The timing of recess! In his old school, physical activity happened just before lunch, but at his new school, recess was at the beginning of the school day. Simply having recess earlier allowed him to release his energy and settle down for learning.

Many kids, especially boys, have a difficult time sitting still. We can point the finger at them and label them as difficult children with behavioral problems. We can diagnose them as having attention issues and recommend medication to fix the problem. But their physical energy is also instructive. It is telling us they have pent-up energy that needs to be released. So, instead of blaming or medicating them, we can introduce physical activities earlier in the day or make our classroom activities more kinetic.

Thinking like an architect fundamentally changes the way we approach the world. We often focus on the *person*, and what *they* generally do wrong. My wife is impractical. My son is impatient. When we do this, we often find the other person *annoying*! I was getting so frustrated at Asher's impatience that I found myself raising my voice: "Just be patient!" By dropping Aden off first, I was setting Asher up to *fail*. By leaving the house together, my wife and I were setting *each of us* up to fail.

The next time you find someone repeatedly failing or find yourself being repeatedly annoyed at someone, ask yourself a few questions: Is the current situation setting them up to fail, or setting me up to be annoyed? What can I do to set this person up for success?

A simple change in drop-off schedule returned my wife and me into more loving spouses. A simple change in drop-off order allowed my sons to be more supportive brothers. A simple change in recess time turned a troublemaker into a model student. These examples all show how a simple change in a daily task can move people from the infuriating to the inspiring end of the continuum.

Another design decision that has a surprising impact is what to wear. Let's see how our attire matters more than we may realize.

INSPIRING FASHION

NOBEL PRIZE–WINNING AUTHOR Isaac Bashevis Singer once asserted, "What a strange power there is in clothing." Research shows he's right. We have long known, intuitively and scientifically, that the clothes we wear powerfully affect how we are perceived by others. It's why we wear our best suits to impress at a job interview or an alluring outfit to attract a first date.

But Hajo Adam of the University of Bath and I have shown that Singer was even more prescient. The clothes we wear also have a profound effect on how we see ourselves. Hajo and I coined the phrase *enclothed cognition* to capture the idea that the clothes we wear not only affect how others view us, but they also impact our own thoughts and behaviors. The principle of enclothed cognition is simple: when we wear a certain piece of clothing or outfit, we psychologically take on its symbolic properties.

In our seminal study, Hajo and I tested whether what we wear (in this study, a lab coat) affects even something as cognitive as attentional focus. We chose to use a white lab coat to test our enclothed cognition theory for three reasons. First, lab coats are associated with doctors and scientists, and we associate these professions with careful attention. Second, a white lab coat can also be used for other purposes, including protecting our clothes when painting artistically, a task Hajo and I found is associated with creativity and not attentional focus. And finally, it was easy to buy lab coats in bulk!

In two of our conditions, we described the lab coat as a medical doctor's coat. In the seeing-a-doctor's-coat condition, participants simply saw the disposable white lab coat displayed on a table. In the wearing-a-doctor's-coat condition, participants were asked to wear the doctor's lab coat throughout the experiment. We also had a third condition—the wearing-a-painter's-coat condition—in which participants were also asked to wear the same disposable white lab coat, but we described it as an artistic painter's coat. In all three conditions, participants gave us their impressions of the coat.

We next tested our participant's attention to detail. To do so, we used the spot-the-difference task. In this task, there are two nearly identical photos except each pair contains four minor differences. In our experiment, we recorded the number of differences participants found across four sets of photos.

We predicted that only when the coat was described as a doctor's coat *and* our participants were wearing the coat would they spot more differences. They had to be wearing the "doctor's" coat to take on its symbolic properties of careful attention. That's exactly what we found. The wearing-a-doctor's-coat condition spotted 20 percent more differences than the seeing-a-doctor's-coat condition and the wearing-a-painter's-coat condition.

Since our initial experiments, dozens of studies have explored how our clothing designs steer our psychological orientations. When my doctoral student Blaine Horton, Hajo, and I analyzed every study ever conducted on enclothed cognition, including 105 effects involving almost 4,000 participants, we found strong support for our core principle that what we wear influences how we think, feel, and act.

Notice that clothing is particularly powerful because it travels through both interpersonal and self-perception. A series of studies by

Mark Frank and Tom Gilovich of Cornell University demonstrates how both processes can occur at the same time. In their research, they examined whether wearing darker uniforms, especially black ones, would lead people to behave more aggressively *and* be perceived as more aggressive. To test these hypotheses, they analyzed whether the darkness of uniforms predicted penalties in the National Football League and the National Hockey League over a sixteen-year period. They found that teams with black uniforms had higher rates of penalties in both sports. What was particularly fascinating is what happened when the Pittsburgh Penguins and the Vancouver Canucks switched to black uniforms: their penalties immediately increased. But Mark and Tom didn't stop there. They conducted experiments to show that the increased penalties traveled through both social perception (the referees saw the same behavior as more aggressive from players wearing darker versus lighter uniforms) and self-perception (people became more aggressive when wearing black T-shirts versus white T-shirts).

Like a map, a barrier, or a change in schedule, what we wear opens or closes off certain psychological channels. Enclothed cognition explains why wearing a nurse's uniform opens the compassion channel, but wearing a military uniform increases aggression. It explains why Wall Street is known for its strict dress code of expensive suits and even more expensive accessories: investment banks want both careful attention and a competitive status hierarchy based on individual effort. And it explains why Silicon Valley takes a dressed-down approach, symbolically captured by Mark Zuckerberg's infamous hoodie, to open psychological pathways toward new ideas and innovation.

When exploring Inspiring Practice (Chapter 7), we discussed how the military often does mission debriefs in civilian clothing to help lower-ranked personnel feel more comfortable sharing their perspective. At the same time, uniforms prominently displaying rank are essential on the battlefield because a clear hierarchy increases effective coordination. The military is selecting the right attire for the right task: military uniforms for coordination and civilian clothing for idea sharing. Note that the military also uses a *change* in attire to help its members change their typical mindset. It's why even investment bankers often dress down during retreats to encourage outside-the-box thinking.

Sometimes clothes can also open the wrong channels. We saw how black uniforms can produce too much aggressiveness in teams. I have noted a similar effect from outfitting local police officers in military-style uniforms. The symbolic association to the military creates what I have called *enclothed blue aggression*, putting officers on the offensive rather than orienting them toward protecting and serving their community.

The strange power of clothing means attire opens and closes channels even when no one is watching us. During the COVID-19 pandemic, my former student Erica Bailey, now at UC Berkeley, Blaine, and I studied the effect of clothing on remote workers. As COVID turned the work and home worlds upside down, it also turned our wardrobe choices inside out. The decision of what to wear for remote work was and is particularly interesting because the *content* of the work is office-based but the *context* is the home. Some remote workers decided to stay the course and kept wearing power suits. Others went the other direction and never shed their pajamas and sweats. And a few donned the Zoom mullet: suit on top and PJs on the bottom.

To understand how these different clothing choices might affect remote work, we went into people's homes and conducted two multiday experiments. We randomly assigned more than four hundred remote workers, who came from a wide variety of industries, to wear one of three types of attire during their remote workday. Some were told to wear what they would wear to the office, others were asked to wear what they normally wear at home, and a third set of workers were directed to wear work attire on top and home attire on the bottom. At the end of each workday, our remote workers reported how engaged and productive they had been at work. We also asked them about two key psychological variables that we discussed in Inspiring Exemplars (Chapter 4): how authentic they felt and how powerful they felt.

The clear winner from our experiments was *home attire*. It consistently made people feel more authentic. Because these workers felt more like themselves, they were more engaged and productive workers. In contrast, clothing did not consistently affect sense of power. And despite being lauded as the perfect pandemic uniform, the Zoom mullet had no positive effects.

To open the right channels for engagement and productivity, we need to match our clothes to the context. This principle also explains why the Zoom mullet still has its place. When I give an online talk to a professional audience, I personally wear the Zoom mullet. I would feel inauthentic looking too casual for a professional presentation. But as soon as I turn the camera off after the talk, the shirt and jacket now feel inauthentic and get quickly replaced with a T-shirt, an outfit more consistent with the home setting.

Erica, Blaine, and I coined the phrase *enclothed harmony* to describe the psychological experience of fitting in when our clothes appropriately match the context or culture. For example, we may feel just right in a business suit at an important meeting, but we would sweat with awkwardness wearing the same outfit at a yoga class. Local cultures also determine what attire produces a sense of enclothed harmony vs. enclothed dissonance. For example, when I was at Northwestern University, not many faculty wore high-end suits in the classroom, and my teaching uniform was a button-down shirt, sweater, and khakis. But when I moved to Columbia Business School, the norm was to wear an investment-banking-style suit. When I tried to be "authentic" by wearing my Northwestern teaching uniform, I instead felt inauthentic. My casual attire made me feel out of place, and it didn't matter whether anyone judged me harshly for it.

My experiences with different teaching attire in different contexts illustrates a breakthrough idea that Erica had: the feeling of authenticity isn't just about expressing yourself. Feeling like who you are also requires fitting into the current context. It's why she and I have found that status predicts feelings of authenticity more than power. Feeling respected matters more for authenticity than how many resources we control. The key to feeling the most authentic is wearing an outfit that both represents who we are *and* fits the current context. It's why I wear a suit when I'm teaching at Columbia, but I still refuse to wear a tie!

WHEN LESS IS MORE

MY UNDERSTANDING OF architectural designs changed dramatically in 2022, when Columbia Business School moved into a brand-new building. The new building was perfect on almost every dimension, except for one.

In contrast, the design of its prior building, Uris Hall, had few redeemable features. I used to refer to it as a Greyhound terminal. But the worst part was that its cramped spaces limited interaction and discouraged collaboration. The need for collaboration and community was top of mind as architect Charles Renfro began sketching his vision for Columbia's newest building. The goal was for the building's design to naturally lead to serendipitous interactions that can foster a sense of community.

Diversity of space was also at the core of the design. In Uris, the public spaces all looked the same. In the new campus, the spaces reflected the wide range of activities that faculty and students engage in. For example, more cozy spaces near windows were designed to encourage close-knit collaboration, but more open, double-height spaces were created to facilitate dynamic interactions.

Although the public spaces were all similar in Uris, faculty offices weren't; some were much better than others. In contrast, a sense of equity was built into the new building. Every faculty office is the same size, which was designed to prevent competition and reduce resentments. And there are no corner offices, literally and figuratively. Even the dean didn't get one. Instead, the corner spaces are exclusively reserved for collaboration spaces.

But not all the building's design features have been successful in facilitating community. In the decrepit Uris Hall, there were few amenities, but there was one that brought everyone together: a prized espresso machine in the faculty lounge. Although the machine itself was not equipped to handle anything fancy, it was a gravitational force that drew faculty from different floors and in different departments to interact with one another.

In the spectacular new Kravis Hall, every faculty floor has not one but two fancy coffee machines. Amazing coffee is just a few steps away. But that's the problem: no one ever leaves their floor. In our new building, the goal of cross-discipline collaboration has been crushed by local amenities. The lack of interaction across floors created such a crisis that I attended multiple brainstorming sessions on how to get people to leave their floors to interact with one another. Most of the ideas were expensive, from catered lunches to daily bagels. Although the numerous coffee machines were the real culprit, taking them away now would be met with protests. In retrospect, the school should have replicated the only bright spot in Uris, a single place for people to get their high-end caffeine fix.

Google understood the benefits of a centralized amenity when they designed their famous cafeteria. By offering a cornucopia of free food, the cafeteria looks like a simple yet generous perk. It's true that the free food is an amazing benefit, and many people talk about it as a gravitational force that attracts them to Google. But its ultimate purpose isn't just to produce well-being or to motivate people to put in a little more effort. By being the sole source of high-quality food, the cafeteria lures people in and becomes an epicenter of impromptu interactions and spontaneous conversations, the kind that might lead to new ideas and promising innovations. The culinary benefits are a bonus for sure, but the cafeteria was designed to create the type of interactions that seed innovation.

Now imagine if every department at Google had their own mini cafeteria. People would never leave their area and spontaneous collaboration would wither. By forcing people to leave their Google neighborhood and venture into the town square, this design feature opens the right channels that enable interactions between a diverse cross section of the Google universe. As Google and Columbia's new buildings teach us, sometimes offering less leads to more. And the key to understanding why is to think like an architect.

INSPIRING REDESIGNS

INSPIRING LEADERS ARE great architects. But here's the thing: it's a lot easier to remake a policy than it is to remodel a building. For example, it only took a couple of days for my wife and me to revise our morning routine to make our marriage more fulfilling. Like marriages, processes and policies are never perfect. As process architects, we need to build in procedures for changing practices.

When I was chair of the Management Division at Columbia Business School, I instituted the first ever Search and Voting Procedures for faculty hiring. Our detailed plan was designed to decrease conflict by preventing periodic fights over our processes. We spent months designing our system and carefully crafted the precise wording through numerous edits. When we finally ratified the document, I thought it was pretty close to perfect. So did the dean's office: they required every other department to create their own Search and Voting Procedures.

The first time we used our new plan, everything went smoothly, from forming the committee to identifying a set of criteria to creating a short list to picking the interviewees. But after we finished all the interviews, we encountered a situation we hadn't faced in the recent past. None of the prospective faculty members we interviewed had generated sufficient enthusiasm to warrant an offer.

We didn't know what to do next. Unfortunately, our carefully crafted document was silent on what to do following a failed search. It turns out our perfect document wasn't so perfect. And we now faced a situation that the document was created to avoid—conflict. We argued vigorously over whether we could reopen the search and interview more candidates.

Eventually, we decided to take a vote on whether to reopen the search. Given the contentious nature of the discussion, we set a higher threshold of 60 percent. Later that summer, we decided to officially amend our Search and Voting document. We institutionalized that reopening a failed search required a 60 percent vote of the faculty. But we also recognized that our document could not foresee all future circumstances. So we built into our system the ability to change the procedures in any given year due to unforeseen circumstances with a 60 percent threshold for approval.

Here's the key insight. Our detailed processes were designed, in part, to help resolve conflict. Because we couldn't foresee all possible scenarios, an unexpected situation arose that created the potential for conflict. As architects, we can solve this inherent issue by designing processes for changing procedures. Like constitutions, we need to have a system for considering and ratifying amendments. Inspiring architects establish processes in advance to deal with the unforeseen circumstances that may populate our horizons.

Of course, changing procedures, processes, and rules shouldn't be too easy. Indeed, they are often purposely designed to be difficult though not impossible to change. For example, amending the US Constitution requires either a two-thirds majority of both the House of Representatives *and* the Senate *or* ratification by three-fourths of the state legislatures. These are high bars to pass, and they explain why there have been only twenty-seven amendments in the 235-year history of America, and only one in the last 50 years.

THINK LIKE AN ARCHITECT

INSPIRING LEADERS THINK like architects. They understand the power of psychological channels, and how opening and closing off the right channels can move us closer to our goals. Thinking like an architect can even help us turn people problems into design solutions.

We began our architectural journey by going through a casino floor. We saw how casinos design their spaces to increase the frequency of gambling. But their goal of increasing gambling isn't very inspiring. As a result, their architectural designs can be seen as manipulative attacks on the well-being of their customers.

Here's the thing: architectural designs are agnostic to goals. Whether you are being inspiring by working for the greater good or acting more selfishly and nefariously, the same principles apply. You want to open psychological channels that make your hoped-for behaviors more likely to occur and to close off psychological channels to make undesired behaviors less likely to occur.

For casinos, the desired behavior is frequent gambling. For medicine, it's encouraging people to seek treatments that make themselves and everyone else healthier. For political campaigns, it's getting people to vote for your candidate. For organizations, it's promoting innovation and cooperation while reducing conflict. For married couples, it's increasing affection and decreasing bickering.

If you pick infuriating goals, your design decisions will make you an infuriating manipulator. To be an inspiring architect, your designs need to be geared toward inspiring visions.

At the heart of *Inspire* is the simple yet profound idea that you can, with forethought and wisdom, design policies and processes that inspire others to better outcomes. In the chapters that follow, we will apply the VEM Diagram of Inspiring Leaders and our think-like-an-architect framework to help us be better negotiators, wiser decision-makers, fairer resource allocators, and more inclusive leaders.

CHAPTER 9

Inspiring Negotiations

WHAT WOULD YOU do if a person was aiming a gun at you? Or a bomb?

Like most people, you would probably run for cover. Or if you were feeling particularly bold, you might try to overwhelm the person and forcefully seize and disarm the weapon.

Here's a different approach: instead of trying to disarm the *weapon*, try to disarm the *person*. To disarm a weapon, we need to know how it works. The same is true for humans. To disarm a person, we need to know what makes that person tick. And knowing how another person works requires taking their perspective and looking at the world from their vantage point.

So, how do we disarm a person? It requires *listening* to them and *observing* them.

That's what Antoinette Tuff did when Michael Hill stormed into an elementary school and fired shots. By really listening to Michael, she was able to understand the source of his desperation, which allowed her to make a connection through her own vulnerability. By observing him, she was able to identify when he was ready to give himself up. By listening and observing, Antoinette guided Michael to lay down his assault rifle with zero injuries.

Let's see how listening and observing can save people from other high-stakes situations.

LISTENING

AT 4:00 P.M. a man walked into a bank in Watsonville, CA, and declared, "I have a bomb in my backpack. I want $2,000 or I'm blowing the whole bank up."

What would you do?

Most of us would probably take the safest action and hand over the $2,000. But that's not what the bank manager did. She mentally took a step back and really *listened* to what fifty-nine-year-old Mark Smith had to say. When she did, she noticed something interesting about his seemingly straightforward request. Unlike most bank robbers, Mark Smith did not ask for *all* the money in the bank. Instead, he had asked for a very specific amount. And that amount was surprisingly small.

By really *listening* to Mark Smith, she guessed that he needed the money for a specific purpose. So she asked, "Why do you need $2,000?" He explained his best friend was about to be homeless unless he got $2,000 to his landlord by the close of business. The clock was ticking, and he needed the money now.

"Oh, you don't want to rob the bank. You want to take out a loan! Why don't you come to my office and we can fill out the paperwork and get you all set up to help your friend," replied the bank manager.*

While going to get Mark Smith his paperwork, she surreptitiously called the police. At 4:30 p.m., officers arrived and arrested Mark Smith while he was filling out the loan application. He was charged with attempted robbery and making a *false* bomb threat—it turns out Mark Smith had no weapons or bombs concealed in his bag.

---

* This is not a direct quote, but one implied from her actions.

By really listening to Mark Smith, the bank manager gained insight into his needs and was able to propose what looked like a creative solution. (If you're like me, you wish it really was a creative solution and Mark Smith could have gotten the loan he needed to save his friend from eviction.)

Really listening to a person can be key to disarming them. But so can simply observing them.

OBSERVING

WHEN NATHALIE BIRLI woke up, she realized she was no longer on her bike. As she tried to get a sense of her surroundings, her head and body throbbed. She suddenly felt an unbearable wave of panic as she grasped that her limbs were bound. When she realized that she had been kidnapped, she was seized by the terrifying thought of her fourteen-week-old son growing up without his mom.

She had to get out of there. But how?

"I thought, I have to convince him that he can get out of this unscathed, because otherwise he wouldn't have released me," Nathalie said about her attacker. "I had to find a way to convince him to trust me."

Her kidnapper promised great suffering if she didn't follow his commands. At one point, he dragged her into the bathtub and forced her head under the water. Another time, he pressed towels over her face. "[Is] he trying to suffocate me?" she wondered.

Suddenly, Nathalie noticed something, an item that had initially struck her attention when she first regained consciousness. Orchids. They were distinctly elegant, yet so out of place in this den of torture.

"I just threw it out there, that his orchids were so beautiful . . . [I] knew how much care went into keeping the delicate blooms alive and thriving."

That simple comment transformed the man from a ruthless tormentor into a hobby horticulturist. As her kidnapper described his routine of floral care, other details of his life poured out, from lost loves to a troubled childhood.

Nathalie eventually asked the kidnapper to take *her* perspective. "I asked him to please not kill me, because the little guy needs me," she said. "I asked him how that would have been for him to grow up without a mother." She also offered to help him. "I told him I could help him find some friends, because it was obvious to me that's what he was missing most," she said. "Then I suggested we could just make the whole thing out to be an accident and say that a deer jumped in front of me and that he found me and brought me home."

Nathalie's kidnapper eventually tried to repair her bike, the one he had purposely crashed into when he kidnapped her. He then drove her all the way home. Ultimately, police were able to locate and arrest Nathalie's attacker using data from her bike's GPS tracking.

THESE TWO HORRIFIC events—a bank robbery and an abduction—highlight two routes for disarming hostile people and defusing volatile situations: listening and observing.

The bank manager in Watsonville, CA, really listened to Mark Smith. By doing so, she realized that he had a specific and prosocial need for demanding a modest amount of money. By simply asking why he was robbing the bank, she was able to introduce an alternative (albeit illusory) path to getting the money he needed.

Nathalie Birli carefully observed the house of her kidnapper. This attentiveness led Birli to notice the tenderly cared for orchids in this otherwise desolate space. She used the orchids to connect with her kidnapper, gain his trust, and convince him to safely take her home.

In these examples, the individuals needed to see the bigger picture in order to protect themselves from potential harm. That visionary insight, driven by necessity, allowed them to be exemplars, courageously offering creative solutions. And by really listening and observing, they were able to connect with their antagonist and mentor them down a nonviolent path.

Listening and observing don't just work in life-or-death situations. They are equally vital in the more mundane aspects of everyday life.

Consider something as simple as getting someone a birthday gift. The problem is we often focus too much on our own preferences. An episode from the television show *The Simpsons* illustrates this point: Homer is beside himself with excitement as he presents his wife, Marge, with a birthday present. What did he get her? A bowling ball . . . with his name on it. That bowling ball epitomizes egocentric gift-giving.

When I first started dating my wife, I gave her a metaphorical bowling ball for her birthday. Jenn and I had begun dating in January and two months later we took our first trip together to celebrate her birthday in Washington, DC. I love stand-up comedy and one of my favorite stand-up comedians, Demetri Martin, was performing that weekend. But there was a problem: the show was sold-out. After a two-day effort, I finally secured tickets. I thought I had hit the boyfriend jackpot, but while I laughed and laughed, my wife stewed and stewed. Turns out, she doesn't like stand-up comedy. I thought I had given her a great gift, and it was a great gift, just not for her.

I should have done what the bank manager did and directly asked Jenn what she wanted to do for her birthday. But birthday presents are often more meaningful when they are surprises. So, like Nathalie, I could have observed which activities made Jenn light up with enthusiasm.

Listening and observing don't just work in high-stakes confrontations or with birthdays. They also work in negotiations more broadly.

PERSPECTIVE-TAKING INSPIRES OPTIMAL OUTCOMES

NEGOTIATIONS ARE A particularly complex social interaction because they represent a vexing mix of self and other interests. To get the outcome *we* want, we need to find ways to help our counterpart get what *they* want. That's what the bank manager presumably did in offering the loan to the bank robber: to peacefully end the robbery, she was offering another way to get the money he needed to avoid his friend's eviction. And that's what Nathalie did when she offered to help her abductor find friends to soothe the loneliness that washed over him.

So how can we meet our needs while also meeting the needs of our counterpart? How can we create a brighter future where each of us is better off?

A key psychological process for meeting both our own and our counterpart's needs is perspective-taking, which we have already discussed throughout *Inspire*. To be an inspiring negotiator we need to see the world from the other side of the table. For the past quarter century, I have created and implemented interventions designed to increase our capacity to get inside the heads of others.

Here is how I have activated perspective-taking in one of my negotiation experiments:

> In preparing for the negotiation and during the negotiation, take the perspective of the other side. Try to understand what they are thinking, what their interests and purposes are in negotiating. [Try] to visualize yourself on the other side of the table, in that role.

In an experiment involving a job negotiation, Will Maddux of UNC and I found that giving negotiators a dose of perspective helped them secure a better deal for themselves. That's amazing, right? But there was another effect that was equally important. The other side also got a better deal when they negotiated with a perspective-taker. Perspective-taking created more value at the bargaining table; it expanded the pie of resources and made both parties better off. Perspective-taking by one negotiator elevated *both* negotiators.

In another experiment, we used a more complex negotiation context involving the potential sale of a private restaurant to a restaurant company. In this negotiation, a deal seems impossible at first because the seller is demanding more money than the buyer is authorized to pay. However, the seller is only demanding a high price for their restaurant because they need the money to pay for culinary school and they won't sell unless they can cover the tuition. As it turns out, the buyer is interested in more than just buying restaurants; they also need to hire a chef with both managerial and culinary experience to oversee their upscale menu. Thus, the buyer can offer to buy the restaurant at a price they can afford but also offer to hire the seller and fund their culinary school education. Without the negotiators discovering each other's underlying interests, a deal is impossible.

Our perspective-taking intervention dramatically increased the probability of discovering this creative solution. In the control condition, only 39 percent of the negotiations reached a deal; without perspective-taking, most of these negotiators walked away with nothing. But when perspective-taking was activated, 76 percent of the negotiations reached a deal. Perspective-taking increased the probability of a deal by nearly 100 percent!

What's going on here? To reach a deal, the buyer first needs to obtain the information about the seller's interest in culinary school. Perspective-taking helps here because it leads negotiators to be more likely to ask the type of questions that will reveal their counterpart's core interests and needs. Like the bank manger did with Mark Smith, the buyer might ask, "Why are you putting your restaurant on the market?" Or to better understand the price demands, "Can you tell me more about why you are asking for this particular price?"

There was another key finding from this experiment. Not only was the negotiation more likely to reach a creative deal when we gave the buyer a boost of perspective-taking, but their sellers also felt more satisfied with how they were treated.

Across our experiments, perspective-taking negotiators were more inspiring. They were visionary, able to see the big picture. They were exemplars of creativity. And they were mentors, encouraging, empathizing, and elevating their counterparts.

———

WE WERE WEEKS away from what was supposed to be the happiest day of our lives, but my wife and I were barely speaking to each other.

We were planning a one-hundred-person out-of-state wedding all by ourselves, and in less than six weeks. That's a recipe for stress and discord, so it's no surprise that Jenn and I found each other to be a bit infuriating as we snapped at any suggestion the other offered.

But there was something deeper going on than time pressure. When we sat down to talk through the tension, we realized what it was. We had competing visions of what a wedding should look like. Neither Jenn nor I had ever been married, and we each had our own perfect wedding dancing in our heads. Our negotiation over the wedding plans had turned into a distributive battle over our seemingly incompatible visions.

We decided to really listen to each other to understand each other's perspective. I asked Jenn what was one thing that she absolutely had to have, even if I found it to be over-the-top. Inspired by her time in Japan, she wanted to hand out *oshibori* towels, cooled and scented in jasmine to honor her Filipino heritage, in between the ceremony and the reception. So we trekked down to Tribeca, bought 120 towels, and carried them down to North Carolina. She asked what I really wanted. I mentioned that I was excited at the prospect of my twin brother and his/our high school friends as the wedding band; although the group had never played publicly, I loved listening to them whenever they jammed together.

We were now like the restaurant owner and the buyer: sharing and integrating what really mattered to each of us. In the end, perspective-taking helped turn our wedding into the happiest day of my life.

PERSPECTIVE-TAKING INSPIRES CONSTRUCTIVE FEEDBACK

PERSPECTIVE-TAKING IS NOT only valuable in negotiations but also when giving feedback. I came face-to-face with this reality when giving feedback to a recently hired administrator. At a former university, the dean's office was trying to expand the research capacity of the faculty and created a new role to help coordinate the behavioral research being done at the school. Given the focus was on faculty research, the associate dean thought faculty should serve as the person's direct supervisor and asked me and a professor to serve in that role.

The efforts to streamline and coordinate the research being done at the school did not go smoothly; in fact, it was filled with more confusion, conflict, and chaos than coordination. These tensions were understandable given this was a novel endeavor and my colleague and I were new to being in a supervisory role. Within a couple of months, the associate dean realized that it would be more effective if the research coordinator reported directly to the dean's office like other administrative units.

When my colleague and I met with the research coordinator, I was prepared to lay down the law and simply inform him of the impending change to the reporting structure. But my colleague chose a more inspiring path. She first asked the lab director for his perspective on how he thought things were going. He clearly understood and eloquently described the issues. She then asked, "Do you have any thoughts on how we can make the situation better?" After some discussion, you could see an idea begin to percolate in his head, and he offered with some enthusiasm, "I just realized that my peers all report to the dean's office. Maybe the solution is to have my role report directly to the dean's office rather than faculty?" My colleague lowered her head in thought and said, "That is a really intriguing idea, why don't Adam and I talk to the dean and see what she thinks." The lab coordinator's solution was the very one we were already planning to implement. But now it was *his* idea! By asking the lab coordinator to share his perspective, a directive was transformed into a collaborative solution.

By asking questions and really listening, we can get inside the heads of others to understand their interests and needs. But sometimes people simply don't want to answer our questions or let us inside their head. Fortunately, we can design our offers in such a way that we can observe what our counterpart truly wants in a negotiation.

OFFERING CHOICE INSPIRES OPTIMAL OUTCOMES

WHEN THERE IS more than one issue at the bargaining table, I have long taught negotiators to make a package offer, which combines all the issues into a single offer, versus trying to negotiate each issue one at a time. But my colleagues and I recently discovered an even more inspiring strategy: presenting more than one package offer at the same time. When we present two or three package offers *simultaneously*, we are giving our counterpart a choice. Earlier we discussed how offering choice makes us a more inspiring mentor. Offering choice also makes us a more successful negotiator.

Geoffrey Leonardelli of the University of Toronto and I conducted numerous experiments where we simply varied whether a negotiator offered a single package or multiple packages as their opening offer. We called these MESOs—multiple equivalent simultaneous offers. To be a MESO, the multiple packages need to be presented *simultaneously*. But the word *equivalent* is equally important. What do we mean by *equivalent*? It means that each of the packages is of equal value to us; that is, we would be equally happy if the receiver accepted proposal one or proposal two.

Here's the example of buying a car we discussed in Inspiring Mentors (Chapter 5). These proposals are equivalent to the dealer, with each year of warranty worth $500 to them.

> *Proposal 1*: $34,875 with a three-year warranty
> *Proposal 2*: $35,875 with a five-year warranty

Here's another example. You're negotiating a job offer and there are three issues on the table: salary, location, and vacation. You prefer NYC, but you'd need more money because it is so expensive to live there. You would be willing to go to Chicago, but you would want more time to travel. You craft two proposals that are of equal value to you. In Proposal 2, you would accept less money but with more vacation time.

> *Proposal 1*: $235,000 in New York with three weeks of vacation
> *Proposal 2*: $200,000 in Chicago with five weeks of vacation

And here's a third example, and one that I have used in my own life when offering negotiation workshops to clients. I offer one price for the standard workshop or a higher price involving a negotiation exercise customized for the client.

Proposal 1: $X for a workshop involving an off-the-shelf negotiation exercise

Proposal 2: $X + $Y for a workshop involving a negotiation exercise tailored to your company's context

Like these examples, our experiments were simple and straightforward: Geoffrey and I randomly assigned our negotiators to one of two experimental conditions. In the single-offer condition, one negotiator offered either proposal one *or* proposal two (randomly assigned) as their opening suggestion. In the MESO condition, the negotiators offered both proposals one *and* two simultaneously.

Notice that the content of the packages isn't changing, the only aspect we are varying is whether a single package is offered or whether both packages are offered at the same time. Despite their equivalence, we have found that offering MESOs fundamentally transforms negotiation dynamics.

The positive transformation happens right off the bat. By offering a choice among first offers, the counterpart sees the offers as a more sincere attempt at reaching agreement. That means the receiver of MESOs is starting the negotiation with an open mind. In addition, offering MESOs objectively increases the probability that one of the offers will meet the counterpart's needs. Given we already designed our MESOs to meet our needs, that means MESOs contain higher joint value right from the very beginning. Because of these two processes—reduced suspicion and having their needs met—the counterpart responds to the first offer by making a less aggressive counteroffer. When we present MESOs, we secure better outcomes than negotiators offering either one of the offers alone.

Another reason why MESOs help us gain better outcomes is they also give us insight into our counterpart's core interests. By presenting MESOs, we can infer our counterpart's needs by observing their reactions to the offers we made. We can then compose an offer that will meet our own needs and also meet theirs.

Given we get a great outcome by presenting MESOs, the counterpart probably gets the short end of the stick, right? Not true! Our counterpart almost always walks away with a fine deal. In fact, in most of our experiments, counterparts who receive MESOs don't get a worse deal than those receiving a single offer. Remember, MESOs are meeting our needs—that's why we offer them. But they are also more likely to meet the needs of the counterpart. By opening the negotiation with more overall value, final agreements also tend to contain more overall value. And by observing our counterpart's core interest, we can meet their needs in our subsequent offers.

MESOs also change how our counterparts *feel* about us and the negotiation. Because MESOs are seen as a sincere attempt at perspective-taking and reaching an agreement, our counterparts are more likely to trust us when we present MESOs versus a single offer. We even start to reciprocate that trust and feel more trusting ourselves. As a result, presenting MESOs starts a chain reaction that produces a more collaborative and cooperative process. We each leave the table trusting the other side more.

Geoffrey and I found that MESOs are especially helpful in difficult situations at the bargaining table. They are particularly valuable when we need to be ambitious and therefore want to make an aggressive offer. In our studies, MESOs were the most beneficial when our offers were the most assertive.

MESOs also help groups that are more likely to face resistance at the bargaining table. We found that MESOs worked equally well for men *and* women. They were also equally effective for negotiators with lots of bargaining power (they had strong alternative offers) *and* negotiators with little bargaining power (they lacked or had poor outside options).

MESOs help us hit the jackpot at the bargaining table: they allow negotiators to be ambitious and achieve better outcomes, but without hurting or infuriating the other side. There's another technique that also helps us hit the negotiation jackpot even when we are negotiating a single issue. Let's learn how a subtle change in presenting our first offer can make us look inspiring rather than infuriating.

MAKING OFFERS (AND NOT DEMANDS) INSPIRES OPTIMAL OUTCOMES

GREECE WAS FACING a crisis in February 2015. Its financial support from the European Union was expiring, and they were desperately seeking an extension. One week before the funding was set to terminate, Greece made a last-ditch proposal: they requested a loan extension in exchange for meeting certain conditions dictated by the eurozone finance ministers. Within five hours, the EU summarily rejected the offer, declaring that the request "was not a substantial proposal to resolve matters." Four months later, Greece made a "new" proposal, but it was virtually identical to their original offer. This time, however, the EU reacted positively, viewing the proposal as "a basis to really restart the talks." A few weeks later, an agreement was officially announced.

What changed from the first proposal to the second? You might think that key difference was time, that the European Union had softened their position because their perspective had changed in the ensuing months. Or you might think they were now feeling more pressure to get a deal done. But there was another factor besides time and pressure that varied from the first proposal to the second one: how the proposal was framed.

In February, Greece was *requesting* cash; they were asking to get something from the European Union. But asking someone to give up something is painful. Scientists call it concession aversion, and it leads us to hold on tightly to what we have. In contrast, in June, Greece was *offering* reforms. Now the European Union was getting something, and in exchange, all they had to do was transfer a little cash. Even though the offers were nearly identical in substance, framing it around what Greece could offer helped melt away the European Union's resistance.

Johann Majer of Leuphana University and I turned this Greece example into a series of experiments. In our experiments, we simply varied a few words in how negotiators presented their opening proposals. In one condition, we had negotiators make proposals like the Greeks did in February: they made a *request*; for example, in a negotiation involving the sale of stocks, we had negotiators in the request condition open with "I am requesting $___ for ___ stocks." In the other condition, our negotiators did what the Greeks did in June, they made an *offer*: "I am offering ___ stocks for $___."

This change is tiny, right? But it produced dramatically different reactions and radically different outcomes. When a negotiator made a request, their counterpart took umbrage at the demand, and the counteroffers were stingy and skimpy in response. But when negotiators made an offer, the counteroffers were larger and more generous. In the end, offerers got much better outcomes than requesters. In one experiment, sellers who presented an offer earned 100 percent more than sellers presenting a request!

There were two other fascinating findings from our series of experiments. First, when negotiators were instructed to make an offer, they made more ambitious proposals than when negotiators were asked to make a request. Our negotiators intuitively knew making an offer would create less resistance and that gave them confidence to ask for more. Second, negotiators were seen as less demanding and aggressive when making an offer versus a request. Although they were demanding more, they were instead seen as demanding less. Like with MESOs, making offers helps us hit the negotiation jackpot: we get inspiring outcomes without infuriating the other side.

Perspective-taking, MESOs, and presenting offers make us look like good guys. These strategies also *turn* us into good guys. When we present MESOs, we leave the negotiation with higher cooperative intentions. When we take the perspective of our counterpart and more deeply understand their interests, we feel more connected to them. And when we are seen as good guys, we become eligible for the good-guy discount.

WHY GOOD GUYS RECEIVE OPTIMAL OUTCOMES

THERE IS ALMOST nothing more frustrating than waking up to a dead car battery, especially on a freezing morning in Chicago. Fifteen years ago, I face this very situation. The good news was my car was a manual, and so it didn't need to be towed. All I needed was a little push to pick up enough speed so I could pop the gear into second and be on my way to the auto shop.

A few hours after dropping off my car, I got a call with bad news. The mechanics had found the problem, but it wasn't the battery and it wasn't the starter. It was the alternator, which was going to be quite expensive to replace!

An hour later, I got a second call. The mechanic said, "I have two more pieces of bad news." The mechanic explained the concept of a "parasitic draw" and how my battery was getting a one-two punch of no charge and rapid draining. I needed to replace both the alternator and another part, which was going to cost an additional $400. He then said, "The second piece of bad news is now we can't finish the car today. I'm sorry, but it won't be ready until tomorrow."

After I fully grasped the situation and the total cost, I did something I had never done before. I spontaneously said, "So what's the final price with the good-guy discount?" He was confused. "The good-guy what??" I responded, "I thought since I'm a good guy, maybe you could give me a discount." He laughed and said, "I am really sorry, but I can't." I responded, "No worries at all. I totally understand."

Three hours later, he called me back. "I now have two pieces of good news to share. First, we moved your car up in the [queue], and it is ready today. Second, we decided to give you the good-guy discount and aren't charging you for the second part we replaced."

My spontaneous comment became known in the world as "the

good-guy discount." I shared this story with Sonari Glinton, a business reporter at NPR News, and it turned into a full-fledged feature on NPR's *This American Life*. Here are some excerpts from the segment.

IRA GLASS: Okay, here's what intrigued Ben. His friend Sonari told him that he'd come up with this thing. And there's no way to say this without sounding like an infomercial. But Sonari was doing this thing that was saving him lots of money.

SONARI GLINTON: I remembered this thing a guy that I had interviewed had talked about: the good-guy discount.

IRA GLASS: The good-guy discount?

BEN CALHOUN: The good-guy discount. This is the thing. Sonari, he'd interviewed this negotiations expert from [Columbia Business School].* And the guy told him about this technique where you say, can I get a good-guy discount on that? You're a good guy, I'm a good guy—come on, just, you know, a good-guy discount.

SONARI GLINTON: And I go, hey, is there a good-guy discount? And he goes, what? You've seen me here all day. You know I want these shoes. It's tough for me, blah, blah, blah. And he looks at me, and he goes, I'll tell you what, brother [and gives him a discount].

BEN CALHOUN: Yeah. I think it's kind of smarmy . . . I don't know. I find it to be not the behavior of a good guy.

IRA GLASS: I go with Ben as he tries to find out whether or not he has what it takes to get free stuff by claiming to be a good guy, even though he worries that doing that, trying the entire exercise, means that he is not a good guy at all.

---

* In Inspiring Mentors (Chapter 5) and The Vicious Cycle of Infuriation (Chapter 6), we discussed how not receiving credit for one's ideas can be especially infuriating. Notice that neither Sonari nor Ben credited me by name for the good-guy discount concept, only mentioning "this negotiations expert from [Columbia Business School]." It still irks me a little bit.

Ben tried asking for a good-guy discount four times on the show and it *never* worked for him. Yet, it worked for me with the car mechanic. And it worked for Sonari with the shoe salesperson. What's going on?

It didn't work for Ben for all the VEM reasons. First, he never bought into the vision of asking for a good-guy discount. Second, because he didn't buy into the good-guy vision, he presented it inauthentically; he was not a good-guy exemplar. And finally, he introduced it immediately without building any rapport with the salesperson; he wasn't a good-guy mentor.

Notice that Sonari and I already had budding connections with our salespeople before we sprung the request for a discount. Because my good-guy discount request flowed naturally from our back-and-forth, it was both expressed genuinely and received as playful.

Sonari and I came across as good guys because of *when* we introduced the potential discount. And by waiting until we had listened and observed our salespeople, it also changed *how* we made the request. In contrast, by rushing the request and making it awkwardly, Ben didn't come across as a good guy at all.

Ben's experience speaks to a larger issue around influence and persuasion. I always tell people to never use a negotiation or influence technique that makes them uncomfortable. Our discomfort will make us act unauthentically, and our awkwardness will make others feel uncomfortable. As a result, we will come across as an infuriating manipulator, and not a good guy.

DESIGNING OPTIMAL OUTCOMES TODAY AND TOMORROW

INSPIRING NEGOTIATORS THINK like architects. They design their offers to produce better deals today and tomorrow. Presenting MESOs and presenting offers (and not requests) lead our counterparts to walk away more satisfied with the negotiation and their outcomes. They leave the bargaining table having greater trust in us. They see us as good guys.

But here's the thing, these strategies also lead our *counterparts* to become good guys. In most negotiations, the interaction isn't over after a deal is reached. We still need to worry about whether the deal gets implemented smoothly or whether we will face ongoing disputes. This is why it is so important to ensure that our counterparts walk away inspired by the negotiation. When they walk away feeling satisfied and seeing us as good guys, they are more likely to efficiently implement any deal we reach, which lowers our costs both psychologically and economically.

But there's a second benefit to our counterparts walking away satisfied. When they walk away clicking their heels, they will want to negotiate with us again in the future. This matters because, as my research shows, having lots of potential negotiation partners is one of the biggest sources of power at the bargaining table. Alternatives give us options, and options give us leverage. By producing satisfied counterparts, perspective-taking, MESOs, and offers not only help us get great outcomes today, but give us future power. In contrast, Ben's salespeople likely didn't want to deal with him again, which lowered his future negotiation potential.

There's even better news from inspiring our counterparts' satisfaction. We can parlay their satisfaction today for good-guy discounts tomorrow. Let's say we present MESOs in a negotiation and our counterpart walks away feeling like their needs were met. The next time we negotiate with them we can ask for the good-guy discount: "Remember that great deal I gave you last time. Hopefully you can move a little more this time."

Negotiations are often defined as a decision-making process. However most decisions aren't made at the bargaining table but in collaborative teams. Let's learn how to inspire and design wise decisions.

CHAPTER 10

Inspiring Wise Decisions

I N 2008, THE worldwide economy nearly collapsed. Trillions of dollars vanished, billions of jobs disappeared, and millions of people suddenly found themselves homeless. All because one man—Joseph Cassano—silenced the voices of those around him.

Cassano played an outsized role in the global financial crisis because his team was responsible for issuing credit default swaps, which essentially served as insurance policies on mortgage-backed securities. Cassano, as head of AIG's financial-products unit, invested heavily in credit default swaps. It was amazingly profitable . . . until suddenly it wasn't.

When these mortgage-backed securities became virtually worthless, AIG was responsible for covering those losses. Because AIG had issued these credit default swaps with almost no collateral, it didn't have the money to cover its tens of billions in losses. The world economy stood on the brink of complete collapse until the government bailed out AIG to the tune of $182 billion.

Cassano continued to collect $1 million a month in compensation even after AIG was bailed out. But his traders weren't so lucky. Because many of them had been required to defer nearly half their pay for years, they were left holding an empty bag.

Cassano's employees, however, didn't just suffer financially. They also endured years of infuriating abuse. Here's how author Michael Lewis described Cassano's leadership style: "[He had] a real talent for bullying people who doubted him . . . The fear level was so high that when we had these morning meetings you presented what you did not to upset him. And if you were critical of the organization, all hell would break loose . . . The way you dealt with Joe was to start everything by saying, You're right, Joe." The father of one of my students had firsthand experience with Cassano's rageful reactions, telling me that "Joseph Cassano is pretty much the only person that ever made my dad cry. Not once, but like all the time. He put my dad in a pretty dark place."

It's no wonder Cassano's traders didn't share their concerns when fundamental problems with mortgage-backed securities started to emerge. They had learned to keep any info that contradicted Cassano's rosy market predictions to themselves. By silencing the voices of his team, Cassano created a collective disaster that almost detonated the entire worldwide economy.

THE LEADER SILENCING EFFECT

AIG MADE THE wrong decision. They kept investing in credit default swaps long after it was wise to do so. Making wise decisions is complex and multifaceted, but it requires something fundamentally simple: *getting all the information on the table*. To make wise decisions, we need all the relevant data, facts, and figures at our fingertips. When we don't get all the information on the table, like Cassano and AIG failed to do, collective ignorance results and collective disasters follow.

The foundation of wise decisions is simple, but it's hard to get all the information needed to make informed choices. People may actively hide or hoard information, while others may not recognize its relevance. But a key driver of missing information is *fear*. That's exactly why AIG was missing critical information about the declining value of mortgage securities: Cassano instilled fear in all his employees.

The leader amplification effect plays a major role in percolating this fear. The idea that the words and behavior of leaders loom large in the minds of others leads to an insidious variant, what I call the *leader silencing effect*.

The leader silencing effect captures the fact that people feel uncomfortable sharing their honest and unvarnished perspective to those in positions of authority. Power, by its very nature, makes it risky for the less powerful to speak up. This is especially true when the powerful, like Cassano, don't want to listen.

But the leader silencing effect doesn't just create financial disasters. It also produces deadly outcomes too. In research led by my former student Eric Anicich, now at the University of Southern California, we analyzed every expedition that went up the Himalayas over the span of one hundred years; that includes more than five thousand expeditions involving over thirty thousand mountain climbers from fifty-six countries. Furthermore, we were able to gather key details about these expeditions: what route they took, whether they used oxygen, if Sherpas joined the expedition, the types of ropes they had, etc.

When we analyzed the data, we found a fascinating result. When an expedition came from a country that was more hierarchical—like South Korea, France, and Venezuela—it was more likely to have people *die* on the mountain.

Importantly, we established that this harmful effect of hierarchy was a *team* failure by showing that the higher fatality rates of climbers from hierarchical countries occurred only for group expeditions but not for solo expeditions. Only when the expedition was a team that needed to share and integrate the perspectives of its members (to get all the information on the snow-covered mountain) did expeditions from hierarchical countries have a greater probability of fatal disaster.

We speculated that expeditions from hierarchical countries produced more fatalities because climbers from hierarchical cultures were more hesitant to share their concerns with expedition leaders about worsening conditions or impending problems. In hierarchical countries, deferring to authority is a foundational value. Citizens in these countries believe "authority (the right to lead or command) is of supreme importance," and "employees [are] afraid to express disagreement with their managers." Like Joseph Cassano's traders, people with less power in hierarchical cultures learn to keep their mouths shut. By not speaking up, these climbers played it safe. But they also put the team, and their own lives, at risk.

The leader silencing effect creates a wide range of avoidable tragedies. Consider how the King family's lives changed forever on January 30, 2001. While her siblings were watching TV, the youngest child, eighteen-month-old Josie, got bored and decided to head upstairs. Suddenly, the television sound was pierced by traumatic screams of pain. Josie had turned on the hot water in the bathtub and crawled inside, burning almost 60 percent of her body. Her parents rushed her to Johns Hopkins Hospital, widely ranked as one of the best hospitals in the world. But the severity of Josie's burns created difficulty in finding veins for intravenous lines. To give her life-sustaining fluids and nutrients, the hospital inserted what is called a central line into her neck just below the collarbone; this way, the doctors could administer medicine and draw blood without having to find a vein each time.

After a few days of recuperating from skin transplants and grafts, Josie looked like she had turned the corner. As Valentine's Day approached, she was transferred out of intensive care, and Josie's siblings excitedly planned her return home.

But Josie never made it home. As her skin on the outside healed, her insides were in turmoil. A fateful dose of narcotics led Josie's heart to stop. It never started again.

Josie's fate was put on its precipitous course because the central line got infected. This infection created a cascading set of problems that would ultimately overwhelm her system. Tragically, it's not just Josie—nearly eighty thousand patients suffer from intravenous infections each year.

Peter Pronovost, a critical care specialist at Johns Hopkins, thought he had found a way to reduce intravenous infections to zero with a five-step sterilization checklist:

1. Wash your hands with soap or alcohol before the procedure.
2. Clean the insertion site with a chlorhexidine antiseptic solution.
3. Completely cover the patient with sterile sheets, and wear a sterile hat, mask, gown and gloves.
4. Avoid placing the catheter in the groin if possible because it has a higher infection rate.
5. Remove catheters as soon as they are no longer needed.

This five-step checklist had it all: it was scientifically valid while being simple and straightforward. So Pronovost was absolutely stunned when infections persisted. Was his checklist rife with miscalculations? Was he missing a step? Were the steps in the wrong order?

It turns out the checklist was perfect, but the doctors implementing it weren't. Some doctors didn't buy into the checklist, while others made mundane errors—born of fatigue or stress—and accidentally skipped an item.

But the problem went deeper, one embedded in the very structure of the typical hospital. Other people were present when the central line was inserted and could have pointed out that one of the sterilization steps had been skipped. The most likely candidates would have been the nurses. But the immense power difference between nurses and doctors didn't make the nurses feel comfortable challenging the doctors when they made a mistake. Even with the potential for life-and-death consequences, the nurses couldn't find their voice. Their insights were left off the operating table.

Due to the toxic mix of fatigued doctors and fearful nurses, a checklist step was skipped for almost one-third of all patients. Infections persisted. Unnecessary deaths continued.

It doesn't matter whether it's a financial collapse, an expedition fatality, or a hospital error, these tragedies all resulted from the same issue: valuable information and insights were left off the table. Note that the source of the problem was the same across these various disasters: the leader silencing effect. People with less power in the team didn't feel comfortable sharing their perspective. Even when imparting their insights could have saved lives, including their own, the presence of more powerful others silenced their voices.

If we want to make the best decisions, we need to find ways to reduce the leader silencing effect and help the less powerful feel comfortable sharing their perspective. Let's learn how to get all the information on the table.

INSPIRING ENCOURAGEMENT

WHEN SOMEONE WITH less power speaks up and shares their perspective, how do you respond? Do you praise them: "Paula, that's a great point"? Do you express gratitude for them speaking up: "Rashad, thank you so much for sharing your perspective"? Do you build off their idea: "I want to follow up on the great insight that Kentaro had"?

Or do you show disgust or displeasure in your face, like a sneering Simon Cowell? Do you say what Nobel Prize winner Danny Kahneman said to me: "That's not right at all"? Do you go off on an employee in a company-wide meeting like the senior executive of a multinational company did? Or maybe you simply don't respond, and just move the conversation forward as if the person had never said a word.

As a leader, all our gestures—from the encouraging (praise, gratitude, and acknowledgment) to the dismissive (silence, displeasure, and open criticism)—get amplified. It's why the leader amplification effect is the foundation of the leader silencing effect. Whenever someone less powerful speaks up, our reaction will be noticed, and it will either encourage them and others to share their perspective or silence future voices.

When we lack power, speaking up is scary. It is why the reactions of leaders matter so much. I have asked people all over the world to tell me about a time when they felt comfortable speaking up even when they didn't have a lot of power. One of the two most frequent answers is feeling supported. Knowing others have our back lowers the risk of speaking up. That's why our reactions as leaders, verbal and nonverbal, matter so much. They either signal support or rejection.

The leader amplification effect not only explains why the leader silencing effect occurs, but it also tells us why encouragement is necessary to turn silence into voice. Our discouragement becomes DISCOURAGEMENT that keeps information off the table. But our encouragement also becomes ENCOURAGEMENT that releases people to share their perspective. It can even produce Tour de France champions.

SIR DAVE BRAILSFORD was knighted by the Queen for taking England from a cycling cellar dweller to a pedaling juggernaut, and in a remarkably short period of time. In 2003, he was named performance director of Britain's national cycling team. A year later in 2004, Britain had their best Olympic performance in nearly a century, winning two gold medals. In the 2008 and 2012 Olympics, Britain won the most cycling gold medals of any country.

But Sir Brailsford wasn't content with just conquering the Olympics. In 2010, he became the manager of the new British-based professional cycling team, Team Sky. Almost immediately they became the best racing team in the world, winning *six* Tour de France victories between 2012 and 2018.

How did Sir Brailsford achieve such remarkable success? Most people point to his innovative concept of marginal gains, the idea that "if you broke down everything you could think of that goes into riding a bike, and then improved [each one] by 1%, you will get a significant increase when you put them all together."

But Brailsford's success, especially with Team Sky, also depended on another concept he embraced. Cycling is complicated: it's a team sport, but only one person gets the glory. Brailsford recognized that to maximize team success, the supporting cast needed to feel valued and respected. Because he understood the fundamental human need for status, he would go out of his way to recognize the effort of each team member and how it contributed to the team's victory.

Brailsford's team-building efforts represent a concept I have labeled *expanding the status pie*, which we discussed in Inspiring Mentors (Chapter 5). Expanding the status pie is surprisingly straightforward: we simply highlight the unique expertise, contributions, and skills of each member of our teams. We can, for example, note someone's experience when asking for their thoughts, e.g., "I know Claudia has worked in the housing industry and I want to get her thoughts on subprime liquidity." That type of encouragement lets people know that you consider their voice essential for making a good decision. It helps you get all the information on the table.

Highlighting expertise is so critical because people feel more comfortable speaking up when they possess unique knowledge or insights. When people feel they know what they're talking about, they're more likely to talk about what they know. Along with feeling supported, having expertise is one of the biggest predictors of speaking up when in a low-power position. In fact, when people feel they have a unique and relevant perspective, they are often *compelled* to put their insights or information on the table. It's why expanding the status pie is a key solution to making wise decisions.

Another way to expand the status pie is to ask those with less power for *advice*. My research with Katie Liljenquist of the University of Utah shows that asking others for advice is so effective because it accomplishes so many interpersonal goals at once. It makes others feel like experts. It signals our own humility, further reducing the power distance between us and others. It induces perspective-taking; for someone to give us effective advice, they need to look at the problem from our vantage point. And their advice serves as a psychological investment in us; as a result, they become more committed to helping us solve our dilemmas. Asking others for advice inspires others while also giving us more loyal supporters.

Your encouragement is necessary to get all the information on the table. But it's not sufficient.

WHY ENCOURAGEMENT AND *LEANING IN* AREN'T ENOUGH

HAVE YOU EVER wondered how a television episode comes to fruition? It starts in the writers' room, and it begins in the pitch meetings where writers pitch their ideas for an episode. If there is enthusiasm behind your pitch, you're given the opportunity to write a draft. And if that draft gets selected, it's *your* name on it, front and center.

One day Glen Mazzara, executive producer of the Emmy Award–winning television show *The Shield*, walked out of a pitch meeting feeling upset. Why? Because not a single female writer pitched an idea that day. He said to himself, in effect, "I'm going to be an inspiring leader; I'm going to go encourage them to speak up." When he did, he was stunned by their reaction: the female writers didn't feel inspired by his encouragement; instead, they dismissed it. They told him to come to the next writers' meeting and watch what happened when they did pitch ideas.

At that next meeting, Mazzara quickly understood why the female writers had scoffed at his encouragement: Whenever a female writer started to pitch an idea, she was immediately interrupted by her male colleagues. Sometimes it was to brutally criticize the idea; other times the male writer was trying to present his own idea. Encouragement wasn't sufficient to help women find their voice in the writers' room. Glen needed to come up with another plan to help the women get their ideas on the table.

Encouragement isn't sufficient and neither is leaning in. The "lean in" movement, popularized by Sheryl Sandberg, presents the idea that women can tackle gender inequality by overcoming their own internal barriers that prevent them from being assertive. It has been widely embraced as an incredibly self-empowering ideology: women can take control of their own lives to get ahead. "Lean in" and rise up.

But it turns out there's a hidden cost to the "lean in" anthem. Researchers from Duke University found that the "lean in" messaging ironically points the finger *at* women. It makes *women* responsible for gender inequality. It makes women responsible for *solving* gender inequality.

Encouraging others to speak up is necessary for getting all the information on the table. But it's not enough. We also need to think like an architect and design the processes that reduce the leader silencing effect and allow everyone to speak up.

DESIGNING WISE DECISIONS

LET'S TRAVEL BACK to the surgery room and the thousands of tragedies that resulted from central line infections. I want you to stop and put yourself in the shoes of Dr. Pronovost. Your five-step sterilization checklist is a home-run strategy: it's simple, straightforward, and life-saving. But the checklist isn't being faithfully followed by doctors, and the nurses aren't comfortable challenging the doctors when they skip a step. How would you solve this problem and ensure the checklist is faithfully followed every time?

Dr. Pronovost and his team did something radical. They put the *nurses* in charge of the checklist.

This simple yet revolutionary redesign of the checklist protocol was effective on many levels. First, because the nurses had been given this solemn responsibility, they meticulously fulfilled each step, reducing the number of checklist mistakes. But what happened if a nurse accidentally skipped one of the checklist items? Well, the powerful doctors had no problem speaking up when a low-powered nurse failed to properly adhere to protocol. This simple design solution of putting nurses in charge of the checklist was such an amazing success that the infection rates for central line catheterization went down to *zero*. By putting nurses in charge of the checklist, Johns Hopkins Hospital saved numerous lives.

But it wasn't just the patients who were better off—so were the nurses. Giving people responsibility fulfills three of the core needs that drive the inspiring visionary and mentor archetypes: the need for status, the need for control, and the need for meaning. The nurses felt respected when the hospital deemed them worthy of the solemn responsibility of the checklist. It also gave them control over an important task, something they lacked when doctors were in charge. And they could take great pride in the zero-infection rate knowing that they played a key role in the larger purpose of saving lives.

The Johns Hopkins redesign offers a simple but powerful lesson: when we share responsibility with our team members, we are expressing faith *in* them and encouragement *of* them. We are empowering them and reducing the leader silencing effect. We are being inspiring mentors.

Another design choice is the language that we use. When Korean Airlines was trying to understand a series of accidents and near misses, they noticed copilots were afraid to speak up when the captain made a mistake. Rather than challenge the authority of the captain, copilots sat tight, even when their plane was in a downward spiral. One of the contributing factors to this dynamic is the Korean language, which is inherently hierarchical. To reduce the grip of hierarchy and the leader silencing effect, the airline made English the official cockpit language. This change was easy to implement because all pilots were already required to know English. Changing the language to English transformed the cockpit culture, not only because English is less hierarchical than Korean, but also because it helped to create a new team identity within the cockpit.

Thinking like an architect means always considering the roles and responsibilities we are giving people, and the language that we're using. But we can do even more: we can carefully design how we run our meetings to ensure all perspectives get on the table.

When you walk into a meeting, where do you sit?

If you sit at the head of the table, you have just reinforced your authority and highlighted your power. Sitting at the head of the table may seem subtle, but it contributes to the leader silencing effect. By allowing others to sit at the head, we can offer them a powerful dose of authority and involvement, just like the nurses in the operating room. Where you sit helps determine how much information gets shared and put on the table.

I discovered the power of musical chairs with a very smart doctoral student who couldn't find his voice with me. No matter how encouraging I was, he was flustered and incoherent. It was clear my status as a professor made him anxious. Then one day I had an idea: What if we *switched* seats? He could sit in my professor chair while I sat in the student chair. This simple change in seating made all the difference. Sitting in the taller chair gave my student the boost he needed to find and express his brilliant insights.

Where we sit can also determine *when* we speak. And when we speak as a leader has a huge effect on the leader silencing effect. By speaking first, we set a powerful anchor that weighs the whole discussion down. It makes it much harder for people to share their perspective, especially if it doesn't align with what we just said. In contrast, when we speak last, others are less likely to feel that they are contradicting their leader when they share their thoughts. By speaking last, we minimize the leader silencing effect.

A good example is the behavior of the European Central Bank. The president of the bank from 2003 to 2011, Jean-Claude Trichet, was "known for being rigid and domineering," while his successor, Mario Draghi, was "applauded for encouraging discussion." Trichet was said to start every meeting by sharing his perspective before turning to the other members on the council to get their perspective. In contrast, the Draghi-led meetings had a dramatically different feel. Instead of speaking first, he waited to hear from everyone else before he shared his views. Speaking first turns us into domineering silencers, whereas speaking last encourages more robust discussions.

Even when we don't sit at the head of the table, and even when we speak last, the weight of our presence is still felt. That means sometimes, the only way to help your team members openly share their viewpoint is to not be present at all. When President John F. Kennedy faced the Cuban Missile Crisis, he needed creative ideas to avoid the looming possibility of nuclear war. But he realized that whenever he joined the brainstorming meetings, his mere presence had a silencing effect on the voices in the room. Every time someone spoke, everyone would look to his expressions for signs of approval or disapproval. He knew the only way to get every possible idea on the table was to remove himself from the room.

What we wear to the meeting can also be the difference between making wise decisions and collective disasters. As we discussed in Inspiring Practice (Chapter 7), the goal of mission debriefs in the US Army is to better understand what really happened and what can be done better next time. To paint a complete picture, it's important that everyone shares their insights, but the military is beset by hierarchy, which is reinforced in their uniforms. The solution to this problem? Mission debriefs are conducted in civilian clothing. By wearing civilian outfits, hierarchical cues are reduced, and a broader range of voices is encouraged.

Clothes can be constraining, and so can rules. In fact, most people hate rules. Some leaders try to implement as few rules as possible to give people a sense of freedom and autonomy. But the absence of rules often offers chaos instead of liberation. The key is having the right rules.

Let's revisit the writers' room from *The Shield* television series to understand why. The female writers didn't pitch many ideas because they quickly got interrupted when they did. Executive Producer Glen Mazzara came up with an unbelievably simple solution. The only change he made was the introduction of a new rule, the "no-interruption rule." The rule states that during a pitch, *no one can interrupt the writer until they have finished pitching their proposed episode*. Pretty simple, right? But it was utterly transformative. It helped level the gender playing field, as female writers finally felt more comfortable pitching ideas knowing they would not be interrupted. Importantly, the rule was inclusively liberating. It wasn't just the female writers but all the writers who benefited from the rule. Everyone came up with better pitches because they had the space to share and develop their ideas. *The Shield* highlights how designing the right rules allows people to develop the best ideas and make the best decisions.

The product design firm IDEO also understands the creative power of a simple rule. IDEO is famous for their inventions and innovations, from the first computer mouse to the *Free Willy* mechanical whale. How do they achieve so many breakthrough ideas, again and again? They have a simple rule during brainstorming called the "no-criticism rule." When they are *generating* ideas, IDEO prohibits criticizing any idea at all. Of course, there is a time and place for evaluation, but the brainstorming period is not it. Why? Because if I criticize Maeda's idea, it might also shut down David's ideas as well. Criticism, even when it's directed at others, leads to self-censorship. The other thing IDEO does during brainstorming meetings is they write down *every* idea. This solves the problem of playing favorites or emphasizing some ideas more than others.

A final way to lower the risk of speaking up is to collect ideas anonymously. By collecting information privately, we get a true temperature of where people stand. This is what IDEO does when they *evaluate* ideas: they do so anonymously. People can voice that an idea is terrible even if it comes from the CEO because their comment isn't attached to them. Knowing that anonymity lowers the risk of sharing one's perspective led to one of my first actions as chair of the Management Division at Columbia Business School: I changed our voting procedure from public to private voting. That way, even our more junior faculty would feel comfortable sharing their opinion.

Making wise decisions involves getting and integrating all the information on the table. No interruption, no criticism, write down everything, anonymous voting—these rules liberate people to generate and share their insights. But even when we have made a wise decision, we still need to get other people to buy into and follow us down our chosen path. If people think our decisions are unfair, they will experience a seething cauldron of infuriation. Let's turn to how we can design our decision-making process to inspire fairness.

CHAPTER 11

Inspiring Fairness

YOU ARE A member of a transplant review board, and a single kidney has suddenly become available. You must assign the kidney from a forty-three-year-old woman to one recipient in the next twenty-four hours. There are four eligible candidates. Who would you select as the recipient of this scarce resource?

> *Candidate A*: A sixty-two-year-old engineer who is on the verge of a revolutionary breakthrough that would transform fuel cell technology to make clean energy abundantly available. She is the only person with the requisite knowledge and expertise who can bring this project to fruition. Given its potential to replace fossil fuels, its impact would be felt globally, potentially raising the standard of living worldwide. The kidney is a better than average match, but not a perfect one.
>
> *Candidate B*: A fifty-one-year-old rancher who suffers from a kidney disease because of his lifelong diabetes. He has been on the transplant wait list for over four years and has worked his way to the top of the list. Despite his seniority on the list, he has been passed over several times due to more urgent cases

and better matches. He is currently unable to work and desperate to regain his health to support his family. The available kidney is not an ideal match, but he could do well with a post-transplant treatment regimen of immunosuppressant.

Candidate C: A thirty-eight-year-old mother with four young children, she has suffered from high-blood pressure but has been inconsistent in taking her medication. As a result of her lack of medication adherence, she has now experienced renal failure. Although she has only been on the wait list for five months, the available kidney is an exact match, which would make the transplant a likely success.

Candidate D: A twenty-three-year-old law student, he donated a kidney to his brother shortly after his eighteenth birthday. Although he knew there was a small risk that he might develop the same kidney disease as his brother, he insisted on helping his brother because his kidney was an excellent match. Now, five years later, he has developed the same disease as his brother. Although his case is less severe, his only remaining kidney is beginning to falter. He is a poor match and would require extensive immunosuppressant medications.

There is a compelling case for each candidate. Utilitarians love Candidate A because she offers the greatest potential value to society, but those who care about the lifetime of the kidney are concerned with her age. Others feel Candidate B deserves the kidney because he has been in the queue the longest and he has a family that depends on him, but he's not a great match, calling into question the success of the transplant. Efficiency followers endorse Candidate C because she offers the greatest chance of transplant success, and she also has four young children, but others blame her for her compromised kidney because she didn't consistently take her medicine. People who want to reward and encourage sacrifice are drawn to Candidate D, who courageously donated his own kidney; although he is also the youngest candidate, potentially offering the longest life to the kidney, he is a particularly poor match, decreasing the odds of a successful transplant.

Notice that I asked *who* you would select as the recipient. But maybe a better question is *how* would you make your decision? To help answer that question, let's travel back to Greek mythology.

DESIGNING FAIRNESS THROUGH PRESELECTED CRITERIA

ODYSSEUS WANTED TO do the impossible. He had heard the legendary tales of the Sirens, a group of gorgeous women who sang the most alluring and exquisite melodies to passing ships. Because their music was so beautiful, sailors were unable to resist its magnetic appeal; they would immediately abandon ship upon hearing the Sirens' harmonies and swim desperately toward shore. But the captivating music was a ruse. Beautiful women did not await the sailors on shore, but hideous monsters leading them to their death.

Odysseus desperately wanted to hear the Sirens' music with his own ears. But he knew no amount of training or self-control would be sufficient to resist their beckoning. He needed to think like an architect and design a process that would allow him to listen to the enchanting music and stay safe while doing so. His process involved two steps. First, he tied himself to the mast so tightly that no matter how much he strained and struggled, he would be unable to escape. Second, he filled the ears of his sailors with wax so densely that they could hear neither the music nor his pleas to be set free.

You might be wondering what Homer's famous tale has to do with fairness? Well, consider this study by Eric Uhlmann of INSEAD. Imagine you are evaluating two candidates for police chief: Greg and Emily. Each officer is superior on one criterion: Emily has more education, while Greg has more experience in the field. Who would you pick?

That was just one of the conditions in Eric's study. In the other condition, Greg has more education while Emily has more experience in the field. *Now* who would you pick?

Eric found that people picked the male candidate in both cases. In the first condition, people pointed to experience in the field and why it was so important. But in the second condition, people highlighted the value of education as the key to chiefly success.

What's really going on here? People were biased in favor of the male candidate, and they could easily explain their decision, even to themselves, by focusing on whichever criterion in which the male was superior. When the man had stronger field experience, people talked about the importance of field experience. But when the man had more education, suddenly credentials really mattered. It's an example of the subtle forms of bias that unfairly prevent some groups from getting hired and getting promoted.

Given people are often unaware of their biases, many companies have tried to increase fairness and reduce bias with unconscious bias training. But that's a problem because unconscious bias training doesn't seem to work. Betsy Levy Paluck of Princeton analyzed 985 studies conducted on the effects of anti-bias training and found almost no effect. Making people aware of their bias also does not seem to prevent bias from infiltrating their decisions. Odysseus and the Sirens reveal why unconscious bias training is mostly ineffective. Like Odysseus, it is almost impossible to unhear our biased reactions once they enter our minds. Just as willpower training would not have helped Odysseus overcome the allure of the Sirens, unconscious bias training doesn't undo biased preferences.

But it gets worse. Unconscious bias training is not only ineffective, but it is often counterproductive. When Frank Dobbin of Harvard analyzed the promotion rates of over seven hundred companies over a thirty-year period, he found that the introduction of unconscious bias training *decreased* the promotion rates of women and minorities across the companies he studied. What's going on here? Well, White employees often emerge from bias training sessions both confused and frustrated. They walked in biased and walked out biased *and* angry.

Why do many people leave these trainings angry? Because unconscious bias training involves finger-pointing. No one likes being singled out with scorn. As my research shows, making people feel ashamed leads them to reject the message and put their head in the sand. Unconscious bias training activates our fight-or-flight system.

But Odysseus also offers a solution: if we tie ourselves to the criteria mast before seeing candidates, it is harder for us to shift the criteria to fit our preferences. That's exactly what Eric Uhlmann found. When he asked evaluators to commit to selecting criteria *before* viewing the applicants, gender bias disappeared.

When I became chair of my department at Columbia University, I put Eric's research into practice. As I mentioned in Inspiring Architects (Chapter 8), I created the first Search and Voting Procedures for faculty hiring at Columbia Business School. These guidelines required that search committees discuss and draft the criteria to be used to evaluate candidates *before* reviewing any candidates. And to reinforce these preselected criteria, we also design our post-interview surveys around those criteria.

Since we have instituted preestablished criteria, the Management Division has doubled its number of female faculty and tripled its number of faculty of color. By committing to criteria in advance, we have produced a fairer process, one that reduces the possibility that biases and preference will dominate our principles.

Preselecting criteria before reviewing candidates can also help us solve the kidney dilemma we just discussed. Notice that I exposed you to the candidates before asking you to select the criteria. As a result, lots of incidental and biasing information could have influenced your decision. Let's see how the organ transplant system in the United States was designed to avoid these types of biases and inspire greater fairness.

———

ORGANS ARE A scarce resource. The number of people needing transplants far outstrips the number of available organs. In February of 2024, 103,223 people were desperately waiting for a transplant. To create a system that distributes available organs fairly, we need to think like an architect.

In 1984, the United Network for Organ Sharing (UNOS) was created to facilitate the organ transplant process in the United States. Their first task was to establish the criteria they would use to match patients to available organs.

There are many different values that can underlie any system of resource allocation. We could look to the future and distribute resources to the person or group who will create the most value for society, what utilitarians call "the greatest good for the greatest number." We could look to the past and reward those who have lived according to our values and punish those who have deviated from the righteous path. We could focus on the present and offer the resource to those who currently need it most. We could focus on the resource itself and seek to use it most efficiently; in this case, we would select a person who would make best use of the resource. And finally, we could use a market approach and offer the resource to the highest bidder.

UNOS rejected the utilitarian, moralizing, and market approaches. They explicitly state on their current website, "Only medical and logistical factors are used in organ matching. Personal or social characteristics such as celebrity status, income or insurance coverage play no role in transplant priority." When the system was created, its primary focus was on the *efficacious* use of the organ. Because transplants are more successful when the patient and the donated organ are immunologically compatible, patients got higher scores when there was a stronger match. Similarly, transplants are more successful when transport time is low; thus, patients received higher scores when the distance between the donor and transplant hospitals was shorter.

UNOS's second-most-important criterion was the *need* of the patient. Patients with greater medical urgency, e.g., a lack of alternatives such as dialysis, get a higher priority score. Finally, UNOS also incorporated the fact that some patients are biologically disadvantaged, i.e., it is harder for them to find matches. The system was designed to offer compensatory points for patients that are difficult to match.

For example, UNOS used the following point system when the kidney allocation system was originally established.

Efficacy: 2 points for each of the six possible antigen matches + a bonus of up to 6 points if the logistics of getting kidney to patient are favorable. An organ found to be a perfect match for a patient on the waiting list must be allocated to that patient.

Need: 6 points for medical urgency.

Disadvantage: 1 point for each 10 percent of population against which they have antibodies.

Since its original framework, the UNOS system has evolved to further maximize efficacy. Immunological compatibility and geography still matter a lot, but now body size has emerged as important because doctors learned over time that the transplanted organ should be close in size to the original organ; e.g., don't give a child an adult-sized organ. For kidneys and lungs, waiting time matters, but not for hearts or livers. Past behavior can matter, but only for kidneys and only in a positive way: Living donors, those who have previously donated a kidney, are given priority.

One controversial issue is whether age should make a difference, with younger individuals being given priority over older ones. For those who value efficacy, or the life of the organ, age should matter. But currently kidneys in the US are as likely to go to an elderly person as a teenager.

Fair allocation systems aren't just the province of internal organs. Consider the difficult decision that the US military faced after Germany surrendered in 1945. Some soldiers would be demobilized and get to go home, while others would travel to Asia and continue the battle with Japan. The military did something that was simple and straightforward,

but also quite brilliant: they surveyed the soldiers to determine the factors they considered to be most important. The factors they initially
included in the survey were: length of time in the army, length of time
overseas, age, and number of dependents. But soldiers were allowed to
write in additional criteria, and "exposure to combat" emerged as an
important one. Through a variety of survey methods, they eventually
settled on a straightforward point system similar to the UNOS organ
allocation system.

Length of time in the army: 1 point per month
Length of time overseas: 1 point per month
Campaign star or combat decoration: 5 points per decoration
Dependents: 12 points per child under 18, up to three children

The system was not only easy to implement and administer, but it
was also perceived as fair. It's not surprising that 82 percent of the soldiers who got to head home gave the system a thumbs-up. But what is
more remarkable is that even among the soldiers who had to continue
fighting, 65 percent rated the system as "good or fairly good." Because
the system was based on their overall preferences, even the soldiers who
got the short end of the stick didn't feel infuriated.

The essence of fairness is ensuring that even those who don't get
great outcomes still think the system is reasonable. And research shows
that inspiring fairness involves four factors. First, we need to be visionary and identify the values that underlie the criteria. Second, we need to
be good mentors and incorporate the voices of those who will be most
impacted by the allocation system. Third, we need to select criteria
that are based on those values and those voices. And finally, we need to
ensure that the system is consistently and transparently applied, i.e., an
exemplar of fairness.

That is exactly what the army did in the demobilization situation.
They were deluged with requests for special treatment but explained
that they were simply following the stated preferences of the soldiers

themselves, and that violating the system would only infuriate the servicemen.

The organ donation and soldier demobilization systems were both simple point-based symptoms. But a point system wouldn't always work in the job hiring process because in many cases we need to interview potential job candidates to select the best people. Let's explore how to design fairness in the interview process.

DESIGNING FAIRNESS THROUGH
STRUCTURED INTERVIEWS

COMMITTING TO CRITERIA in advance is a first step toward creating fairer selection processes. But the interview stage is often rife with other potential biases. And one way that applicants get treated differently in interviews is in the questions they are asked.

When we review résumés, we often get excited by candidates who went to the same school or majored in same subject as us. But we get really excited by people who share our hobbies. "You play squash??? I play squash! You will be a great addition to our team." Lauren Rivera of Northwestern University found that the entire hiring process is different for a candidate that shares the passions of their interviewers. Let's consider the situation where the interviewer and interviewee don't share the same hobbies. It will likely be more formal and follow a familiar script. In contrast, when they share a hobby, the interview is transformed into a casual conversation.

It's not just incidental information on résumés that can lead to different types of interviews. It also turns out that men and women get asked a different set of questions in interviews. To understand how, let's travel to the high-stakes world of venture capital. In 2016, 40 percent of all privately held companies in the United States were founded by women, but only 2 percent of venture capital funding went to female founders. Former Columbia student Dana Kanze, who is now at London Business School, had an idea why.

Before getting her PhD at Columbia, Dana had spent five years raising money for her own start-up. As she pitched her venture to investors and at various funding competitions, she noticed that she was getting asked a very different set of questions than her male cofounder. He got questions that focused on the venture's upsides. In contrast, Dana's questions highlighted everything that could go wrong with the venture. At first, Dana thought *she* was doing something wrong; maybe her presentations had unwittingly focused on the downsides. But when she realized that her presentations didn't really differ from her cofounder's presentations, she began to wonder whether women more generally were being asked a different set of questions than men.

When Dana arrived at Columbia, she analyzed every funding competition run by TechCrunch in New York City since its inception in 2010. TechCrunch is a big deal: it's where both Dropbox and Fitbit got their starts. Importantly, Dana got the videos of not only the presentations but also the six-minute Q&As that followed.

When she analyzed her data, she found a shocking result. Although there were no differences in how start-ups were presented by male and female founders, male-led start-ups raised five times more funding than female-led ventures. This disparity held when she controlled for other variables that typically affect funding outcomes, including the age of the start-up, the founder's past experience, etc.

However, when Dana analyzed the six-minute Q&A with the venture capitalists *after* the pitch, it became clear why women were being underfunded. Just like with her cofounder, male founders were asked to elaborate on the upside, e.g., "How many new customers do you plan to acquire this year?" In contrast, the female entrepreneurs were asked pessimistic questions that put them on the defensive, e.g., "How do you plan to retain your existing customers?" In fact, 67 percent of the questions given to male entrepreneurs focused on the potential upside of their venture, while 66 percent of those posed to female founders were flooded with downside queries.

These Q&A sessions had a huge effect on funding outcomes. When a start-up was asked mostly upside questions, it went on to raise *seven times more* than start-ups peppered with pessimistic questions.

But it gets even more interesting. The questions mattered so much because they constrained the answers. An upside question led to an answer focused on potential, but a downside question produced answers focused on risks. Starting off with a question focused on the downside created a six-minute spiral of gloom and doom.

We all tend to give answers that match the structure of the questions we are asked. My advisor Joel Cooper conducted a groundbreaking study back in the '70s. He found that Black applicants were often dinged in interviews for answering questions with poor grammar. But when he analyzed videotapes of interviews, it turned out that the *questions* that White interviewers were asking Black applicants contained more speech errors. Because of the tendency for our answers to match the style of questions, the Black applicants appeared to lack communication skills. However, they were only mirroring the poorly phrased questions of the interviewers. Joel even showed that when White individuals were asked questions with speech errors, their answers were also grammatically compromised.

So, what's the solution?

We could train female founders to always focus on the upside in their answers. And Dana found that this approach is certainly helpful. When founders responded to downside questions with upside answers, they raised fourteen times more funding than if they responded to downside questions with downside answers. But that's unfair as it places the burden of solving gender bias on women. Instead let's think like an architect. How can we design a fairer process?

The answer is amazingly simple. To create great fairness in funding, all founders should be asked the exact same questions. Indeed, research finds that structuring interviews so interviewees all get asked the same questions dramatically increases fairness compared to unstructured interviews.

Notice that asking everyone the same questions doesn't just solve gender bias, but also solves the similarity bias that Lauren Rivera discovered. Rather than spending the whole interview talking about shared passions with some candidates but not others, everyone gets treated similarly. When we let interview interactions develop organically, bias creeps in. Different applicants get asked very different questions. By using a structured interview, we level the playing field and create more equal opportunities.

To select the most talented candidates, we can extend the idea of structured interviews even further. To choose the right person for a particular job, we also need to use *structured tasks* in the application process.

When I was chair of the Management Division at Columbia, I oversaw the hiring of divisional staff. But when it came to selecting our computer and technology specialist, I had to rely on the broader tech team. When we needed to hire a new specialist, the tech team came to me and said, "We found the perfect person, someone with lots of experience. Do you want to meet him?" I not only wanted to meet him, but I also wanted to meet the top three candidates. I also insisted on putting all three candidates through a test. Instead of just having a casual conversation with the top candidate, we had the top three applicants come in and perform two or three tasks that they would routinely face on the job. This way we could measure their speed and accuracy on the activities they would deal with daily.

Giving the applicants similar assignments to complete saved us from making a terrible mistake. The person the tech team had lauded as the perfect match wasn't so perfect on the assigned tasks. In fact, he bombed them. He talked a good game, but it quickly became clear that he lacked the necessary knowledge to be effective at the job. In contrast, one of the other three aced the tests. He ended up being so good that he was promoted out of my department within six months.

My decision to use work-related tasks in the interview process wasn't a random hunch. I knew that the traditional interview method is very good at selecting people who are good at, well, interviews. But interviews rarely tell how well a person will do on the *job*. A fair process not only asks all applicants the same questions but also includes the same work-related tasks. It's why consulting companies ask potential applicants to solve cases that represent the type of problems they will be solving for clients.

DESIGNING FAIR PROMOTIONS

WE NEED FAIRNESS in selecting the candidates to be interviewed. We need fairness in the interviews themselves. But once we hire someone, we also need fairness in how they are evaluated and promoted.

When Ann Hopkins came up for partnership at Pricewaterhouse-Coopers, she was the only female among the eighty-eight candidates. She had billed more hours and brought in more business than any of the other eighty-seven candidates. She received praise touting her as an "outstanding professional" with a "strong character, independence, and integrity." However, she was told she needed "a course in charm school" and she was too "macho," with many of these comments coming from partners who barely worked with her.

Ann was not selected as one of the forty-seven candidates promoted to partnership. She sued. The Supreme Court decided in her favor and elevated her to partner. The Supreme Court opinion stated, "An employer who objects to aggressiveness in women but whose positions require this trait places women in an intolerable Catch 22: out of a job if they behave aggressively and out of a job if they don't."

Ann Hopkins was treated differently than the male partner candidates. She faced a double bind, where the behavior required for success—assertiveness—was prohibited for her gender. She declared, "That's not fair."

The key to designing a fairer promotion system involves the same solutions we discussed for hiring, and for allocating organs and demobilizing soldiers. We need preselected criteria that are uniformly applied to every person up for promotion. In the case of Ann Hopkins, there

was an objective marker of success: business brought into the organization. Furthermore, the criticisms of her behavior were primarily driven
by those partners who worked with her the least. To design a fairer process, we can ensure that the opinions given the most weight come from
those who worked most closely with the promotion candidate.

When we think like architects, we can design fairer systems at
every stage of the employment process, from applicant screening to
interviews to promotions. We can also design fairness by expanding
the set of criteria we consider.

DESIGNING FAIRNESS BY EXPANDING THE CRITERIA PIE

PRESELECTING CRITERIA BEFORE making allocation decisions—from
interview slots to promotions to organ donations—produces more fair
and less biased decisions. But true fairness only occurs if the selected
criteria themselves are fair, i.e., when the criteria accurately reflect the
attributes needed for success in a role.

In Inspiring Wise Decisions (Chapter 10), we discussed how Sir
David Brailsford produced six Tour de France victories in seven years,
in part, by acknowledging the varied and unique contributions of each
team member. I call this *expanding the status pie*. We can use a similar
logic for selecting criteria that represent the complete set of attributes
that contribute to job success.

Consider the fascinating research of Felix Danbold of University
College London. Felix immersed himself in the world of firefighting
by spending dozens of hours observing and interviewing firefighters
in multiple stations throughout Southern California. Not surprisingly,
he observed that heroic actions and physical strength were essential to
the job. But he also saw how traits like compassion, which are stereotypically feminine traits, were also necessary to be a great firefighter.
The problem was that compassion was routinely devalued in formal
and informal evaluations. Felix wondered what would happen if these

equally necessary but feminine traits were put on equal footing with the stereotypically masculine ones.

Felix conducted an experiment with over four hundred active-duty firefighters to test his hypothesis. Everyone watched a videotape of a male fire captain responding to this question: "What are the most important characteristics for modern firefighters to have in order to succeed in the fire service?" In the traditional criteria condition, physical strength was highlighted as the key to firefighter success. But in the expanded criteria condition, the captain emphasized the importance of compassion in addition to physical strength and explained why compassion was so important to be a successful firefighter. Notice that this condition emphasized the importance of feminine traits but without denying the necessity of masculine attributes.

What did Felix find? The expanded criteria condition led firefighters to see women as legitimate colleagues while lowering their concern that recruiting women would compromise safety. By emphasizing an expanded set of diagnostic criteria, Felix helped open up opportunities for female firefighters.

Felix's research extended work that I had conducted with Laura Kray of UC Berkeley nearly two decades earlier. Like Felix, we analyzed the traits necessary for successful negotiators. We found that some attributes that predicted negotiator success were stereotypically masculine traits like being assertive and being rational. But others were stereotypically feminine traits like being a good listener, a perspective-taker, and a verbally facile communicator. Like Felix, we then conducted an experiment where novice negotiators (MBA students on the first day of class) were randomly assigned to a control condition or to a positive feminine traits condition. In the positive feminine traits condition, we told our negotiators that "Highly skilled negotiators have: (1) a keen ability to express their thoughts verbally; (2) good listening skills; and (3) insight into the other negotiator's feelings." We then had a man and a woman negotiate over the sale of a pharmaceutical plant. In our control condition, men outperformed their female counterparts, consistent with prior research. But when we emphasized the importance of feminine traits, we reversed the gender gap, with women outperforming men at the bargaining table. In this condition, women thought they had what it takes to be a great negotiator and men felt they didn't measure up.

Note that our experiment didn't expand the criteria, like Felix did, but focused only on a subset of attributes predictive of negotiation success that were stereotypically feminine. Instead, we would have created a fairer set of criteria by listing all the attributes of effective negotiators, some of which are stereotypically masculine and others stereotypically feminine.

Expanding the criteria doesn't just lower bias but also expands the pool of interested applicants. Let's consider job advertisements, whose copy helps determine who applies and who doesn't. Aaron Kay of Duke University found that job ads in male-dominated industries for engineers and computer programmers tended to emphasize masculine attributes (e.g., ambitious, assertive, competitive), and rarely mentioned equally important feminine traits (e.g., supportive, committed). Women have little interest in applying to jobs that only emphasize stereotypical male attributes; essentially, these ads are saying to women, "You don't belong." But when Aaron changed the wording of the ads for a sales manager position to emphasize less masculine wording (e.g., he changed "challenging" to "motivating"), he found women were more eager to apply.

For the past five years, I have worked with a male-dominated industry—the wine and spirts wholesale industry—to increase the number of successful women. This industry holds up industry experience as a foundational criterion, especially for high-ranking positions. They even emphasize it in ads, "fifteen years of industry experience required." The problem is that in a male-dominated industry, the men are much more likely to have experience within that industry and therefore access to high-status opportunities. So, what's the solution? In this case, I recommend asking why *industry* experience is so important and to consider whether other industries could provide comparable experience and skill building. In addition to expanding the experience criteria, we can also consider trainings that can compensate for differential levels of experience and get everyone up to speed.

By expanding the set of criteria we use to recruit, evaluate, and promote candidates—from firefighters to negotiators to computer programmers—we can ensure that all the necessary skills are represented. And in doing so, we can produce more fair hiring and promotion systems.

There is one more piece to the fairness puzzle we need to consider. Note that the point systems for organ allocations and demobilizing soldiers only record values on the preselected criteria. This ensures that they are blind to other factors that might be biasing. For example, it doesn't matter if you are a parent or not, or what occupation you hold, when allocating kidneys. To truly inspire fairness, we also need to make ourselves blind to potentially biasing information.

DESIGNING FAIRNESS THROUGH BLINDNESS

LET'S GO BACK to the sailors on Odysseus's boat. They were protected from the Sirens' hypnotic melodies because they simply couldn't hear them. One protection against potentially biasing information is to limit exposure to that information.

That's what symphony orchestras did in transforming one of the most gender-segregated industries into one of the most gender diverse. In the 1970s, 45 percent of the class at Juilliard, one of the top feeders into symphony orchestras, were women, but less than 5 percent of the top US orchestras were female. Today, these same orchestras are approaching gender parity; the New York Philharmonic in 2022 even had more female than male members: forty-five women to forty-four men. What led to this dramatic change in gender parity?

Blind screens.

For an industry ostensibly based on musical merit, beliefs about gender played an outsized role in evaluations. Some conductors simply didn't think that women belonged in orchestras. Others just couldn't fathom that the smaller female frames could handle heavy and lung-dependent instruments like the tuba and trombone. In the late 1970s and early '80s, orchestras in the US began to audition candidates onstage, but behind a screen. The judges could no longer listen with their eyes and only had sound to infer what the musician had to offer. As Nobel Prize–winning economist Claudia Goldin showed in her research, "[The] blind audition procedure fostered impartiality in hiring and increased the proportion [of] women in symphony orchestras."

The blind screens of orchestra auditions also reveal how powerful cues to gender are. Even though the evaluators couldn't see the candidates, they could hear them come onstage and get into position. And the click, click, click of heels was a telltale sign that a woman was performing. The judges needed the same wax the sailors had on Odysseus's boat. Fortunately, there was a straightforward solution: put down carpeting or have all the candidates perform without shoes.

There are other ways we can make people blind to biasing information. For example, Lauren Rivera has suggested that we can remove hobbies from résumés. She argues that their presence on résumés is mostly biasing because outside hobbies are unlikely to be predictive of future job performance.

Speaking of résumés, the way the traditional one is structured puts people with employment gaps at a severe disadvantage. Many of us have employment gaps on our résumé, but women are particularly vulnerable given they are more likely to have gaps after having kids. The traditional résumé highlights these gaps by listing previously held jobs with dates of employment, e.g., Northwestern University faculty, January 2002–September 2012. With this format, employment gaps scream off the page.

My colleague Ariella Kristal at Columbia University came up with an ingenious alternative format that makes these gaps less apparent. She created résumés that only list years of experience, e.g., Northwestern faculty, 10.5 years. This format truthfully conveys an applicant's job experience, but it simply makes employment gaps less visible. When Ariella conducted a large-scale field experiment in the United Kingdom, she found that when applicants with employment gaps listed their job history with the number of years worked (and without employment dates), their callback rate increased by 15 percent. Listing years of experience and not employment dates not only helped women, but it helped anyone with an employment gap achieve higher callback rates.

THE INSPIRING VEIL OF IGNORANCE

JOHN RAWLS CREATED the concept of the veil of ignorance to prevent our preferences from overriding our principles. Rawls noted that because our preferences are inherently biasing, any system we design, even when we think it is truly fair, will always be constructed to benefit ourselves. His solution was to create systems where we are blind to our position in that system, i.e., we don't know if we will be a CEO or a homeless person. What rules and structures would we create knowing we had equal odds of being poor versus rich? For Rawls, he would maximize the well-being of the worst-off member of that world. But, more broadly, he felt that the veil of ignorance was the only path toward a just society.

At a former university, my colleagues and I used the veil of ignorance to design a more perfect system of faculty recruitment, and to decrease the pervasive conflict that was tearing the department apart. We used to fight mercilessly over the voting rules at every hiring meeting. We argued over voting thresholds (e.g., majority vs. supermajority), veto options, and even voting format (private or public). Each of us was trying to manipulate the voting procedure to maximize hiring our own preferred candidates. This perennial battle over process was not only inefficient, but it was also exhausting and corrosive. It led me to be filled with unrelenting resentment toward some of my colleagues.

As we reached our breaking point, one of my colleagues suggested we use the veil of ignorance. He proposed a summer retreat to create processes and voting principles for our faculty searches at a time when no searches were taking place. Because of the timing, none of us had a preferred candidate we were fighting for; we would truly be behind the veil of ignorance. In the absence of competing preferences, we were able to construct voting principles that could be applied to all hiring situations.

Because the system created under the veil of ignorance was universally seen as fair, it offered numerous benefits. Our meetings became efficient as we made decisions quickly and seamlessly. Our meetings became less volatile; the conflict and rancor of our past meetings dramatically decreased as mutual attempts at manipulation were taken off the table. But maybe the most surprising effect was that our commitment to a predetermined process also created acceptance of all outcomes. When I lost votes during our all-out slugfests, I seethed at the unfairness of the process. But after we installed our principled process, I accepted outcomes even when they went against my preferences. I was disappointed but never infuriated. And I found the process itself to be inspiring.

Fair processes reduce infuriation. They also decrease bias and increase more equal opportunities. As a result, fairness is a key lever for increasing diversity. Diversity, in turn, is a catalyst for new ideas and innovation. But diversity is also a recipe for conflict and division. Let's see how diversity can produce both the best and worst outcomes, and how we can design diversity to inspire more innovation without conflict.

CHAPTER 12

Inspiring Diversity and Inclusion

I N INSPIRING PRACTICE (Chapter 7), we discussed the incredible story
of how Coach Ek inspired his teenage soccer team to survive with no
food and no water for ten days while trapped in the flooded Tham Luang
caves. Equally remarkable were the rescue efforts that took place outside
the caves.

The search for the boys began immediately when they didn't return
home that first evening. Their panicked families contacted their local governor, Narongsak Osottanakorn, who quickly alerted the Thai military.
However, by the time the military arrived at the cave the next morning, the
water was already too high and the current too forceful for the Thai Navy
SEALs to make any headway.

Three days into the ordeal, Governor Osottanakorn pleaded to the
world for help: "Yesterday, we said every minute counts. Today, every
half a minute, every ten seconds counts for the boys. But we are losing
our battle against the water."

Vernon Unsworth, a British financial consultant known locally as the
"crazy foreign caver," quickly realized that the rescue was going to require divers expert in the most dangerous version of the sport: cave diving.
The international community of cave divers is astonishingly small, with

estimates of less than one hundred divers globally. Vern bluntly told the governor, "Sir, you have one chance at this rescue," and gave the minister of the interior a handwritten note: "Time is running out! 1. Ron Harper, 2. Rick Stanton, 3. John Volanthen. They're the world's best cave divers. Please contact them through the UK EMBASSY ASAP."

Within hours, Rick, a retired firefighter, and John, an IT consultant, were on a plane from England to Thailand. Four days into the ordeal, Rick and John made it to the site and immediately attempted to enter the cave. But the Thai Navy SEALs prevented them from passing. As John noted, "If you are the Thai Navy SEALs and suddenly two scruffy-looking middle-aged men turn up, I can see how that really is a bad start to a relationship." Eventually, Rick and John were given permission to dive, but not without a warning from a local commander: "If you die in there, don't [expect] us to go fetch your body."

Because the current was so strong, it took Rick and John almost a day to finally reach the cave's third chamber. As they surfaced, four figures came into focus. Excitement was quickly replaced with confusion—it wasn't a group of teenagers but four fully grown men. They were pump workers who had fallen asleep on the sandbank when the sudden flood had trapped them; no one even knew they were missing. Given the chamber was at risk of flooding any minute, Rick and John immediately dove the pump workers out.

After four days of brutal diving (and eight days since the boys were trapped), John felt defeated. "The conditions in the cave felt impossible . . . There was a very strong feeling that the children couldn't be still alive. It just didn't seem possible. We lost hope . . . We started to wonder, 'do we actually need to be here?'" John and Rick asked the British consulate to look into flights to take them home.

As Rick and John questioned their commitment, rescue efforts didn't cease. A global team of engineers was able to divert enough water from the cave to slow the current and allow the Thai Navy SEALs to build the critical dive line necessary for any rescue. After forceful prodding from the British consulate, Rick and John decided to dive back into the rescue efforts. But they were now banned from the cave. The American military had to intervene to convince the Thai military to let them back in.

Because of the pumping success, Rick and John were able to reach Pattaya Beach on day ten. This was the area of the Tham Luang caves where everyone hoped the boys would be. But they weren't. The area was just too flooded.

As they pressed on, Rick and John came to a small opening in the narrow passages and were immediately overcome by a foul stench. "It was instantaneous. A pungent smell. Silence. We both assumed we were smelling decomposing bodies." But then they saw a light coming from the darkness with the words "Thank you. Hello, thank you."

As each boy hugged the divers, Rick and John made a promise that they would come back for the boys. But they had no idea how to get them out. As they dove back out, they realized that "we may be the only ones that ever see them [alive]."

The rescue team explored a wide range of options. They considered drilling holes into the cave to try and pull the boys out, but the rock was too deep. They discussed leaving the boys in the cave until the long monsoon season ended, but bodily waste would create unsanitary conditions. But an even more pressing concern was the cave's oxygen was rapidly diminishing. On day thirteen, John noticed the air was stale and turned on his oxygen monitor. It immediately sounded an alarm as the oxygen level (15 percent) was below the level of sustaining life! They had to get the boys out *now*.

One idea was to dive the boys out. That might seem simple enough, but when inexperienced divers are suddenly placed underwater, they are overtaken by terror. Rick had witnessed this firsthand when he dove out the four pump workers. "It's highly disorienting being led, basically blind, underwater . . . I described it as an underwater wrestling match. The four water workers were underwater for only 30, 40 seconds, but they still panicked, and they were adults. Now we were talking about a group of children [and a two-and-a-half-hour dive]. We didn't think it was possible for us to dive the children out."

As Rick contemplated how to keep the boys' underwater terror at bay and the thrashing to a minimum, his first thought was to sedate them, but he realized that would be insufficient to fully prevent them from panicking. He quickly concluded that the boys would need to be fully anesthetized.

Improbably, one person in the tiny community of cave divers happened to be an anesthetist. But Dr. Richard Harris was far away in Australia tending to his ailing father. On day twelve, Rick messaged Dr. Harris, "Is it possible to anesthetize the children?" Dr. Harris's immediate response: "Absolutely not. It's not possible."

Dr. Harris elaborated, "I could think of 100 ways a child would die very quickly . . . At any time during the dive, their masks could fill with water, and they'd drown . . . [or] their sinuses could fill up with blood [and] they could drown in their own saliva . . . Their airway would obstruct and they would suffocate . . . the temperature of the water and the air in the cave, over the course of three hours, under anesthesia . . . they would slowly freeze to death."

Dr. Harris decided to fly to Thailand and dive out to see the boys firsthand. He was shocked by what he saw. "I was horrified at how thin they looked. And I could hear a couple of them coughing, pretty wet coughs." On the dive back out, he finally accepted that the alternative to an anesthetized dive was certain death for the boys. "I think in the end, I justified it to myself by saying, 'if I do this anesthetic, they are probably going to die, but at least they will be asleep when they die.'"

Even if the boys were successfully anesthetized, there was still the problem of their masks possibly filling up with water and drowning them. The rescue required a special type of mask—positive pressure masks—that would allow any leak to flow outward rather than inward. The good news was that the Americans possessed these special masks. The bad news was they only had four of them. That meant the rescue would have to be a multiday affair, raising the stakes even higher.

Similar to SEAL Team Six's raid on Osama bin Laden's compound, the divers understood the need to practice their mission from start to finish. The American military helped them simulate the rescue on land as best they could, practicing with local volunteers.

As they began their final preparation, the team encountered a familiar roadblock. The Thai Navy SEALs wouldn't give them the green light to dive. After hours of discussions, the Thai officers finally relented, but with another warning. According to an Australian foreign affairs official, Thai prison potentially awaited if anything went wrong. Rick took this threat seriously enough that he had "a James Bond–esque" plan in place to escape the country if things went south.

On day sixteen, the rescue operation was ready to go once the second doses of the anesthetic—along with fifteen body bags—were brought into chamber three. Dr. Harris made sure each diver knew that "this is a one-way trip. Once you start . . . you can't come back to me. There's nothing I can do. If you end up taking a body out of the cave, then that's what you take out of the cave."

After putting the first boy in a wet suit and attaching a tank, Dr. Harris and a Thai doctor were ready to administer their carefully crafted cocktail. First came a tablet of Xanax to quell anxiety. Next, atropine, an anti-salivation drug to reduce the potential for drowning on one's own saliva, was injected into one leg. Finally, the general anesthetic was injected into the other leg.

After the boys were unconscious, Dr. Harris forced their faces underwater and tied their hands behind their backs. "It was basically trying to put a mask on [a rag doll]. I didn't feel comfortable in [any way, shape, or form] about what we were doing. It felt like euthanasia to me."

The first boy finally arrived, alive and breathing, at the unflooded area of the cave, where a line of two hundred people was waiting to pass him to the cave entrance. The first day of the operation was an unimaginable success as all four boys were safely extracted from the cave. Day two went equally well. But more heavy rain arrived the night before day eighteen of the ordeal, making diving not only incredibly hazardous, but also the last chance they would get to complete the rescue. Despite a variety of close calls, the final five people emerged alive. All thirteen members of the trapped soccer team miraculously survived.

DIVERSE TEAMS HAVE THE BEST *AND* WORST OUTCOMES

THE BREATHTAKING THAI cave rescue illustrates the power of diversity. But it also highlights its pitfalls. It also speaks to a scientific truth. Diverse teams have the best *and* the worst outcomes.

Diverse teams have the best outcomes because they tend to be more creative and make better decisions. That's why diverse markets experience fewer price bubbles and greater value equilibrium and why diverse leadership teams produce higher firm value. Even geographic diversity within towns predicts greater economic prosperity.

The cave rescue illustrates the creative and synergistic benefits of diversity. The operation brought together personnel from all over the world. For example, along with civilian rope specialists, the dive ropes team consisted of Thai, American, Australian, and Chinese military personnel. A diverse set of Thai and foreign engineers helped enhance the pumping to reduce the raging current and make building the dive line possible. Four Thai Navy SEALs spent nearly a week with the boys in chamber nine. The final team of rescue divers included five Thai and thirteen international divers.

The successful rescue integrated not only the diverse skill sets but also the diverse experiences of the larger team. Without Rick Stanton's experience with the pump workers, he might not have recognized the need to fully anesthetize the boys during the dive. Without Dr. Harris's experience as an anesthetist, it would have been impossible to execute the plan.

Diverse teams, however, also have the worst outcomes. We see the roots of this reality in the cave rescue, despite the surprising smoothness and remarkable outcome of the final mission. The Thai military viewed the foreign cave divers as interfering interlopers rather than collaborators, which led to multiple confrontations. This tension, which persisted throughout the rescue efforts, illustrates the core downside of diversity; it creates distinctions, and distinctions often lead to discord. Not surprisingly, research shows that diverse neighborhoods have lower trust among neighbors and less community engagement. And diverse teams have less confidence in their performance, even when their decisions and outcomes are superior to those of homogenous teams.

So how do we solve the problem of diversity? How do we get the best outcomes while avoiding the worst ones? How can we make diversity truly inspiring?

The problem of diversity is solved through two seemingly contradictory ideas: *diversity* and *uniformity*. Although the concepts of diversity and uniformity may seem incongruous, they work in concert to help diverse teams become the best teams.

DIVERSITY SOLVES THE PROBLEM OF DIVERSITY

AT FIRST BLUSH, the idea that diversity is solved through diversity sounds absurd. But diversity doesn't just represent differences in demographics (gender, race, age, socioeconomic status, etc.); it also includes other dimensions on which people vary.

One area of diversity that has taken prominence recently is in acknowledging that not everyone processes information in the same way, what psychologists call *neurodiversity*. The team of elite cave divers illustrates this neurodivergence. The divers were very different from many of their peers growing up, but this difference allowed them to find solace in the tight spaces underground that they couldn't find on playgrounds. Richard Harris summed up the value of their cognitive differences this way: "Last to be chosen for the cricket team, first to be chosen for the cave rescue." Without the unique talents of these cave divers, a set of skills born from their distinct cognitive orientation, the miraculous rescue never would have happened.

But we can expand the concept of diversity even further by looking beyond differences *between* people. We can also conceive of diversity as occurring *within* people, i.e., the diversity of their experiences. In fact, it is this diversity that lies *within* people that is the key to solving the diversity *between* people. Diverse experiences give us direct access to new ideas and new perspectives. That's what happened with Rick Stanton and his underwater wrestling match with the pump workers. He witnessed that it took only thirty seconds underwater for panic to seize the pump workers. Without that experience, Rick would never have recognized the need to anesthetize the boys, and certainly not in time to save them. His experience with the pump workers helped him generate a creative lifesaving solution. But diverse experiences do more than just change *what* we think. They also change *how* we think.

MY INSIGHT THAT diverse experiences change how we think began on a Monday evening in the winter of 2005. Will Maddux, a recently hired postdoctoral fellow, and I were preparing a lecture on cross-cultural communication to hundreds of MBA students embarking on two-week international trips when I was suddenly struck by an idea. I turned to Will and said, "I wonder if people who have spent time abroad are more creative." We quickly searched the scientific literature but didn't find any research that had even asked the question. So we decided to put our idea to a test.

That night, Will and I put together a simple survey consisting of only three questions and sent it to the 250 MBA students coming to my lecture two days later.

1.   Have you ever traveled abroad? If so, how many months: _____
2.   Have you ever lived abroad? If so, how many months: _____
3.   Please solve the problem below.

Here's the problem we gave the students to solve:

You have three objects on a table next to a cardboard wall: a candle, a pack of matches, and a box of tacks. Using only the objects on the table, how would you attach the candle to the wall so that it would burn without dripping wax on the table or the floor?

This is a classic measure of creative insight—called the Duncker candle problem—and it's not an easy problem to solve. When I gave Princeton undergraduates this problem in the 1990s, only 6 percent could solve it without any intervention.

Here's the correct solution: empty the box of tacks, tack the box to the wall, and place the candle inside. It seems so straightforward, right? So why could only 6 percent of Ivy League students solve it? It's because we get stuck or fixated on the usual functions of objects and have a difficult time seeing their many other uses. In this case, the box is not just a repository for tacks; it can also be used as a candle stand.

The candle problem may seem a bit esoteric, but it represents a larger phenomenon called *functional fixedness*. When we get stuck looking at a problem or situation from only one angle, we often can't see the many other possibilities that lie before us.

When Will and I looked at our survey, we found no difference in solving the candle problem between people who had traveled abroad and those who had not. That's not surprising given almost everyone (99 percent) had visited another country. Furthermore, we found that the amount of time traveling abroad actually had a *negative* relationship with creativity. The more time people had spent traveling abroad, the *less likely* they were to solve the candle problem.

We next analyzed whether living abroad mattered. A little more than half of the students had lived in a foreign country at some point in their life. We found that those students were 40 percent *more likely* to solve the problem than those who had not lived abroad. And we found time spent living abroad *positively* predicted solving the candle problem.

We were stunned by these results, especially because the candle problem was unrelated to their experiences living abroad. The solution didn't require any specialized cultural knowledge; it didn't depend on *what* people thought. Instead, our results suggested that diverse experiences change *how* people think. Our findings that only living abroad increased solution rates also suggested that those diverse experiences needed to be particularly deep for this creative transformation to take place.

To ensure that our results weren't a fluke and that they weren't unique to the candle problem, Will and I conducted dozens of studies using a wide variety of creativity tasks over the next fifteen years. In one study, we used the same restaurant negotiation as when we discussed Inspiring Negotiations (Chapter 9). This negotiation might seem very different from the candle problem, but it is structurally similar: in both cases, we need to think about alternative functions to find a solution. In this negotiation, a deal seems impossible at first because the seller's asking price is higher than what the buyer is willing to pay. But when we look deeper, we see the seller is seeking a higher sum to fund culinary school and the buyer is looking to hire amazing chefs. To solve this negotiation, we need to stop fixating on sale price and consider other sources of value. A deal can be reached if the buyer pays their walkaway price but hires the seller as a chef and offers to fund their culinary education.

The results of this study were remarkable: When neither the buyer nor the seller had lived abroad, 0 percent of them solved the negotiation. But when both the negotiators had lived abroad, they reached a creative deal *70 percent of the time*!

Across many studies using many different creativity tasks, we have discovered three important findings. First, our negative effect of traveling abroad was never replicated. Traveling abroad just didn't matter for predicting creativity in our studies. Second, people who have lived abroad tend to be more creative than those who remained homeward bound. Third, time spent living abroad positively predicts creativity. Having deeper experiences abroad changes *how* people approach the world. It frees their minds from well-worn conceptual ruts to look at the world in new ways.

In our research, living abroad consistently mattered more for changing how we think than traveling abroad. But Will and I also discovered that the secret ingredient isn't really about living abroad. Living abroad is just a proxy for having a deep, meaningful interaction with another culture. For example, in a longitudinal study involving MBA students, where we measured creativity at orientation and then again at graduation, we found that dating someone from another culture increased a student's ability to generate creative ideas and solve creative problems like the candle one. Similar to travel, cross-cultural friendships didn't predict increased creativity.

But like living abroad, the effect isn't about dating. The key ingredient is forming *deep* connections to someone who is from a different culture. When we examined the surveys of J-1 work visa holders (foreign individuals participating in work- and study-based programs in the US), we found that the more frequently they connected with their American friends after returning home, the more likely they were to start their own business in their home country. It's the depth, not the type of connection, that matters for changing how we think.

Importantly, the creative benefits of deep intercultural experiences are not confined to laboratory or classroom settings. In a project led by Frédéric Godart of INSEAD business school, we analyzed the creative output of 270 top fashion houses over 21 seasons. We focused our attention on the creative director because as the top executive in charge of design, they control every aspect of their house's biannual collection, from idea generation to runway presentation during the fashion weeks in Milan, Paris, New York, and London. To measure international experience, we exhaustively studied the work history of these creative directors and carefully identified the countries and time spent working abroad. To measure creativity, we were lucky to find that a French fashion trade newspaper, *Le Journal du Textile*, asked fashion experts to evaluate the creativity, and not the consumer potential, of every collection shown during each of the four fashion weeks. Even in the context of high-end fashion, we replicated our findings. The longer a creative director had worked outside of their home country, the more creative the collections they designed were.

GLOBAL LEADERS INSPIRE GLOBAL TEAMS

FORMING DEEP CONNECTIONS with other cultures expands our minds and changes how we think and approach the world. It turns out we can solve the paradox of diverse teams—that they produce the best and worst outcomes—by ensuring that our leaders have experienced deep connections with other cultures. To better understand why, let's travel to England.

As you likely know, the British are nuts about soccer. Their main soccer league, the English Premier League (EPL), is the most watched sports league in the world; in the 2019 season alone, more than 3.2 billion people watched a Premier League game. The EPL is also one of the most diverse soccer leagues, with foreign players accounting for more than two-thirds of the players.

In a study led by my former student Jackson Lu, now at MIT, we set out to see if the diversity of teams predicted their on-field performance. We collected data from every season of the EPL since its inception. That included twenty-five seasons from 1992 to 2017 involving forty-seven unique teams and 4,781 unique soccer players. We measured the national diversity of each team by identifying the home country of every player and creating a team level measure of diversity, where the more countries represented on the team, the more diverse the team was. We measured team performance using the same point system the EPL uses to determine their rankings and their champions (this is the same point system used in the group stages of the World Cup): teams get 0 points for a loss, 1 point for a tie, and 3 points for a win.

When we analyzed whether team national diversity (i.e., the number of nationalities of the players) predicted team performance, we found that it did not. Some teams high in national diversity won a lot, and other diverse teams lost all the time. Diversity had produced some of the best teams but also some of the worst ones.

Our research didn't end there. We explored whether the team leader would determine when diversity won and when it lost. The leader of an EPL team is the manager and this role carries a lot more responsibility than professional coaches in the US. Essentially, an EPL manager is the coach, general manager, and team president all rolled into one.

Our analyses revealed two fascinating findings. First, the more countries a manager had worked in before a given season, the more points his team won that season. If a manager worked in one additional foreign country, his team's performance increased by an extra 3.42 points, or more than one extra win.

Those three-plus points might seem insignificant, but that number can be the difference between winning it all and being stuck in second place. For example, Manchester City beat Arsenal by just two points in 2024. And those points can also be the difference between staying in the Premier League versus getting relegated down to a worse league, the Championship League. Leicester City, who won the EPL championship in 2016, was relegated in 2023 after finishing a mere two points behind Everton. Being relegated is not only humiliating, but also financially disastrous. A typical relegated club will lose more than 50 percent of its revenues, a sum that can approach £100 million.

Deep experiences with other cultures make us more inspiring for all the VEM reasons. By removing ourselves from our conventional contexts and daily habits, we can take a step back and see the bigger picture. And being exposed to the values of other cultures helps us decipher what really matters to us and articulate a more vivid vision. It's why Michael Crichton, the author of *Jurassic Park*, proclaimed, "Often I feel I go to some distant region of the world to be reminded of who I really am." Deep experiences abroad make us an exemplar of desired behavior by activating our sense of passion and curiosity, while also making us feel more authentic and more human. And we become a more inspiring mentor because it increases our sense of empathy and appreciation of others.

The second result was even more interesting. We found that the effect of team diversity on performance *depended* on the foreign experience of its manager. Let's unpack this finding. When managers had worked in multiple countries before that season, team national diversity strongly and positively predicted performance. But when managers had little to no foreign experience, team national diversity had a small negative effect on performance. Diverse teams had the best outcomes, but *only* if they had a manager who had a diverse set of international experiences. Diverse teams tended to have worse outcomes, however, when their managers spent their whole coaching life stuck in England.

LEARN THE *WHY* OF CULTURES

WHY DID THE foreign experience of the EPL managers matter so much for harnessing the benefits of diversity? When we deeply engage with another culture, we *learn* about that culture's behavioral tendencies and customs. But more importantly, we often learn *why* these foreign practices and customs exist. And we come to understand their underlying cultural function. It is learning the many whys of another culture that transforms how we think.

Take something as simple as food on a plate. In different cultures, it carries different meanings. When I lived with a family in Indonesia in high school, I learned that leaving food on your plate is an insult there because it suggests the food wasn't very good. But in China, leaving food on your plate is a compliment because it communicates that you were given enough to eat. Like the box of tacks, whose form has many functions, the same form (food on a plate) has different meanings in different cultures.

Let's go back to the EPL managers. Working in many different countries required these managers to learn how to communicate with individuals from different backgrounds by understanding the different ways that people share and receive information in different countries. Experiences abroad helped these managers understand the nuances and underlying values of the different nationalities on their team, which made them better overall communicators. Consider the concept of time, which, like food on a plate, has different meanings in different cultures. Arsène Wenger, who won three EPL titles as manager of Arsenal, described how his time managing in France and Japan helped him understand the cultural nuances of time and adapt his communication style to the context and to the player. "Being on time isn't the same for a Japanese man as it is for a Frenchman—when a Frenchman arrives five minutes late, he still thinks he is on time. In Japan, when it's five minutes before the set time he thinks he is too late."

In later research, Will Maddux and I confirmed that it is learning the *why* of other cultures—what we called *functional learning*—that is the key piece for catalyzing the power of cross-cultural experiences to change *how* we think. In contrast, observing a behavior in another country without understanding its function leaves people trapped inside conventional boxes.

Here's how Will and I demonstrated the transformative power of learning the *why* of other cultures. We asked everyone to write about a multicultural experience in which they noticed something novel about another culture, but we varied whether they were *able* or *not able* to figure out the underlying reasons *why* the novel behavior existed. The people who were able to understand the *why* behind the novel behavior were 40 percent more likely to solve the candle problem.

Learning the *why* of other cultures changes not only how we think but also how we communicate. In a longitudinal study, Will and I asked graduating MBA students the extent to which they had learned about new cultures during their graduate program. At both the beginning and end of their MBA, these students were also asked to write an essay discussing "the pros and cons of working in multicultural teams." We coded these essays for their ability to integrate different perspectives on the topic. Not surprisingly, integrative thinking at time one predicted integrative thinking at time two. But here is what was fascinating: learning more about other cultures during one's MBA *increased* integrative thinking from time one to time two. Further, we found that by changing how people think and communicate, learning the *why* of other cultures helped them be more effective during their job interviews: those students who had deeply learned about other cultures while pursuing their MBA received more job offers. Even more interesting, the effect of learning on job interviews occurred because of their increased ability to integrate different perspectives. Learning the *why* of other cultures helped give these students the vision they needed to inspire during their job interviews.

DIVERSE TEAMS PRODUCE a paradox: more diverse teams result in both the best and worst outcomes. The good news is we can broaden our understanding of diversity to solve the very problem of diversity. It is the diversity within leaders that helps inspire diverse teams to reach the mountaintop. From soccer to fashion, diverse teams achieve greater success when their leaders have had more diverse experiences.

Before you pack your passport, it's important to remember that you don't need to hop on a plane to be a more creative thinker, a better communicator, or a more effective leader. You only need to invest in *learning* about other cultures, especially the *why* behind their cultural practices. That means you can engage deeply with other cultures right here at home. When we understand and appreciate the *why* behind different cultural practices, we help free our minds from conventional boxes to harness the power of diversity.

The first key to solving the problem of diversity is diversity. The second key is uniformity. Let's see how uniform processes can help make everyone on a diverse team feel truly included.

INSPIRING DIVERSITY AND DESIGNING
INCLUSION THROUGH UNIFORM PROCESSES

WHEN DISCUSSING HOW to inspire fairness (Chapter 11), we noted that creating and leading diverse teams requires uniform processes. Putting everyone through a similar process during applicant selection, interviews, and promotions inspires both fairness and diversity. But uniform policies don't just increase diversity. Policies that are uniformly applied to everyone also inspire a sense of inclusion within diverse groups that prevents differences from leading to discord.

Inclusion is intertwined with diversity. Concerns with ensuring inclusion are often motivated by the need to increase feelings of acceptance by employees of color and women who are often underrepresented in organizations. But to create truly inclusive practices, we need to uniformly apply them to everyone. Instead of creating policies designed to benefit one demographic group or applied to only some employees, we need to ensure that these practices are company-wide efforts applied to all its members. Indeed, as we will see, the most successful practices for creating a sense of inclusion in employees of color are ones not designed specifically for those employees.

DESIGNING AN INCLUSIVE UNIFORM VISION

EVERY TEAM NEEDS an inspiring vision, but this is especially true of diverse teams. Without an inspiring vision, diverse teams quickly veer toward division and conflict. In contrast, a clear vision helps keep diverse teams on track toward the best outcomes.

We saw the value of a shared vision in the Thai cave rescue. Having the shared goal of saving the boys allowed the broader rescue team to overcome the tensions created by differences in nationality and expertise. When conflict erupted, bringing the shared goal back to the forefront allowed everyone to get past any hard feelings to focus on the task at hand.

Diversity can only thrive when everyone is on the same page. That's why a diverse team needs an *inclusive* vision that resonates with *all* its members. To understand why a uniformly uniting vision is so important, imagine you are the CEO of GO Consulting and are considering two different mission statements. Which one do you think will increase the engagement and commitment of all your employees?

Vision 1: At GO Consulting, we believe that our clients receive the highest-quality consulting services when our workforce mirrors the increasingly diverse marketplace. Our employees also benefit from our dedication to this diversity: their own backgrounds are recognized and celebrated. We foster an inclusive and open-minded workplace that values diverse backgrounds and experiences, which, in turn, benefits our employees, clients, and the industry at large. At GO Consulting, our commitment to diversity contributes to our success as a company.

Vision 2: At GO Consulting, we believe that our clients receive the highest-quality consulting services when our workforce is composed of the most qualified individuals. Our employees also benefit from our dedication to merit: they have equal opportunities to succeed and be rewarded. We seek the most qualified individuals to join our company and reach their potential, which, in turn, benefits our employees, clients, and the industry at large. At GO Consulting, our commitment to merit contributes to our success as a company.

It's a trick question: you shouldn't choose either one! In my research with Seval Gündemir of the University of Amsterdam, we found that neither is very effective.

Let's look at the first vision: it makes a commitment to and celebrates diversity. Unsurprisingly, it increases the engagement and involvement of employees of color, while also increasing their sense of self-efficacy. Sounds great, right? The problem is this vision turns off White employees, and it leads them to view their minority colleagues in more stereotypical terms. But it's also not perfect for the employees of color either because it increases their tendency to conform to existing stereotypes about their group.

Now let's consider the second vision: it makes a commitment to merit. Seems fair, right? The problem is employees of color often feel a color-blind approach doesn't acknowledge the stereotypes and obstacles they continue to face, or the unique perspectives they bring to the table. As a result, they are suspicious of missions that focus on merit.

In looking at these two archetypal visions, Seval and I had an idea. What if we combined and integrated them? What if we never mentioned merit without diversity? We called this type of vision *multicultural meritocracy*. Here is the multicultural meritocracy vision we created.

At GO Consulting, we believe that our clients receive the highest-quality consulting services when our workforce is composed of the most qualified individuals who also mirror the increasingly diverse marketplace. Our employees also benefit from our dedication to merit and diversity: our employees have equal opportunities to succeed while their own diverse backgrounds are recognized and celebrated. We seek the most qualified individuals to be part of an inclusive workplace that values differences, which, in turn, benefits our employees, clients, and the industry at large. At GO Consulting, our commitment to merit and diversity contributes to our success as a company.

It turns out our vision that combined both merit and diversity was a home run. All employees expressed greater engagement under the multicultural meritocracy vision. Employees of color felt more engaged under this vision than even from the pure commitment-to-diversity vision, and they felt it was more inclusive than any other vision. White employees also felt more engaged from the multicultural meritocracy vision than from the commitment-to-merit vision, and they felt it was fairer than any other vision. Overall, by both celebrating diversity *and* highlighting fair and equal-opportunity treatment, our multicultural meritocracy vision achieved the benefits of each of these separate visions but without their limiting downsides. The implication is clear: to lead a diverse team, we need to make sure our vision resonates with all its members.

Having an inclusive vision not only engages a diverse set of employees and group members, but it also attracts a diverse set of potential applicants. As we saw when discussing fairness (Chapter 11), having uniform processes can help increase diversity. Uniform processes can also make our mental Rolodexes more inclusive.

EXPAND YOUR MENTAL ROLODEX

IMAGINE YOU'RE A film producer and you need to generate a list of potential actors for an upcoming action-thriller film. Write down three names.

Great, now I want you to expand your short list by adding three more names.

Now imagine you are a board member of a technology start-up looking for a new CEO. Write down a list of three people who should be interviewed for the role. Okay, now add three more names.

In both cases, you generated three names, and then were asked to generate three additional names. Seems simple, right? But my former student Brian Lucas of Cornell University found that this technique has transformational effects on creating more equal opportunities. Asking people to expand their short list dramatically increased the gender diversity of applicant pools. In fact, it nearly doubled the number of women who made the cut. I call this technique *expanding our mental Rolodex*.

Why does expanding our mental Rolodex have such a powerful effect on increasing diversity? Making the short list longer leads responses to diverge from the typical prototype in an industry. When we think about a film director or the CEO of a technology company, an image of a man pops into our head. But when we are asked to expand our short list, our mind naturally breaks out of this narrow perspective and actively shifts to thinking of less prototypical examples.

The effect isn't just about male prototypes. If an industry or role is populated by women, then expanding the short list will lead people to include more male candidates. Brian ran a clever study to demonstrate this finding. He asked parents to list three role models for their child, and then to expand their short list by adding three more names. When their child was a boy, expanding the short list increased the number of female role models. But when their child was a girl, expanding the short list increased the number of male role models!

The lesson is clear: by uniformly expanding our short lists, we get unstuck from the same narrow faces and open our minds to a more diverse set of possibilities.

DESIGNING INCLUSION THROUGH UNIFORMLY APPLIED RULES AND VALUES

HAVING UNIFORM PROCESSES not only helps increase diversity, but it helps manage diversity effectively because it reduces both the possibility and the appearance of bias. Let's go back to the TV show *The Shield*, which we discussed in Inspiring Wise Decisions (Chapter 10). The writing team was diverse on gender but unequal in participation; the women rarely pitched ideas because they were immediately interrupted by the men when they did. But when one of the show's executive producers installed a no-interruption rule, gender equity in the pitching process increased.

Note that the no-interruption rule was not directed at men interrupting women. Although the rule was inspired to create more equal opportunities for women, it was not applied to only one gender. Instead, it was applied equally to men *and* women. As a result, it helped everyone produce better ideas. This simple rule was so effective because it was uniformly and inclusively applied to everyone.

To increase feelings of inclusion from underrepresented members of a group, we often emphasize how much we want these individuals to feel comfortable sharing their authentic selves. But as we saw with research on unconscious bias training in Inspiring Fairness (Chapter 11), inclusive efforts that put minorities in the spotlight only make these employees feel exposed, while also leaving White employees feeling disgruntled. Furthermore, these efforts don't fully address the uncertainty that historically marginalized employees feel in whether they can authentically express themselves.

When my former student Cindy Wang, now of Northwestern University, and I surveyed and interviewed Black employees, we found that they felt an acute tension between being authentic and fitting in. They were concerned that authentically expressing their identities would only highlight differences and reinforce negative stereotypes. One of our interviewees laid out how complex the seemingly simple decision of hairstyle is for Black women: she was unsure if her colleagues would appreciate her for wearing a natural hairstyle or if they would see it as unprofessional.

Cindy and I found that when companies encouraged *all* employees to be authentic, to embrace and share their true selves at work, a reinforcing cycle of inclusion was fostered. Since employees of color were not the focus, White employees felt comfortable expressing the varied aspects of their identities. Seeing their White colleagues authentically express themselves, in turn, provided the Black employees in our study with greater confidence that their own authentic expressions would be embraced rather than rejected. Consider how Keira describes the joy of working in a company that uniformly encourages authentic expressions:

> They come to work as themselves, whatever that is. For example, a friend who was a vegetarian influenced the workplace in a positive way . . . Okay, this person is not wasteful, so this person makes me not want to use paper plates and things like that. So, just showing up and helping them to see, "Look at me, I'm a Black person who is on the South Side [of Chicago], you see me every day, you know how I roll," you talk to me, maybe that can help you better relate to Black people.

As Keira's quote demonstrates, inclusively encouraging authenticity allows each employee, including underrepresented minorities, to feel more comfortable sharing their true self and being a fully engaged member of the team.

The idea of creating a culture of inclusive authenticity may seem vague, but here's a specific practice from my time at Northwestern University. Each year there was an international food competition at the business school where students would make a variety of dishes from their home countries. Each country had a food stall that offered various culinary offerings. Faculty, students, and staff could go from stall to stall and select dishes from different countries to buy. But we didn't use money, we used tickets. Why? Because the tickets were the currency of competition; the country with the most tickets at the end of the fair would be declared the winner! As I walked through the food fair, each stall clamored for my attention, luring me to try their country's cuisine (and give my tickets). Although the competitive nature of the event created a surge of energy, what struck me was the intense pride that everyone felt at sharing their countries' unique dishes. I would see students at each stall beam with pride as they explained how a dish was made or why it was important to their culture. And I would often hear emotion crackle in their voices as they offered personal stories about the joy this dish had brought them during their childhood.

The no-interruption rule, climates of authenticity, and Northwestern's food fair each speak to the power of design, of thinking like an inclusive architect.

DESIGNING INCLUSION BY MAKING
THE INFORMAL FORMAL

NAOMI ASKS TO meet her boss for coffee. She listens to how her boss learned to navigate the hidden obstacle course of the organization. Naomi is mesmerized, soaking up all the inside information. Her boss feels validated. The boss is becoming Naomi's mentor.

Seems simple and straightforward, right? But it's problematic. Wait, what? How could it be wrong for an employee to learn from their boss?

The problem is that other employees may not be aware that they can approach their boss in the same way. They may have had the same thought but dismissed it as inappropriate. Or they were scared their boss would say no to the request and that would feel like a REJECTION because of the leader amplification effect. When individual initiative drives informal interactions, we only promote the people who were taught that this initiative is permissible or encouraged.

But there is a second problem with letting mentoring relationships develop informally: they tend to be divided by gender and race. David Thomas, now the president of Morehouse College and previously a professor at Harvard Business School, found that cross-race and cross-gender mentoring relationships rarely develop naturally. There are also barriers to cross-gender mentorships: male bosses often fear that reaching out to mentor a female employee will be interpreted through the lens of inappropriate intentions.

So, what's the solution? In the example of Naomi above, a wrong lesson would be to ban all coffee chats with the boss. Instead, we can explicitly let everyone on our team know that they can always request a coffee chat. And maybe an even better solution is that we create a uniform and inclusive process of scheduling regular coffee chats with *every* direct report.

I call this *making the informal formal*. Formalizing the informal involves transforming naturally evolving but unequal interactions into uniform processes. It is simply standardizing a process so that the opportunity is uniformly made available to everyone. Like standardized and uniform questions for interviews, making sure everyone has equal opportunities for mentorship levels the playing field.

As I was writing this chapter, a doctoral student asked if I would be willing to use my research funds to cover her expenses for a conference where she would be presenting our research. Instinctively, I said yes. The very next day, however, it dawned on me that my yes wasn't fair and inclusive. What about the other doctoral students who didn't ask and who may not have known they could ask? My research funds are limited, and I can't fund every request. So, the next day I told the student that I couldn't say yes but it didn't mean the answer was no. I needed to think like an architect and design a uniform and fair process for this type of request.

To understand how relying on informal processes creates inequality, here's a story a consultant shared with me in 1997 when I was in graduate school. This consultant was working with a law firm to boost their dismal rate of partnering female associates and associates of color. His team did a deep analysis to determine the key variables that predicted achieving partnership. One variable stood out because it had nothing to do with law or the office.

Golf.

It turned out that the associates who played golf were more likely to make partner. But it wasn't mere cronyism. The golfing associates deserved to make partnership because they had objectively superior records.

What's going on here?

Partners were often looking for golfers to join their outings at fancy country clubs because they needed a foursome to secure a weekend tee time. When they were one golfer short, they would seek out an associate from their law firm to join them.

Golf was an amazing way for a young associate to connect with a powerful partner. Because golf takes forever to play, often more than four hours, the associates had lots of face time with powerful members of their firm. Importantly, that time on the golf course isn't spent constantly short of breath; there is lots of downtime and plenty of conversation. And alcohol is often involved, loosening up the potentially stiff interaction. Although they were away from the office and out in nature, the conversation would inevitably turn to work, and to opportunities. The partner might ask what type of law the associate is interested in and then steer opportunities that fit their passion. Or the partner might describe a high-profile case they were working on and invite the associate to join. As a result, the golfing associates had more high-quality opportunities. With these opportunities leading to new ones, the initial invitations offered on the golf course compounded over time. Then, when it was time to decide on partners, the golfing associates shone the brightest.

Golf is even more problematic because it isn't the most inclusive sport. It's expensive to play, from equipment to lessons to high-priced green fees and country club dues. Because the partners only sought out associates who already played golf, the advantaged were further advantaged.

The problem isn't golf per se but any activity that attracts the passions of some but not others. For one investment bank, it was Sunday-night basketball that created informal mentors. At a consulting company, mentorship was developed over monthly poker tournaments.

What can we learn from these examples? The solution isn't to start playing golf, basketball, or poker. And the solution isn't to actively prohibit any of these shared activities. The key insight is that informal interactions, often undertaken with the best of intentions, can create opportunities for some but not others. But by redesigning these informal interactions into more structured processes, we can create opportunities that are equitably and inclusively offered.

These interactions over shared interests also highlight the other theme of this chapter: the key to solving diversity is *diversity*. In this case, it's crucial to make sure that we offer a diverse set of bonding activities. And it's important to choose some that don't require a particular skill or where people can be included without actively participating. Karaoke is one example. Many people who are tone-deaf, like me, still love to belt out karaoke tunes. And for those who are mortified at the thought of singing in front of others, they can still enjoy listening. We can even diversify the timing of these activities, given that some employees are morning people and others are night owls, and the fact that employees who are parents often have restricted weekend schedules.

THE INSPIRING POWER OF INCLUSIVE MENTORING

IN TACKLING THE problem of unequal promotion rates among women and minorities, many companies designed mentoring programs only for members of these groups. For example, many organizations created mentoring programs where women were matched with a female mentor in the same organization. These programs are well-intentioned, moti-vated by the idea that young female employees can learn key insights from managers who have faced similar problems and experiences. But these programs are limiting as they exacerbate the very problem that David Thomas found in his research where most mentoring relationships are siloed within gender and within race. And they put an incredible burden on the female managers.

So, what's the solution? We need to design a mentoring program that has a few key elements. First, it needs to include all employees. The program can't just target underrepresented groups or be offered as a reward for high potentials; programs structured this way are a breeding ground for division and inequity. Thus, it is critical that our mentoring programs are inclusively applied to everyone.

Second, we should match mentors with mentees based on interests, not demographics. Because shared interests are built on mutual passions, they are inherently motivating and connecting. This type of matching system ensures that the mentor and mentee have something in common.

The benefits of inclusive mentoring programs are clear. When Frank Dobbins analyzed companies over a thirty-year period, mentoring programs that inclusively involved all employees led to higher promotion rates of women and minorities. Importantly, he also observed these mentoring programs didn't decrease the promotion rates among White men.

I recently met with a working group of business school deans to discuss how to design more effective mentoring programs. We recognized the value of having a *diverse* set of mentors, where a mentoring program assigns multiple mentors to each new/junior employee, one within their division and one outside their division. Since many promotion decisions are made within divisions, it is essential people have the internal knowledge they need to succeed. But by having a mentor outside of one's primary area of expertise, young employees can receive a broader organizational perspective, develop a wider social network, and get access to more opportunities.

Second, we highlighted how mentorship programs are less fraught with land mines when there is a rotational system in place, where each employee gets a new set of mentors every year or two. There are two advantages to a rotational system. First, it further expands and diversifies the social ties of both mentors and mentees. Many employees will maintain contact with their initial mentors, while getting access to additional new perspectives. But a rotational system also solves the problem of ineffective or infuriating mentoring relationships. When an employee is dissatisfied with their mentor, they often feel stuck. Remember, they are, by definition, in a low-power position. Many worry that if they attempt to change to a new mentor, they will create an enemy in their old one. But a rotational mentoring system solves this problem. Rather than being based on dissatisfaction or accusations, a change in mentor is simply part of the mentoring program. It takes the informal need for change and turns it into a uniform part of the process. It is why we need to always be thinking like an architect. When we design the right mentoring system, we open the right channels to inspiring relationships and close off the wrong channels toward infuriating ones.

Thinking like an inclusive architect helps us design uniform practices and policies that apply equally to everyone. Remember: creating policies intended to benefit one group not only creates distinctions that lead to accusations of unfairness and discord, but they also don't always end up benefiting the intended target group.

The most effective policies are inclusive practices that apply uniformly to all members of the organization. An inclusive vision that is shared with everyone. A climate of authenticity that is applied to everyone. A successful mentoring program that is open to everyone. True inclusion helps diverse teams reach for the stars, and that is truly inspiring.

A More Inspiring Tomorrow

PRESIDENTS JIMMY CARTER and Donald Trump couldn't be more different. One is a soft-spoken, humble peanut farmer from Georgia and the other a brash self-promoter from the rough-and-tumble world of New York real estate. When each left the White House, they continued down different paths. Carter focused on philanthropy and won the Nobel Peace Prize for his efforts to secure peaceful solutions to global conflicts. In contrast, Trump directed his post-presidency attention toward his commercial enterprises, doubling his business holdings three years after leaving office (while also battling numerous legal challenges).

But there is one thing that Carter and Trump have in common: they each lost their bid for reelection. Their single-term presidencies reveal a key wrinkle in the core premise of *Inspire*—that leaders exist on an enduring inspiring-infuriating continuum that is made up of three universal factors (visionary, exemplar, mentor). Both Carter and Trump speak to a frequent set of questions I get asked. Am I only inspiring if I am high on all three of these factors? What happens if I am an amazing mentor and shining exemplar but lack a vision? What about if I am profoundly visionary and courageous but a wire-mesh mentor? Carter and Trump were inspiring *and* infuriating, but at different times and to different people.

Animated by his born-again Christianity, Jimmy Carter was passionate about governmental integrity and human rights. He campaigned on a promise to bring honor and dignity back to the Oval Office and to support the rights of all individuals. These commitments resonated with an electorate reeling from the duplicity of the former president Richard Nixon, the only American president to resign in disgrace.

Even though his generosity of spirit was always evident, Jimmy Carter served only one term as president because he never articulated a clear vision during his time in the Oval Office. Writer Stephen Hess perfectly captured the consequences of Carter's visionary failures halfway through his term in 1978: "When a president lacks an overriding design for what he wants government to do, his department chiefs are forced to prepare presidential options in a vacuum . . . neither White House staff nor cabinet officials have been given the predictive capacity that they must have to do their jobs properly. A subordinate—even on the cabinet level—has to be able to plan on the basis of some past pattern." Under Carter, the executive branch lacked a title (remember the power of "doing the laundry"). Even his passionate concern with human rights was never translated into a meaningful and actionable vision during his time in office.

Because Carter lacked a clear and optimistic *why* for his government, his presidency floundered in bureaucratic infighting and confusion. When it was claimed that he personally oversaw the schedule of the White House tennis court, it "came to be a popular symbol of what many felt was the fatal flaw of his presidency: the unwillingness to delegate authority on small matters."

His lack of vision made him seem small. And when he faced the biggest crisis of his presidency, the Iran hostage crisis, he didn't seem up to the task. After more than fifty Americans were taken hostage in Iran on November 4, 1979, exactly one year before the next presidential election, Carter was never able to secure their release. He left his presidency having failed to be a courageous protector of his people. Carter may have satisfied people's need for respect, but he didn't fulfill their need for control or protection. He was infuriating in his apparent weakness.

But Carter found salvation after leaving the Oval Office by dedicating himself to the one overriding passion that drove his original campaign: his vision of human rights for all. He became an inspiring exemplar by personally building houses with Habitat for Humanity. And his graceful ability to treat people like *people* made him an inspiring mentor, even as memories of his one-term presidency continued to linger.

Donald Trump also inspired millions of people. And it's not surprising from a VEM perspective. He is visionary. As we have already discussed, *Make America Great Again* is brilliant in its simplicity, motivating in its optimism, and alluring in its sense of purpose, especially for those disaffected by demographic shifts in the US. Trump also details the many traits that make him an inspiring exemplar. He portrays himself as a courageous protector, declaring in his 2016 convention speech, "Nobody knows the system better than me, which is why I alone can fix it." He explains how his many successes derive from his creative genius. And he is viewed as both passionate and authentic even by his detractors. Although the accuracy of these exemplar characteristics can be debated, Trump presents them as given, and millions of Americans take them as gospel.

At the same time, Trump partly lost his reelection for two VEM reasons. Although Trump is clearly visionary, that vision is not universally embraced. His MAGA vision infuriates many who see it as steeped in division and a reactionary call to roll back the well-deserved gains of women and minorities. Because it is such a divisive vision, many people voted *against* Trump in the 2020 election.

Second, Trump treats people as *objects*, as pawns in his political machinations. It's no wonder that his presidency was marked by staffing turmoil and constant turnover in every major role; for example, he went through four chiefs of staff in less than four years. He notoriously threw his subordinates under the bus, taking sole credit for all successes and accepting zero responsibility for any difficulties.

Trump is particularly fascinating because his infuriating mentorship can also come across as exemplary strength in competitive contexts. In fact, his belittling treatment of his fellow Republican primary candidates helped him rise to his party's nomination in 2016. One strategy he used to undermine his opponents was conferring a demeaning nickname on each candidate that ingeniously captured their greatest weakness. He called Ted Cruz "Lying Ted," to capture his inauthenticity. He called Jeb Bush "Low-Energy Jeb," to highlight his inability to engage others. Marco Rubio was "Little Marco" to magnify not only his physical stature but also his lack of presence and gravitas. He was equally tactical with his Democratic opponent Hillary Clinton, who became "Crooked Hillary," to highlight her suspect morals.

Unlike Carter, Trump was able to rebound and become the second person in U.S. history to win the presidency after losing re-election four years earlier. Trump didn't change in 2024, but our memories of his presidency did. Trump's *Make America Great Again* vision, his authentic passion, and his professed strength continued to inspire millions of Americans. In contrast, the divisiveness of his presidency, his impulsive outbursts, and his tendency to use and discard people receded into the past. Because he wasn't the sitting president, his words and behavior had fewer consequences. And because he was running as a *challenger*, the competitive context helped turn some of his more infuriating comments into a groundswell of voter support.

Jimmy Carter and Donald Trump reveal that few of us are fully and perpetually inspiring. They also show how the inspiring-infuriating continuum always exists in context. Carter was a visionary exemplar and mentor as a private citizen, but not as the symbolic or administrative head of a nation. Carter's inspiring attributes were suited for more contained contexts; for example, he may have been a more inspiring cabinet member than a president. Similarly, Trump's belittling of others could be motivating in the competitive context of a presidential primary but infuriating in many other circumstances.

No leader is perfect. John F. Kennedy and Martin Luther King Jr.

were visionary giants who repeatedly cheated on their spouses. Aung San Suu Kyi's passionate advocacy for democracy in Myanmar led her to win the Nobel Peace Prize after spending a decade under house arrest. But when she eventually became her country's top civilian leader, she played a role in the brutal atrocities committed against ethnic minorities.

Given our inherent imperfections, how do we reach the inspiring end of the continuum and stay there as long as possible?

WE BEGAN OUR journey by recognizing that each and every one of us has the potential to be inspiring. Traveling toward the inspiring side of the continuum, at first blush, seems surprisingly simple. All we need to do is nurture and develop the universal set of inspiring attributes. But the inspiring-infuriating continuum also carries a warning: each of us can slip toward the infuriating side of the continuum at a moment's notice. We lose a little sleep, we miss a meal, we feel a little insecure, our responsibilities overwhelm us, and poof—suddenly we are infuriating.

A fundamental premise of *Inspire* is that we are not born as inspiring or infuriating individuals. Instead, it is our *current* behavior—our words, our actions, and our interactions—that either inspires or infuriates. I have used the term *universal path* to describe the journey toward the inspiring end of the continuum because we never reach a place of inspiring permanence. Each day we are at risk of being infuriating. The drive to remain on the inspiring side is a lifelong endeavor that is never fully achieved.

To be more inspiring more of the time takes practice, reflection, and concrete commitments. As we saw in Inspiring Practice (Chapter 7), expertise comes from deepening our experiences, reflecting on those experiences, and then committing to make our next experience more inspiring. And we can't reflect just once, engage in a single practice, or make a solitary commitment. It's why thinking like an architect is so important: we need to embed these processes into our daily lives.

When we slip to the infuriating side of the continuum, we also need a sense of patience and forgiveness to find our way back to the other side. It requires letting go of our shame while using its poignancy to commit to a more inspiring effort next time. As the character Ted Lasso opined, "I hope that [we] are not judged by the actions we take in our weakest moments, but rather for the strength we show if, and when, we're ever given a second chance." Remember Steven Rogelberg's study on self-talk. Infuriating self-talk, which involved condemning the self for its past infuriations and forecasting future infuriations, predicted less creative leadership. Without self-forgiveness, we risk falling into a vicious cycle of infuriation.

But there's good news. The techniques we outlined in each of the VEM chapters were designed to provide us with an inspiring boost. To get into a visionary state of mind, we discussed three strategies that broaden our perspective. First, we can reflect on our core values. Values reflections not only help us see the big picture, but lift us up in our lowest moments. When my colleagues and I asked unemployed individuals to reflect on their values for fifteen minutes, they were three times more likely to find a job over the next two months. Second, we can reflect on our past and the winding road that led to our present. I have found that reminiscing on the roads not taken infuses our lives with a newfound sense of purpose, helping us satisfy the fundamental human need for meaning. Finally, we can leap psychologically into the future. By vividly imagining tomorrow, we help ourselves and others experience our vision more deeply. Getting into a visionary state of mind helps us craft and communicate a big-picture, optimistic, meaningful, simple vision of tomorrow to inspire those around us.

We can prime the exemplar pump by thinking of a time when we had power, when we felt secure and in control, when we were our best self. Power reflections make us both more exemplary and more visionary. Researchers all over the world have found that simply recalling an experience with power makes us physiologically more calm and psychologically more confident and authentic. It helps us craft more compelling visions by increasing our creativity and helping us see and communicate the big picture. It even makes our voices more dynamic. Getting into an exemplar state of mind helps us meet the moment by being a calm and courageous protector or a creative and passionate superhuman.

To shift into a mentor state of mind we can focus on learning from those below us in the hierarchy. Simply thinking about a time in which we learned from someone with less power turns us into more inspiring mentors by making us more engaged and more likely to offer more thorough advice. Mentees, in turn, rate downward-learning mentors as better encouragers and more empathic supporters. To be an inspiring mentor, we also need to look beyond what makes others similar to us, and instead learn to appreciate what makes each person unique. Remember different people have different needs at different times. Getting into a mentor state of mind helps us elevate, encourage, and challenge others to be the best version of themselves.

These techniques all rely on self-awareness. Just as self-awareness can help us solve the leader amplification effect, it is also a key for spending more time on the inspiring side of the continuum. We need to identify and reinforce our inspiring strengths but also recognize our infuriating weaknesses. And we can reduce those infuriating weaknesses by designing a set of systematic practices, commitments, and habits. But sometimes we can't do it alone. We need to form inspiring partnerships to stay away from the infuriating end of the continuum.

INSPIRING PARTNERSHIPS

I LIVED IN Chicago for more than a decade, and I loved my job and adored the city. Yet I was completely miserable. Within months after moving to New York City, I had never been happier. What changed?

Part of it has to do with love. I moved to Chicago after ending a ten-year relationship and never found an enduring romantic partner in the Windy City. Then I met my now-wife, Jenn, three months after moving to New York. But there's something more going on here.

I am great at seeing the big picture and a pro at logistics, but I'm a horrible planner. It turns out Jenn is an amazing curator of experiences.

Soon after we started dating, she was sketching out interesting plans every weekend. In contrast, when I was in Chicago, I would sit at home, depressed, with nothing to do. And when I would travel internationally for work, I rarely planned any excursions. But the first time Jenn accompanied me for a work trip to Thailand, she organized a culturally immersive and adventurous journey through Cambodia and Laos.

To be fulfilled, I needed a partner who complemented my inspiring elements while compensating for my infuriating limitations. Jenn and I formed the perfect traveling partnership: she curates the trips while I handle the logistics. It's why our sons were each able to visit multiple continents before they were two.

Recently Jenn went on her first solo international trip since we got married. She got in the wrong security line flying over and the wrong immigration line coming back home. Without Jenn, I would be sitting at home doing nothing. Without me, she would be standing in the wrong line. But together, we live a life full of inspiring adventures.

Inspiring partnerships aren't unique to marriage. The idea that two people can complement each other's inspiring strengths and compensate for each other's infuriating weaknesses is a general phenomenon. But that doesn't mean inspiring partnerships are common or easy to form. When my former student Eric Anicich, now at the University of Southern California, and I surveyed over five hundred MBA students, we found out that 87 percent had experiences with co-led teams, but the vast majority declared that their co-led groups were much *less* effective than their solo-led ones. The few people who were part of inspiring partnerships cited their complementary and compensatory nature as the key to their success. Here is how one student described why their co-led team worked so well: "[Our] success stemmed from aligning our goals from the very beginning, separating the workload and leaning on each other's strengths. For instance, she was better at the more creative tasks, while I was better at the project management."

Inspiring partnerships may be rare, but when they work, they can revolutionize the world. That's what the Steves did when they created the world's first personal computer. Steve Jobs was a brilliant strategic thinker and marketing genius, but he lacked engineering skills. His partner Steve Wozniak was a technical savant who could conceive of radical innovations in computing, but he lacked ambition and a strategic vision. Together, their strengths complemented and compensated for each other's weaknesses. The result was a company—Apple Inc.—that has transformed our lives.

For Jenn and me, my MBA student, and Steve and Steve, an inspiring partnership began with a shared vision. It's a key to all successful teams, but as we discussed, it is especially critical for diverse ones. Co-led teams, like diverse teams, have extraordinary potential but are vulnerable to fiery conflict and paralyzing confusion. As a result, they both desperately need a shared vision to survive and to thrive. Jenn and I both bought into the importance of travel adventures. My MBA student and his coleader were aligned on their goals. Steve and Steve were each committed to creating a personal computer. Shared visions create the necessary scaffolding for complementary and compensatory skills to form inspiring partnerships.

Inspiring partnerships also speak to a larger point about leadership. Even at our most inspiring, we can't do everything by ourselves. We need the talents of others to accomplish even our modest goals, let alone our most lofty ones. It's why being inspiring is so important. Through our vision, our example, and our mentorship, we are able to build, ignite, and integrate the many talents of those around us. Through leadership, our teams can be inspiring.

Instilling inspiring skills in others matters not only because we can't do everything ourselves, but also because none of us will live forever. Our bodies break down and our minds begin to fade. It's why we need to teach and inspire others to also inspire others. Inspiring leaders create inspiring leaders. That is the universal path for creating a more inspiring tomorrow.

CODA

I WANT TO end our journey together with an important realization I had about my parents. My mom and dad weren't perfect. My dad had an explosive anger, and his too-truthful teasing would often touch people's most sensitive nerves. My mom was anxious and competitive and a little too stubborn.

This realization isn't unique to me; it's one we all eventually discover about our parents. When we are young, we tend to idolize our parents as superheroes and see them as continually on the inspiring end of the continuum. Eventually, however, we learn that they are human, with a range of flaws. And in adolescence, our parents become purely infuriating in our eyes, mortifying us with their every gesture. The good news is that, for many of us, our perspective rebalances in early adulthood and we come to view our parents as imperfect yet inspiring in their own ways.

That's what happened to me. In my mid-twenties, I found my way back to a more generous appreciation of my mom and dad's many parental talents and learned to accept their flaws with less infuriation. I marveled at my dad's creative solutions and his ability to take criticism with an open heart. And I cherished my mom's little touches of support and connection, from her homemade birthday cards to bringing gifts to restaurants to honor an employee's recent marriage or baby. My siblings and I even began to celebrate her quirky side, describing her offbeat actions as "That's so Maeda."

In writing my mom's memorial speech in 2019, I had an epiphany. I suddenly realized what it was about my parents that truly inspired me. What made my parents truly inspiring is that they each tried to be a better person today than they were yesterday. And they were committed to being better tomorrow than they were today. They were forever reaching for the inspiring end of the continuum. They lived what my wife, Jenn, calls a *kaizen* way of life, the Japanese word for continuous improvement.

My parents' lifelong commitment to be more inspiring is reflected in one of my dad's favorite books, *The Great Gatsby*, whose last page he could recite from heart. As a nod to him, I quoted that page in the salutation speech I gave for my high school graduation:

> And as I sat there brooding on the old, unknown world, I thought of Gatsby's wonder when he first picked out the green light at the end of Daisy's dock. . . . Gatsby believed in the green light, the orgastic future that year by year recedes before us. It eluded us then, but that's no matter—tomorrow we will run faster, stretch out our arms farther. . . . And one fine morning——So we beat on, boats against the current . . .

Gatsby's and my dad's green light speaks to the universal inspiring-infuriating continuum. The life worth living is one where we perpetually strive toward the inspiring end. Although we can reach the green light and be deeply inspiring for a moment, we never find full purchase there. None of us is always inspiring. We are forever leaning toward, and sometimes falling onto, the infuriating end of the universal continuum. But like my parents, each of us can strive to be more inspiring today than we were yesterday.

My hope is that this book inspires you to take a *kaizen* approach to life, to always be reaching for the green light of a more inspiring tomorrow, even as we beat against the infuriating current of daily life.

Every month, let's ask ourselves a set of critical VEM questions: When was I and when was I not visionary? When did I fail and when did I succeed in being an inspiring exemplar? What were the conditions that led me to an inspiring versus infuriating mentor recently? Now let's make a specific commitment for how we will be more visionary, more exemplary, a better mentor the next month.

If we turn these reflections and concrete commitments into a lifelong habit, our days, and the days of those around us, will be full of inspiration.

Acknowledgments

THIS BOOK REPRESENTS my heart and soul, and I am so grateful for the inspiring efforts of the many who helped bring it to life. Jim Levine has been my agent for over a decade and his exquisite combination of brutal honesty and compassionate encouragement always steers me in the right direction. I am so lucky to have had such a fearless editor in Hollis Heimbouch. She helped me harness my vision and simplify it into a digestible form. She also accepted my perfectionism while also helping me let the book go when it was ready.

My two copilots every step of the way were my research coordinator, Chloe Levin, and my writing coach, Rena Setzer. Chloe is brilliant and creative, and the best editor I have ever seen. She not only helped find so many amazing examples, but she also never hesitated in letting me know when an example or a thread line didn't work. She has the wisdom of an old soul despite enjoying the benefits of youth. I met with Rena every week for almost three years, and I would have been lost in an intellectual maze without her structured guidance, challenging queries, and generative ideas. Chloe and Rena embodied the very essence of *Inspire*: their visions and authentic insights both encouraged me but also challenged me to write the best book I could. Simply put, *Inspire* would not exist without them.

I am grateful to Nikhil Saldana whose generative examples inspired me to get started. Roslyn Raser's passion and insights helped push me toward the finish line. Special thanks to Janet Rosenberg, who copy-edited the final version of *Inspire*. Her attention to detail and insightful questions sharpened my arguments. She was a word wizard who made my musings seem more magical.

Inspire would also not exist without my inspiring teaching partners at Columbia. For more than a decade, I have collaborated with Modupe Akinola, Ashli Carter, Sandra Matz, Michael Morris, Kathy Phillips, and Rebecca Ponce de Leon on teaching leadership to our MBA students. Our collective conversations over the years sharpened my thinking on what it means to be inspiring. They are the brightest, wittiest, funniest, and most generous colleagues I could have ever hoped for.

I am grateful for Lisa Andujar and Ana Campoverde, my partners in making Columbia Business School a more inclusive and equitable place to be. They not only offered their constant support, but also lifted me up as I navigated writing a book while still doing my day job.

I am most indebted to my family—Jenn, Asher, and Aden, and my mother-in-law Vicki aka Lola—who encouraged me throughout this process. Jenn is not just a marriage partner but an intellectual one, always pushing me to be clearer and more inclusive in my writing and examples. Our boys tolerated my late night and weekend writing sessions and cheered me on as I got close to the finish line. Lola made sure I had the energy to write with a boundless supply of delicious Filipino cuisines. Without them I would be forever stuck on the infuriating end of the continuum. Instead, their belief in me inspired me to keep going.

Notes

INTRODUCTION

ix The jolt was so forceful: R. Minutaglio, "How Southwest Pilot Tammie Jo Shults Landed Fatal Flight 1380," *Elle*, October 8, 2019, https://www.elle.com/culture/books/a29355725/tammie-jo-shults-book-interview/.

ix "My first thought": T. J. Shults, *Nerves of Steel: How I Followed My Dreams, Earned My Wings, and Faced My Greatest Challenge* (Nashville, TN: Thomas Nelson, 2019).

ix "an unscripted combination of emergencies . . .:" Interview on *The 700 Club*, October 19, 2019, https://www.youtube.com/watch?v=RjJXxurSZ8o.

x "bought WiFi as the plane was going down": Marty Martinez, Facebook post, April 17, 2018.

x "a few minutes can seem like an eternity": Shults, *Nerves of Steel*.

xi "what it took to fly the crippled airplane safely to the ground": Ibid.

xi "you're completely calm": Ibid.

xi prevent "any falsehoods about the incident from taking root": Ibid.

xii "a foundation of trust that we critically needed after the engine failed": Interview on *CBS Mornings*, May 23, 2018, https://www.cbsnews.com/news/southwest-flight-1380-captain-tammie-jo-shults-crew-live-interview/.

xii on the *Costa Concordia*: B. Little, "The Costa Concordia Disaster: How Human Error Made It Worse," History.com, June 23, 2021, https://www.history.com/news/costa-concordia-cruise-ship-disaster-sinking-captain.

xiii "I have said that we had . . . a blackout": Ibid.

xiii while sitting in the lifeboat: Francesco Schettino, "Telephone call between Costa Concordia Captain and Italian Coast Guard," 2012, https://youtu.be/WX_o8zcCmx8?si=HbRT8_KPY8-eTWDV.

xv Schettino ended up paying a price: S. Ognibene and I. Binnie, "Costa Concordia captain sentenced to 16 years for 2012 shipwreck," Reuters, February 11, 2015, https://www.reuters.com/article/idUSKBN0LF12H/.

CHAPTER 1: THE LEADER AMPLIFICATION EFFECT

6 dramatically fell one thousand feet in twelve seconds: "Flight Attendant Critically Hurt as United Jet Hits Turbulence," NBC News, February 18, 2014, https://www.nbcnews.com/news/us-news/flight-attendant-critically-hurt-united-jet-hits-turbulence-n32506.

9 louder, bolder, and stronger: J. R. Pierce, G. J. Kilduff, A. D. Galinsky, and N. Sivanathan, "From glue to gasoline: How competition turns perspective-takers unethical," *Psychological Science* 24 (2013): 1986–94.

9 others feel dependent: J. C. Magee and A. D. Galinsky, "Social hierarchy: The self-reinforcing nature of power and status," *Academy of Management Annals* 2 (2008): 351–98.

10 compared to viewing that stimulus alone: G. Shteynberg, J. B. Hirsh, E. P. Apfelbaum, J. T. Larsen, A. D. Galinsky, and N. J. Roese, "Feeling more together: Group attention intensifies emotion," *Emotion* 14 (2014): 1102–14.

12 make us feel invisible: A. D. Galinsky, "Research on power teaches why Blagojevich did what he did," Huffington Post, August 23, 2012; A. D. Galinsky, J. C. Magee, D. H. Gruenfeld, J. A. Whitson, and K. A. Liljenquist, "Social power reduces the strength of the situation: Implications for creativity, conformity, and dissonance," *Journal of Personality and Social Psychology* 95 (2008): 1450–66.

14 others may not be privy to that same knowledge: B. Keysar, D. J. Barr, J. A. Balin, and J. S. Brauner, "Taking perspective in conversation: The role of mutual knowledge in comprehension," *Psychological Science* 11, no. 1 (2000): 32–38; G. Ku, C. S. Wang, and A. D. Galinsky, "The promise and perversity of perspective-taking in organizations," *Research on Organizational Behavior* 35 (2015): 79–102.

14 What number is on the table?: J. A. Yip and M. E. Schweitzer, "Losing your temper and your perspective: Anger reduces perspective-taking," *Organizational Behavior and Human Decision Processes* 150 (2019): 28–45.

14 when we are in positions of leadership: J. C. Magee and A. D. Galinsky, "Social hierarchy: The self-reinforcing nature of power and status," *The Academy of Management Annals* 2, no. 1 (2008): 351–98.

15 power *causes* a loss of perspective-taking: A. D. Galinsky, J. C. Magee, M. E. Inesi, and D. H. Gruenfeld, "Power and perspectives not taken," *Psychological Science* 17 (2006): 1068–74.

19 powerful leaders are often impulsive: B. E. Pike and A. D. Galinsky, "Power leads to action because it releases the psychological brakes on action," *Current Opinion in Psychology* 33 (2020): 91–94.

CHAPTER 2: UNIVERSAL INSPIRATION

26 identify and more deeply internalize principles and insights: M. L. Gick and K. J. Holyoak, "Analogical problem solving," *Cognitive Psychology* 12, no. 3 (1980): 306–55; D. Gentner, J. Loewenstein, and L. Thompson, "Learning and transfer: A general role for analogical encoding," *Journal of Educational Psychology* 95, no. 2 (2003): 393–408.

CHAPTER 3: INSPIRING VISIONS

30 life gets worse when you have kids: D. Kahneman, A. B. Krueger, D. A. Schkade, N. Schwarz, and A. A. Stone, "A survey method for characterizing daily life experience: The day reconstruction method," *Science* 306 (2004): 1776–80; M. Luhmann, W. Hofmann, M. Eid, and R. E. Lucas, "Subjective well-being and adaptation to life events: A meta-analysis," *Journal of Personality and Social Psychology* 102 (2012): 592–615; J. M. Twenge, W. K. Campbell, and C. A. Foster, "Parenthood and marital satisfaction: A meta-analytic review," *Journal of Marriage and Family* 65 (2003): 574–83.

30 "a why to live can bear almost any how": F. Nietzsche, *Twilight of the Idols: Or How to Philosophize with a Hammer* (Indianapolis, IN: Hackett Publishing, 1997).

31 this simple yet profound experiment: J. D. Bransford and M. K. Johnson, "Contextual prerequisites for understanding: Some investigations of comprehension and recall," *Journal of Verbal Learning and Verbal Behavior* 11 (1972): 717–26.

32 predicts faster recovery times: A. Luck, S. Pearson, G. Maddem, and P. Hewett, "Effects of video information on precolonoscopy anxiety and knowledge: A randomized trial," *The Lancet* 354, no. 9195 (1999): 2032–35; E. B. Ertürk and H. Ünlü, "Effects of pre-operative individualized education on anxiety and pain severity in patients following open-heart surgery," *International Journal of Health Sciences* 12 (2018): 26–34.

32 "how I got home": J. Lebovich, "Faithful see Mary on underpass wall," *Chicago Tribune*, April 19, 2005.

33 "the image that's portrayed in the Bible": Ibid.

33 explanations for *unexpected* events: B. Weiner, "'Spontaneous' causal thinking," *Psychological Bulletin* 97, no. 1 (1985): 74–84.

33 the identification of a coherent and meaningful interrelationship among a set of *unrelated* stimuli: J. A. Whitson and A. D. Galinsky, "Lacking control increases illusory pattern perception," *Science* 322 (2008): 115–17.

34   more elaborate rituals than their fellow shallow-water fishermen: B. Malinowski and R. Redfield, *Magic, Science and Religion, and Other Essays* (Boston: Beacon Press, 1948).

34   not when they are still on the ground: P. V. Simonov, M. V. Frolov, V. F. Evtushenko, and E. P. Sviridov, "Effect of emotional stress on recognition of visual patterns," *Aviation, Space, and Environmental Medicine* 48, no. 9 (1977): 856–58.

34   more likely to believe in conspiracies than second-year students: R. M. Kramer, "The sinister attribution error: Paranoid cognition and collective distrust in organizations," *Motivation and Emotion* 18 (1994): 199–230.

35   images of visual static: Whitson and Galinsky, "Lacking control increases illusory pattern perception," 115–17.

35   a conspiracy among their coworkers: J. A. Whitson, A. C. Kay, and A. D. Galinsky, "The emotional roots of conspiratorial perceptions, system justification, and belief in the paranormal," *Journal of Experimental Social Psychology* 56 (2015): 89–95.

35   biased their investments: Whitson and Galinsky, "Lacking control increases illusory pattern perception," 115–17.

35   superstitions increase during periods of economic uncertainty: S. M. Sales, "Threat as a factor in authoritarianism: An analysis of archival data," *Journal of Personality and Social Psychology* 28, no. 1 (1973): 44–57.

36   more autocratic forms of government: A. C. Kay, S. Shepherd, C. W. Blatz, S. N. Chua, and A. D. Galinsky, "For god (or) country: The hydraulic relation between government instability and belief in religious sources of control," *Journal of Personality and Social Psychology* 99 (2010): 725–39.

36   the result of 5G phone towers: K. M. Douglas, "COVID-19 conspiracy theories," *Group Processes & Intergroup Relations* 24, no. 2 (2021): 270–75; M. Lynas, "COVID: Top 10 current conspiracy theories," Alliance for Science, April 20, 2020, https://allianceforscience.org/blog/2020/04/covid-top-10-current-conspiracy-theories/.

37   a *universal midlife crisis*: A. D. Galinsky and L. J. Kray, "How COVID created a universal midlife crisis," *Los Angeles Times*, May 15, 2022, https://www.latimes.com/opinion/story/2022-05-15/covid-universal-midlife-crisis.

37   mean something even after it was over: K. Wade-Benzoni, H. Sondak, and A. D. Galinsky, "Leaving a legacy: Intergenerational allocations of benefits and burdens," *Business Ethics Quarterly* 20 (2010): 7–34.

38   to secure better outcomes: A. D. Galinsky, T. Mussweiler, and V. H. Medvec, "Disconnecting outcomes and evaluations: The role of negotiator focus," *Journal of Personality and Social Psychology* 83, no. 5 (2002): 1131–40; A. D. Galinsky, G.

J. Leonardelli, G. A. Okhuysen, and T. Mussweiler, "Regulatory focus at the bargaining table: Promoting distributive and integrative success," *Personality and Social Psychology Bulletin* 31 (2005): 1087–98.

38   were the most likely to be forwarded: J. Berger and K. L. Milkman, "What makes online content viral?," *Journal of Marketing Research* 49 (2011): 192–205.

39   courage and fortitude: Franklin Delano Roosevelt Inaugural Address, March 4, 1933, https://historymatters.gmu.edu/d/5057/.

39   "what you can do for your country": John F. Kennedy Inaugural Address, January 20, 1961, https://www.jfklibrary.org/learn/about-jfk/historic-speeches /inaugural-address.

39   "peace among ourselves and with all nations": Abraham Lincoln Second Inaugural Address, March 4, 1865, https://www.nps.gov/linc/learn/historyculture /reece-second-inaugural.htm.

40   infuses it with validity: A. Hassan and S. J. Barber, "The effects of repetition frequency on the illusory truth effect," *Cognitive Research* 6 (2021).

40   focus only on a few values: A. M. Carton, C. Murphy, and J. R. Clark, "A (blurry) vision of the future: How leader rhetoric about ultimate goals influences performance," *Academy of Management Journal* 57 (2014): 1544–70.

40   Zoom's vision is "deliver happiness": https://www.zoomgov.com/about; J. Luna, "Eric Yuan on Keeping Customers and Employees Happy," Insights by Stanford Business, November 29, 2022, https://www.gsb.stanford.edu /insights/eric-yuan-keeping-customers-employees-happy.

41   Every year, I give this scenario . . . to my students: A. Tversky and D. Kahneman, "Extensional versus intuitive reasoning: The conjunction fallacy in probability judgment," *Psychological Review* 90, no. 4 (1983): 293–315.

42   Consider another experiment: Carton et al., "A (blurry) vision of the future," 1544–70.

42   by using vivid imagery: V. Akstinaitė and A. D. Galinsky, "Words matter: The use of vivid imagery in convention speeches predicts presidential winners," working paper.

44   think that it is true: I. M. Begg, A. Anas, and S. Farinacci, "Dissociation of processes in belief: Source recollection, statement familiarity, and the illusion of truth," *Journal of Experimental Psychology: General* 121 (1992): 446–58.

44   a boost in competitive markets: C. B. Horton, S. S. Iyengar, and A. D. Galinsky, *Say Your Name; The Competitive Advantages of Name Repetition*, working paper.

47   "whatever that slogan is they're working on": M. Kelly, "The minimally acceptable man," *The New Yorker*, August 5, 1996, https://www.newyorker.com/magazine /1996/08/05/the-minimally-acceptable-man.

48   *difficult for others to understand*: Z. Brown, E. A. Anicich, and A. D. Galinsky,

"Compensatory conspicuous communication: Low status increases jargon use," *Organizational Behavior and Human Decision Processes* 161 (2020): 274–90.

49 a visionary state of mind: A. M. Carton and B. J. Lucas, "How can leaders overcome the blurry vision bias? Identifying an antidote to the paradox of vision communication," *Academy of Management Journal* 61 (2018): 2106–29.

49 (see endnotes for the link): "Sample Value Words for Reference," https://tinyurl.com/2yrn89nt.

50 a Swiss governmental employment agency: J. Pfrombeck, A D. Galinsky, N. Nagy, M. S. North, J. Brockner, and G. Grote, "Self-affirmation increases re-employment success for the unemployed," *Proceedings of the National Academy of Sciences* 120 (2023). e2301532120.

51 boosted the GPAs: G. L. Cohen, J. Garcia, N. Apfel, and A. Master, "Reducing the racial achievement gap: a social-psychological intervention," *Science* 313 (2006): 1307–10; G. L. Cohen, J. Garcia, V. Purdie-Vaughns, N. Apfel, P. Brzustoski, "Recursive processes in self-affirmation: intervening to close the minority achievement gap," *Science* 324 (2009): 400–403.

51 middle school students: G. L. Cohen and D. K. Sherman, "The psychology of change: Self-affirmation and social psychological intervention," *Annual Review of Psychology* 65 (2014): 333–71.

52 tended to *decrease* well-being: S. Lyubomirsky, K. M. Sheldon, and D. Schkade, "Pursuing happiness: The architecture of sustainable change," *Review of General Psychology* 9 (2005): 111–31.

52 asked in one of our studies: L. J. Kray, L. G. George, K. A. Liljenquist, A. D. Galinsky, P. E. Tetlock, and N. J. Roese, "From what might have been to what must have been: Counterfactual thinking creates meaning," *Journal of Personality and Social Psychology* 98 (2010): 106–18.

54 (i.e., "Describe all the ways that your company might not have come into being"): H. Ersner-Hershfield, A. D. Galinsky, L. J. Kray, and B. King, "Company, country, connections: Counterfactual origins increase organizational commitment, patriotism, and social investment," *Psychological Science* 21 (2010): 1479–86.

CHAPTER 4: INSPIRING EXEMPLARS

57 in our voice, in our arms, and in our body: J. M. Jachimowicz, C. To, S. Agasi, S. Côté, and A. D. Galinsky, "The gravitational pull of expressing passion: When and how expressing passion elicits status conferral and support from others," *Organizational Behavior and Human Decision Processes* 153 (2019): 41–62.

57 "'I must have this stock now'": B. Mishkin, "One on 1 Profile: Wall Street Executive Carla Harris Forges Unique Path to the Top," Spectrum Local News,

June 8, 2015, https://spectrumlocalnews.com/one-on-1/2015/06/8/one-on
-1-profile-wall-street-executive-carla-harris-forges-unique-path-to-the-top.

61 Jacinda Ardern, prime minister of New Zealand: "New Zealand's PM stays
calm during an earthquake on live TV – BBC News," October 7, 2020, https://
www.youtube.com/watch?v=qCycOM8YsuU.

62 "She isn't a politician, she is a leader": Ibid., first comment from
@muskansahay2645, second comment from @ryanphillips4448.

62 onstage giving a national press conference: "'Sorry, a slight distraction':
Jacinda Ardern unruffled as earthquake interrupts press conference," *The
Guardian*, October 21, 2021, https://www.theguardian.com/world/2021
/oct/22/earthquake-shakes-new-zealand-parliament-during-jacinda
-ardern-press-conference.

64 twenty ideas in the first ten minutes: B. J. Lucas and L. F. Nordgren, "The
creative cliff illusion," *PNAS* 117, no. 33 (2020): 19830–36.

64 the final version of his famous design: Interview in *Harvard Business Review*,
July–August 2010, https://hbr.org/2010/07/lifes-work-james-dyson.

65 "an invention with 1,000 steps": N. Ramkumar, "The Greatest Inventor 'Thomas
Alva Edison's' vision on Failures," LinkedIn, 2019, https://www.linkedin.com
/pulse/greatest-inventor-thomas-alva-edisons-vision-failures-narayanan/.

66 dedication to practice and greater task effort: A. Duckworth, C. Peterson,
M. D. Matthews, and D. Kelly, "Grit: Perseverance and passion for long-term
goals," *Journal of Personality and Social Psychology* 92 (2007): 1087–101.

66 grit has been called "overrated" and "overhyped": J. Useem, "Is grit overrated?,"
Atlantic, May 15, 2016, https://www.theatlantic.com/magazine/archive/2016/05
/is-grit-overrated/476397/; J. Barshay, "Grit under attack in education circles,"
U.S. News & World Report, April 18, 2016, https://www.usnews.com/news
/articles/2016-04-18/grit-under-attack-in-education-circles; D. Denby, "The limits
of 'grit,'" *The New Yorker*, June 21, 2016, https://www.newyorker.com/culture
/culture-desk/the-limits-of-grit.

66 two inspiring exemplar attributes: J. M. Jachimowicz, A. Wihler, E. R. Bailey,
and A. D. Galinsky, "Why grit requires perseverance and passion to positively
predict performance," *PNAS* 115, no. 40 (2018): 9980–85.

67 "Too much Superman, not enough Clark Kent": L. Rottenberg, *Crazy Is a
Compliment: The Power of Zigging When Everyone Else Zags* (New York: Port-
folio, 2016).

67 "so I let it all out": Ibid.

70 some experiments I had just started conducting: A. D. Galinsky, D. H. Gruenfeld,
and J. C. Magee, "From power to action," *Journal of Personality and Social Psychology* 85 (2003): 453–66.

71 into the eye of the hurricane: P. C. Schmid and M. S. Mast, "Power increases performance in a social evaluation situation as a result of decreased stress responses," *European Journal of Social Psychology* 43 (2013): 201–11.

71 write more persuasive job applications: J. Lammers, D. Dubois, D. D. Rucker, and A. D. Galinsky, "Power gets the job: Priming power improves interview outcomes," *Journal of Experimental Social Psychology* 49 (2013): 776–79.

72 when the stakes are high: S. K. Kang, A. D. Galinsky, L. J. Kray, and A. Shirako, "Power affects performance when the pressure is on: Evidence for low-power threat and high-power lift," *Personality and Social Psychology Bulletin* 41, no. 5 (2015): 726–35.

72 an experiment with four stages: S. J. Ko, M. S. Sadler, and A. D. Galinsky, "The sound of power: Conveying and detecting hierarchical rank through voice," *Psychological Science* 26 (2014): 3–14.

73 it makes people feel more *authentic*: Y. Kifer, D. Heller, W. E. Perunovic, A. D. Galinsky, "The good life of the powerful: The experience of power and authenticity enhance subjective well-being," *Psychological Science* 24 (2013): 280–88.

73 it makes us more *compelling*: Lammers et al., "Power gets the job," 776–79.

73 it makes us more *creative*: Galinsky et al., "Social power reduces the strength of the situation," 1450–66.

73 by seeing *the big picture*: P. K. Smith and Y. Trope, "You focus on the forest when you're in charge of the trees: power priming and abstract information processing," *Journal of Personality and Social Psychology* 90, no. 4 (2006): 578–96.

73 the ability of each study to detect an effect was only 5 percent: J. P. Simmons and U. Simonsohn, "Power posing: P-curving the evidence," *Psychological Science* 28, no. 5 (2017): 687–93.

73 made people become more super: A. D. Galinsky, T. Turek, G. Agarwal, E. M. Anicich, D. D. Rucker, H. R. Bowles, N. Liberman, C. Levin, and J. C. Magee, "Are many sex/gender differences really power differences?," *PNAS Nexus* 3, no. 2 (2024): 025.

CHAPTER 5: INSPIRING MENTORS

76 how powerful offering a choice is: G. J. Leonardelli, J. Gu, G. McRuer, V. H. Medvec, and A. D. Galinsky, "Multiple equivalent simultaneous offers (MESOs) reduce the negotiator dilemma: How a choice of first offers increases economic and relational outcomes," *Organizational Behavior and Human Decision Processes* 152 (2019): 64–83.

78 numerous field studies showing that involvement is truly inspiring: S. J. Wu

and E. L. Paluck, "Having a voice in your group: Increasing productivity through group participation," *Behavioural Public Policy*, 1–20.

79 the simultaneous need for structure and autonomy: E. Chou, N. Halevy, A. D. Galinsky, and J. K. Murnighan, "The goldilocks contract: The synergistic benefits of combining structure and autonomy for motivation, creativity, and cooperation," *Journal of Personality and Social Psychology* 113 (2017): 393–412.

81 a sense of control and autonomy is for humans: G. A. Nix, R. M. Ryan, J. B. Manly, and E. L. Deci, "Revitalization through self-regulation: The effects of autonomous and controlled motivation on happiness and vitality," *Journal of Experimental Social Psychology* 35 (1999): 266–84.

82 "I've never been in my father's bedroom": "Survive and Advance," *30 for 30* TV episode, ESPN, 2013.

83 the need for status has been classified as a fundamental need: C. Anderson, J. A. D. Hildreth, and L. Howland, "Is the desire for status a fundamental human motive? A review of the empirical literature," *Psychological Bulletin* 141, no. 3 (2015): 574–601.

83 Swain wrote that: C. Swain, "Claudine Gay and My Scholarship," *Wall Street Journal*, December 17, 2023, https://www.wsj.com/articles/claudine-gay -and-my-scholarship-plagiarism-elite-system-unearned-position-24e4a1b1.

84 not only does their status grow, *but so does our own*: M. Hoff, D. Rucker, and A. D. Galinsky, "The Vicious Cycle of Insecurity," working paper.

85 Liu Bang (now going by his emperor name of Gaozu) asked: Q. Sima, *Records of the Grand Historian: Han Dynasty*, vol. 65 (New York: Columbia University Press, 1993).

88 a series of revolutionary studies: H. F. Harlow and R. R. Zimmermann, "Affectional response in the infant monkey: Orphaned baby monkeys develop a strong and persistent attachment to inanimate surrogate mothers," *Science* 130, no. 3373 (1959): 421–32.

88 Ryan Gosling's performance in her movie: Greta Gerwig, Presentation of Kirk Douglas Award to Ryan Gosling, January 13, 2024, https://www.youtube .com/watch?v=LvuNZ3luTFU.

89 I ran with a group of executives: A. D. Galinsky, J. C. Magee, D. Rus, N. B. Rothman, and A. R. Todd, "Acceleration with steering: The synergistic benefits of combining power and perspective-taking," *Social Psychology and Personality Science* 5 (2014): 627–35.

90 terry-cloth doctors: B. Blatt, S. F. LeLacheur, A. D. Galinsky, S. J. Simmens, and L. Greenberg, "Perspective-taking: Increasing satisfaction in medical encounters," *Academic Medicine* 85 (2010): 1445–52.

95 valuable sources of knowledge: T. Zhang, D. Wang, and A. D. Galinsky, "Learning down to train up: Mentors are more effective when they value insights from below," *Academy of Management Journal* 66 (2023): 604–37.

97 power tends to decrease perspective-taking: Galinsky et al., "Power and perspectives not taken," *Psychological Science*, 17 (2006), 1068–74.

97 people who are similar to us: J. Launay and R. I. M. Dunbar, "Playing with strangers: Which shared traits attract us most to new people?," *PLOS ONE* (2015): 10.

97 She turned her research into a useful exercise: K. W. Phillips, "Why Diversity Matters," https://www.youtube.com/watch?v=lHStHPQUzkE.

98 an experimental test: A. R. Todd, K. Hanko, A. D. Galinsky, and T. Mussweiler, "When focusing on differences leads to similar perspectives," *Psychological Science* 22 (2011): 134–41.

CHAPTER 6: THE VICIOUS CYCLE OF INFURIATION

101 a critical distinction between power and status: Magee et al., "Social hierarchy," 351–98.

101 from bouncers to custom agents to reimbursement clerks: A. R. Fragale, J. R. Overbeck, and M. A. Neale, "Resources versus respect: Social judgments based on targets' power and status positions," *Journal of Experimental Social Psychology* 47, no. 4 (2011): 767–75.

102 status is a fundamental need: Anderson et al., "Is the desire for status a fundamental human motive?," 574–601.

102 little tyrant that demeaned others: N. J. Fast, N. Halevy, and A. D. Galinsky, "The destructive nature of power without status," *Journal of Experimental Social Psychology* 48, no. 1 (2012): 391–94.

105 a vicious cycle of infuriating behaviors: E. M. Anicich, N. J. Fast, N. Halevy, and A. D. Galinsky, "When the bases of social hierarchy collide: Power without status drives interpersonal conflict," *Organization Science* 27, no. 1 (2016): 123–40.

108 their experiences with insecurity: Hoff et al., "The Vicious Cycle of Status Insecurity."

116 a psychological foundation of inspiring leaders: A. R. Todd, M. Forstmann, P. Burgmer, A. W. Brooks, and A. D. Galinsky, "Anxious and egocentric: how specific emotions influence perspective taking," *Journal of Experimental Psychology: General* 144, no. 2 (2015): 374–91.

117 this study by Jeremy Yip of Georgetown: J. A. Yip and M. E. Schweitzer, "Losing your temper and your perspective: Anger reduces perspective-taking," *Organizational Behavior and Human Decision Processes* 150 (2019): 28–45.

119   Steven Rogelberg of the University of North Carolina at Charlotte: S. G. Rogelberg, L. Justice, P. W. Braddy, S. C. Paustian-Underdahl, E. Heggestad,
L. Shanock, and J. W. Fleenor, "The executive mind: leader self-talk, effectiveness and strain," *Journal of Managerial Psychology* 28, no. 2 (2013): 183–201.

119   some of the most seminal work on meditation: Andrew C. Hafenbrack et al.,
"Helping people by being in the present: Mindfulness increases prosocial behavior," *Organizational Behavior and Human Decision Processes* 159 (2020): 21–38.

CHAPTER 7: INSPIRING PRACTICE

122   the armed cavalry outside of it: Full Georgia School Shooting 911 Call with
Antoinette Tuff, 2013, http://www.cnn.com/TRANSCRIPTS/1308/21
/pmt.01.html.

127   the twelve teenagers on the Wild Boars soccer team: This story is a compilation
from multiple documentaries including: *The Rescue* (2021) and *The Trapped 13:
How We Survived the Thai Cave* (2022).

132   "I owe that all to my pastor. He has actually trained us": Anderson Cooper, *360
Degrees*, CNN, August 22, 2013.

133   "and it ricocheted": "How One Woman's Faith Stopped A School Shooting,"
January 31, 2014, https://www.npr.org/2014/01/31/268417580/how-one
-womans-faith-stopped-a-school-shooting.

133   down into the compound below: N. Schmidle, "Al Qaeda and the SEALs," *The
New Yorker*, August 7, 2011.

134   "that first voice report": A. B. Zegart, *Spies, Lies, and Algorithms: The History
and Future of American Intelligence* (Princeton, NJ: Princeton University Press,
2022).

134   "over the last couple of years, night after night": Schmidle, "Al Qaeda and the
SEALs."

135   "more likely to succeed": B. Simmons, "The Sports Guy," ESPN, May 19,
2008, https://www.espn.com/espnmag/story?id=3403820.

136   build reflection into every mission: P. T. Bartone and A. B. Adler, "Event-
oriented debriefing following military operations: what every leader should
know," US Army Medical Research Unit–Europe, Unit, 29218, 1995, 1–9;
G. Hammett, "Military leaders know the power of reflection. Here's how you
too can use the debrief in business," Inc., https://www.inc.com/gene-hammett
/military-leaders-know-power-of-reflection-heres-how-you-too-can-use
-debrief-in-business.html.

137   the foundation of preparation and future practice: K. Epstude and N. J. Roese,
"The functional theory of counterfactual thinking," *Personality and Social Psychology Review* 12, no. 2 (2008): 168–92.

137 one of the scenarios I used in my research: A. D. Galinsky, V. Seiden, P. H. Kim, and V. H. Medvec, "The dissatisfaction of having your first offer accepted: The role of counterfactual thinking in negotiations," *Personality and Social Psychology Bulletin* 28 (2002): 271–83.

140 "one interaction, one person, one day at a time": Chesley Sullenberger, commencement speech at Purdue University, May 15, 2011.

CHAPTER 8: INSPIRING ARCHITECTS

149 experiment conducted at Yale University back in the 1960s: H. Leventhal, R. Singer, and S. Jones, "Effects of fear and specificity of recommendation upon attitudes and behavior," *Journal of Personality and Social Psychology* 2 (1965): 20–29.

151 extols the structure's grandeur: https://www.hudsonyardsnewyork.com /discover/vessel.

151 "free to walk on the High Line": C. Burlock, "Why is it so easy to jump off a bridge," *The Atlantic*, December 21, 2022.

152 "when you build high, folks will jump": A. Wachs, "What do New Yorkers get when privately-funded public art goes big?," *Architect's Newspaper*, December 12, 2016, https://www.archpaper.com/2016/12/heatherwick-hudson-yards-vessel-public-space-art/.

152 they started charging a $10 entrance fee: L. Crook, "Heatherwick's Vessel closes again after fourth suicide," *Dezeen*, August 2, 2021, https://www .dezeen.com/2021/08/02/heatherwick-vessel-hudson-yards-suicide/.

152 "How much time passed between the time you decided to complete suicide and when you actually attempted suicide?": T. R. Simon, A. C. Swann, K. E. Powell, L. B. Potter, M. J. Kresnow, and P. W. O'Carroll, "Characteristics of impulsive suicide attempts and attempters," *Suicide and Life-Threatening Behavior* 32, supplement to issue 1 (2001): 49–59.

152 from their first thought to their actual attempt of suicide: E. A. Deisenhammer, C. M. Ing, R. Strauss, G. Kemmler, H. Hinterhuber, and E. M. Weiss, "The duration of the suicidal process: how much time is left for intervention between consideration and accomplishment of a suicide attempt?" *Journal of Clinical Psychiatry* 70 (2009): 19.

152 nets beneath bridges reduced suicide attempts by 77 percent: A. Hemmer, P. Meier, and T. Reisch, "Comparing different suicide prevention measures at bridges and buildings: lessons we have learned from a national survey in Switzerland," *PLOS ONE* 12 (2017).

157 "What a strange power there is in clothing": I. B. Singer, *The Collected Stories of Isaac Bashevis Singer* (New York: Vintage, 1982).

157 impact our own thoughts and behaviors: J. Adam and A. Galinsky, "Enclothed cognition," *Journal of Experimental Social Psychology* 48 (2012): 918–25.

158 what we wear influences how we think, feel, and act: C. B. Horton Jr., H. Adam, and A. D. Galinsky, "Evaluating the Evidence for Enclothed Cognition: Z-Curve and Meta-Analyses," *Personality and Social Psychology Bulletin* 01461672231182478 (July 17, 2023).

159 be perceived as more aggressive: M. G. Frank and T. Gilovich, "The dark side of self- and social perception: Black uniforms and aggression in professional sports," *Journal of Personality and Social Psychology* 54 (1988): 74–85.

159 wearing a military uniform increases aggression: R. D. Johnson and L. L. Downing, "Deindividuation and valence of cues: Effects on prosocial and antisocial behavior," *Journal of Personality and Social Psychology* 37 (1979): 1532–38; A. Galinsky, "Why Outfitting Police in Military Uniforms Encourages Brutality," *Fast Company*, June 17, 2020, https://www.fastcompany.com/90517517/why -outfitting-police-in-military-uniforms-encourages-brutality.

160 military-style uniforms: Ibid.

160 the effect of clothing on remote workers: E. R. Bailey, B. Horton, and A. D. Galinsky, "Enclothed harmony or enclothed dissonance? The effect of attire on the authenticity, power, and engagement of remote workers," *Academy of Management Discoveries* 8 (2022), 341–56.

161 status predicts feelings of authenticity more than power: E. R. Bailey, J. Carter, S. Iyengar, and A. D. Galinsky, "The Privilege to be Yourself Depends on What Others Think of You: Status Increases Authenticity More than Power," unpublished manuscript.

163 new ideas and promising innovations: D. Burkus, "The Real Reason Google Serves All That Free Food," *Forbes*, July 2, 2015, https://www.forbes.com /sites/davidburkus/2015/07/02/the-real-reason-google-serves-all-that-free -food/?sh=57b4bdc195f6.

CHAPTER 9: INSPIRING NEGOTIATIONS

168 "I have a bomb in my backpack. I want $2,000 or I'm blowing the whole bank up": J. Squires, "Man says he has a bomb, tries to rob Watsonville bank," *Santa Cruz Sentinel*, September 11, 2010.

169 she realized she was no longer on her bike: M. Eddy, "She Thought He Would Kill Her. Then She Complimented His Orchids," *The New York Times*, July 30, 2019.

172 one of my negotiation experiments: A. D. Galinsky, W. W. Maddux, D. Gilin, and J. B. White, "Why it pays to get inside the head of your opponent: The differential effects of perspective taking and empathy in negotiations," *Psychological Science* 19 (2008): 378–84.

176   multiple packages as their opening offer: G. J. Leonardelli, J. Gu, G. McRuer,
      V. H. Medvec, and A. D. Galinsky, "Multiple equivalent simultaneous offers
      (MESOs) reduce the negotiator dilemma: How a choice of first offers increases
      economic and relational outcomes," *Organizational Behavior and Human Deci-
      sion Processes* 152 (2019): 64–83.

179   Greece was facing a crisis in February 2015: J. Kanter and N. Kitsantonis,
      "Greece's request for loan extension is rejected by Germany," *The New
      York Times*, February 19, 2015, http://www.nytimes.com/2015/02/20
      /business/greece-bailout-program-european-union.html; R. Maltezou and
      J. Strupczewski, "Greece offers new proposals to avert default, creditors
      see hope," Reuters, June 22, 2015, https://www.foxbusiness.com/politics
      /greece-offers-new-proposals-to-avert-default-creditors-see-hope.

180   a series of experiments: J. M. Majer, R. Trötschel, A. D. Galinsky, and D. D.
      Loschelder, "Open to offers, but resisting requests: How the framing of
      anchors affects motivation and negotiated outcomes," *Journal of Personality
      and Social Psychology* 119, no. 3 (2020): 582–99.

182   some excerpts from the segment: "Good Guys," *This American Life*, episode
      515, National Public Radio, January 10, 2014.

184   power at the bargaining table: A. D. Galinsky, M. Schaerer, and J. C. Mage,
      "The four horsemen of power at the bargaining table," *Journal of Business and
      Industrial Marketing* 32 (2017): 606–11.

CHAPTER 10: INSPIRING WISE DECISIONS

186   "The way you dealt with Joe": M. Lewis, *The Big Short: Inside the Doomsday
      Machine* (London: Penguin UK, 2011).

187   over the span of one hundred years: E. M. Anicich, R. I. Swaab, and A. D.
      Galinsky, "Hierarchical cultural values predict success and mortality in high-
      stakes teams," *Proceedings of the National Academy of Sciences* 112, no. 5 (2015):
      1338–43.

188   "authority (the right to lead or command) is of supreme importance": S. H.
      Schwartz and K. Boehnke, "Evaluating the structure of human values with confir-
      matory factor analysis," *Journal of Research in Personality* 38, no. 3 (2004): 230–55.

188   "employees [are] afraid to express disagreement with their managers": G. Hof-
      stede, *Culture's Consequences: International Differences in Work-Related Values*,
      2nd ed. (Thousand Oaks, CA: Sage Publications, 2001).

188   the King family's lives changed forever: S. King, "Josie's Story," Oprah.com,
      https://www.oprah.com/relationships/josies-story-by-sorrel-king/all.

188   a five-step sterilization checklist: A. Gawande, "The Checklist," *The New
      Yorker*, December 10, 2007, 86–95.

190 When we lack power, speaking up is scary: A. D. Galinsky, "How to speak up for yourself," TED talk, 2016, https://www.ted.com/talks/adam_galinsky_how _to_speak_up_for_yourself?language=en.

191 "a significant increase when you put them all together": M. Slater, "Olympics cycling: Marginal gains underpin team GB dominance," BBC Sport, https://www.bbc.com/sport/olympics/19174302.

191 the supporting cast needed to feel valued and respected: D. Brailsford, "How to foster a culture of excellence," presentation in Palm Springs, CA.

192 accomplishes so many interpersonal goals at once: K. A. Liljenquist and A. D. Galinsky, "Turn your adversary into your advocate," *Negotiation* 10 (2007): 1–3.

193 walked out of a pitch meeting feeling upset: A. Grant and S. Sandberg, "Speaking While Female," *The New York Times*, January 12, 2015, 12.

193 points the finger *at* women: J. Y. Kim, G. M. Fitzsimons, and A. C. Kay, "*Lean in* messages increase attributions of women's responsibility for gender inequality," *Journal of Personality and Social Psychology* 115 (2018): 974–1001.

194 They put the *nurses* in charge of the checklist: Gawande, "The Checklist," 86–95.

195 copilots were afraid to speak up when the captain made a mistake: M. Gladwell, *Outliers: The Story of Success* (New York: Little, Brown, 2008).

196 "applauded for encouraging discussion": J. Moulds, "Is Mario Draghi the saviour of the eurozone?," *The Guardian*, September 6, 2012.

197 a silencing effect on the voices in the room: R. F. Kennedy, *Thirteen Days: A Memoir of the Cuban Missile Crisis* (New York: W. W. Norton & Company, 1999).

197 a broader range of voices is encouraged: P. T. Bartone and A. B. Adler, "Event-oriented debriefing following military operations: what every leader should know," US Army Medical Research Unit–Europe, Unit, 29218 (1995): 1–9; G. Hammett, "Military leaders know the power of reflection. Here's how you too can use the debrief in business," Inc., 2018, https://www.inc.com/gene-hammett/military-leaders-know-power-of-reflection-heres-how-you-too-can-use-debrief-in-business.html.

197 Let's revisit the writers' room: Grant and Sandberg, "Speaking While Female," 12.

198 they do so anonymously: "Innovative Design to Improve the Shopping Cart," *Nightline*, television broadcast, ABC, February 2, 1999, New York: American Broadcasting Company, ABC News Home Video N 990209-01.

CHAPTER 11: INSPIRING FAIRNESS

199 You are a member of a transplant review board, and a single kidney has suddenly become available: This example is based on D. Austen-Smith, T. Feddersen, A. Galinsky, and K. Liljenquist, "Kidney Case: Negotiation, teamwork, and decision-making exercises," Northwestern University, Kellogg School of Management, Dispute Resolution Research Center, retrieved from drrcexercises.com.

201 Eric Uhlmann of INSEAD: E. L. Uhlmann and G. L. Cohen, "Constructed criteria: Redefining merit to justify discrimination," *Psychological Science* 16 (2005): 474–80.

202 the effects of anti-bias training and found almost no effect: E. L. Paluck, R. Porat, C. S. Clark, and D. P. Green, "Prejudice reduction: Progress and challenges," *Annual Review of Psychology* 72 (2021): 533–60.

202 unconscious bias training *decreased* the promotion rates of women and minorities: F. Dobbin, S. Kim, and A. Kalev, "You can't always get what you need: Organizational determinants of diversity programs," *American Sociological Review* 76, no. 3 (2011): 386–411; F. Dobbin and A. Kalev, "Why doesn't diversity training work? The challenge for industry and academia," *Anthropology Now* 10 (2011): 48–55.

203 reject the message and put their head in the sand: J. J. Gladstone, J. M. Jachimowicz, A. E. Greenberg, and A. D. Galinsky, "Financial shame spirals: How shame intensifies financial hardship," *Organizational Behavior and Human Decision Processes* 167 (2021): 42–56.

203 desperately waiting for a transplant: "Organ Donation Statistics," HRSA, February 2024, https://www.organdonor.gov/learn/organ-donation-statistics.

204 "no role in transplant priority": UNOS, "How we match organs," https://unos.org/transplant/how-we-match-organs/.

205 UNOS used the following point system: T. E. Starzl, R. Shapiro, and L. Teperman, "The point system for organ distribution," *Transplantation Proceedings* 21, no. 3 (1989): 3432.

206 a straightforward point system similar to the UNOS organ allocation system: P. Young, *Equity: In Theory and in Practice* (Princeton, NJ: Princeton University Press, 1994), 23–27.

207 the entire hiring process is different for a candidate that shares the passions of their interviewers: L. A. Rivera, *Pedigree: How Elite Students Get Elite Jobs* (Princeton, NJ: Princeton University Press, 2016).

207 only 2 percent of venture capital funding went to female founders: Amex, "The 2016 state of women-owned businesses report," New York, NY: American Express Pitchbook & National Venture Capital Association, 2016, Pitchbook–NVCA 4Q 2016 venture monitor.

208 since its inception in 2010: D. Kanze, L. Huang, M. Conley, and T. Higgins, "We ask men to win & women not to lose: Closing the gender gap in startup funding," *Academy of Management Journal* 61 (2018): 586–614.

209 a groundbreaking study back in the '70s: C. O. Word, M. P. Zanna, and

J. Cooper, "The nonverbal mediation of self-fulfilling prophecies in interracial interaction," *Journal of Experimental Social Psychology* 10, no. 2 (1974): 109–20.

211 the only female among the eighty-eight candidates: Joseph L. Badaracco Jr. and Ilyse Barkan, 1991, revised 2001, Ann Hopkins (A), Harvard Business School Case, 391-155.

211 "out of a job if they behave aggressively and out of a job if they don't": Price Waterhouse v. Hopkins, 1989, Justia, https://supreme.justia.com/cases/federal/us/490/228/#:~:text=Hopkins%2C%20490%20U.S.%20228%20(1989)&text=Discrimination%20against%20an%20employee%20on,Civil%20Rights%20Act%20of%201964.

212 Consider the fascinating research of Felix Danbold: F. Danbold and C. Bendersky, "Balancing professional prototypes increases the valuation of women in male-dominated professions," *Organization Science* 31, no. 1 (2020): 119–140.

213 nearly two decades earlier: L. J. Kray, A. D. Galinsky, and L. Thompson, "Reversing the gender gap in negotiations: An exploration of stereotype regeneration," *Organizational Behavior and Human Decision Processes* 87, no. 2 (2002): 386–409.

214 consistent with prior research: L. J. Kray, L. Thompson, and A. Galinsky, "Battle of the sexes: gender stereotype confirmation and reactance in negotiations," *Journal of Personality and Social Psychology* 80, no. 6 (2001): 942–58; J. Mazei, J. Hüffmeier, P. A. Freund, A. F. Stuhlmacher, L. Bilke, and G. Hertel, "A meta-analysis on gender differences in negotiation outcomes and their moderators," *Psychological Bulletin* 141, no. 1 (2015): 84–104.

214 Aaron Kay of Duke University and I found: J. P. Friesen, A. C. Kay, R. P. Eibach, and A. D. Galinsky, "Seeking structure in social organization: Compensatory control and the psychological advantages of hierarchy," *Journal of Personality and Social Psychology* 106, no. 4 (2014): 590–609.

215 less than 5 percent of the top US orchestras were female: C. Rice, "How blind auditions help orchestras to eliminate gender bias," *The Guardian*, October 14, 2013, https://www.theguardian.com/women-in-leadership/2013/oct/14/blind-auditions-orchestras-gender-bias.

215 forty-five women to forty-four men: H. Waleson, "Orchestrating gender equity," Curtis Institute of Music, 2022, https://www.curtis.edu/news/feature-story-orchestrating-gender-equity/.

216 "increased the proportion [of] women in symphony orchestras": C. Goldin and C. Rouse, "Orchestrating impartiality: The impact of 'blind' auditions on female musicians," *American Economic Association* 90 (2000): 715–41.

216 we can remove hobbies from résumés: L. A. Rivera, "Hiring as cultural matching: The case of elite professional service firms," *American Sociological Review* 77 (2012): 999–1022.

216 makes these gaps less apparent: A. S. Kristal, L. Nicks, J. L. Gloor, and O. P. Hauser, "Reducing discrimination against job seekers with and without employment gaps," *Nature Human Behaviour* 7 (2023): 211–18.

CHAPTER 12: INSPIRING DIVERSITY AND INCLUSION

219 the rescue efforts that took place outside the cave: This story is a compilation from multiple documentaries, including: *The Rescue* (2021) and *The Trapped 13: How We Survived the Thai Cave* (2022).

224 more creative and make better decisions: S. R. Sommers, L. S. Warp, and C. C. Mahoney, "Cognitive effects of racial diversity: White individuals' information processing in heterogeneous groups," *Journal of Experimental Social Psychology* 44 (2008): 1129–36; K. W. Phillips and D. L. Loyd, "When surface and deep level diversity collide: The effects on dissenting group members," *Organizational Behavior and Human Decision Processes* 99 (2006): 143–60; D. L. Loyd, C. S. Wang, K. W. Phillips, and R. B. Lount Jr., "Social category diversity promotes premeeting elaboration: The role of relationship focus," *Organization Science* 24 (2013): 757–72.

224 diverse leadership teams produce higher firm value: S. S. Levine, E. P. Apfelbaum, M. Bernard, V. L. Bartelt, E. J. Zajac, D. Stark, "Ethnic diversity deflates price bubbles," *Proceedings of the National Academy of Sciences, USA* 111 (2014): 18524–29; V. Hunt, D. Layton, and S. Prince, "Diversity matters," *McKinsey & Company* 1 (2015): 15–29.

224 geographic diversity within towns predicts greater economic prosperity: N. Eagle, M. Macy, R. Claxton, "Network diversity and economic development," *Science* 328 (2010): 1029–31.

225 lower trust among neighbors and less community engagement: R. D. Putnam, "E Pluribus Unum: Diversity and community in the twenty-first century," *Scandinavian Political Studies* 30 (2005): 137–74; A. Alesina and E. La Ferrara, "Ethnic diversity and economic performance," *Journal of Economic Literature* 43 (2005): 763–800.

225 their decisions and outcomes are superior to those of homogenous teams: K. W. Phillips, K. A. Liljenquist, and M. A. Neale, "Is the pain worth the gain? The advantages and liabilities of agreeing with socially distinct newcomers," *Personality and Social Psychology Bulletin* 35 (2009): 336–50.

226 Here's the problem we gave the students to solve: K. Duncker, "On problem solving," *Psychological Monographs* 58, no. 5, serial no. 270 (1945).

227 only 6 percent could solve it without any intervention: A. D. Galinsky and G. B. Moskowitz, "Counterfactuals as behavioral primes: Priming the simulation heuristic and consideration of alternatives," *Journal of Experimental Social Psychology* 36 (2000): 384–409.

227 *functional fixedness*: S. Glucksberg and W. R. Weisberg, "Verbal behavior and problem solving: Effects of labeling in a functional fixedness problem," *Journal of Experimental Psychology* 71 (1966): 659–64.

227 whether living abroad mattered: W. W. Maddux and A. D. Galinsky, "Cultural borders and mental barriers: the relationship between living abroad and creativity," *Journal of Personality and Social Psychology* 96 (2009): 1047–61.

229 solve creative problems like the candle one: J. G. Lu, A C. Hafenbrack, P. W. Eastwick, D. J. Wang, W. W. Maddux, and A. D. Galinsky, "'Going out' of the box: Close intercultural friendships and romantic relationships spark creativity, workplace innovation, and entrepreneurship," *Journal of Applied Psychology* 102, no. 7 (2017): 1091–1108.

229 they were to start their own business in their home country: Ibid., 1091.

229 the creative output of 270 top fashion houses over 21 seasons: F. Godart, W. W. Maddux, A. Shipilov, and A. D. Galinsky, "Fashion with a foreign flair: Professional experiences abroad facilitate the creative innovations of organizations," *Academy of Management Journal* 58 (2015): 195–220.

230 if the diversity of teams predicted their on-field performance: J. G. Lu, R. I. Swaab, and A. D. Galinsky, "Global leaders for global teams: Leaders with multicultural experiences communicate and lead more effectively, especially in multinational teams," *Organization Science* 33, no. 4 (2022): 1554–73.

231 Michael Crichton, the author of *Jurassic Park*: M. Crichton, *Travels* (New York: Vintage, 2012).

231 also making us feel more authentic: H. Adam, O. Obodaru, J. G. Lu, W. W. Maddux, and A. D. Galinsky, "The shortest path to oneself leads around the world: Living abroad increases self-concept clarity," *Organizational Behavior and Human Decision Processes* 145 (2018): 16–29.

233 "when it's five minutes before the set time he thinks he is too late": B. Oakley, *Podium: What Shapes a Sporting Champion?* (Edinburgh, Scotland: A&C Black, 2014).

233 the transformative power of learning the *why* of other cultures: W. W. Maddux, H. Adam, and A. D. Galinsky, "When in Rome . . . learn why the Romans do what they do: How multicultural learning experiences facilitate creativity," *Personality and Social Psychology Bulletin* 36 (2010), 731–74.

233 the extent to which they had learned about new cultures during their graduate program: W. W. Maddux, E. Bivolaru, A. C. Hafenbrack, C. T. Tadmor, and A. D. Galinsky, "Expanding opportunities by opening your mind: Multicultural engagement predicts increases in integrative complexity and job market success," *Social Psychological and Personality Science* 5 (2014): 608–15.

236 neither is very effective: S. Gündemir, A. C. Homan, A. Usova, and A. D.

Galinsky, "Multicultural meritocracy: The synergistic benefits of valuing diversity and merit," *Journal of Experimental Social Psychology* 73 (2017), 34–41.

238 creating more equal opportunities: B. J. Lucas, Z. Berry, L. M. Giurge, D. Chugh, "A longer shortlist increases the consideration of female candidates in male-dominated domains," *Nature Human Behavior* 5 (2021): 736–42.

240 an acute tension between being authentic and fitting in: C. S. Wang, G. Ku, A. N. Smith, E. Scott, B. Edwards, and A. D. Galinsky, "Increasing Black employees' social identity affirmation and organizational involvement: Reducing social uncertainty through organizational and individual strategies," *Organization Science*.

242 cross-race and cross-gender mentoring relationships rarely develop naturally: D. A. Thomas, "The truth about mentoring minorities," *Harvard Business Review* 79 (2001): 98–107.

245 higher promotion rates of women and minorities: F. Dobbin and A. Kalev, "The origins and effects of corporate diversity programs," *Oxford Handbook of Diversity and Work*, Quinetta Roberson, ed. (New York: Oxford University Press, 2013), 253–81.

AFTERWORD: A MORE INSPIRING TOMORROW

251 secure peaceful solutions to global conflicts: "The Nobel Peace Prize 2002," The Nobel Prize, https://www.nobelprize.org/prizes/peace/2002/summary/.

251 (while also battling numerous legal challenges): S. R. Kim, "Trump's new financial disclosure shows his number of business holdings has doubled since leaving White House," ABC News, April 14, 2023, https://abcnews.go.com/US/trumps-new-financial-disclosure-shows-number-business-holdings/story?id=98600900.

252 "forced to prepare presidential options in a vacuum": S. Hess, "Jimmy Carter: Why he failed," Brookings, June 1978, https://www.brookings.edu/articles/jimmy-carter-why-he-failed/.

252 "the unwillingness to delegate authority on small matters": B. Cuniberti, "Stars, athletes, politicians to boost drug abuse fund," *Los Angeles Times*, May 23, 1985, https://www.latimes.com/archives/la-xpm-1985-05-23-vw-8291-story.html.

252 Carter was never able to secure their release: "The Iranian Hostage Crisis," Office of the Historian, https://history.state.gov/departmenthistory/short-history/iraniancrises.

253 personally building houses with Habitat for Humanity: C. O'Kane, "Jimmy Carter has a long history with Habitat for humanity – even pitching in on builds in his 90s," CBS News, February 28, 2023, https://www.cbsnews.com/news/jimmy-carter-habitat-for-humanity-history-the-carter-work-project/.

253 "Nobody knows the system better than me": D. Jackson, "Donald Trump accepts GOP nomination, says 'I alone can fix' system," *USA Today*, July 21, 2016,

https://www.usatoday.com/story/news/politics/elections/2016/07/21 /donald-trump-republican-convention-acceptance-speech/87385658/.

253   for example, he went through four chiefs of staff in less than four years: K. D. Tenpas, "Tracking turnover in the Trump administration," Brookings, https:// www.brookings.edu/articles/tracking-turnover-in-the-trump-administration/.

254   threw his subordinates under the bus: J. Filipovic, "If you work for Trump, expect to be 'thrown under bus,'" CNN, May 8, 2019, https://www.cnn .com/2019/05/08/opinions/stephanie-winston-wolkoff-thrown-under-bus -filipovic/index.html.

254   ingeniously captured their greatest weakness: "From 'Crooked Hillary' to 'Little Marco,' Donald Trump's Many Nicknames," ABC News, May 11, 2016, https://abcnews.go.com/Politics/crooked-hillary-marco-donald-trumps -nicknames/story?id=39035114.

254   brutal atrocities committed against ethnic minorities: A. Taylor, "How Aung San Suu Kyi, arrested Myanmar leader, went from Nobel Peace Prize to pariah," *Washington Post*, February 1, 2021, https://www.washingtonpost.com/world /2021/02/01/aung-san-suu-kyi/.

255   "the strength we show if, and when, we're ever given a second chance": J. Sudeikis, L. Lawrence, and B. Hunt, "Mom City," *Ted Lasso*, season 3, episode 11, May 24, 2023.

255   Remember Steven Rogelberg's study: S. G. Rogelberg, L. Justice, P. W. Braddy, S. C. Paustian-Underdahl, E. Heggestad, L. Shanock, and J. W. Fleenor, "The executive mind: leader self-talk, effectiveness and strain," *Journal of Managerial Psychology* 28, no. 2 (2013): 183–201.

256   three times more likely to find a job over the next two months: J. Pfrombeck, A. D. Galinsky, N. Nagy, M. S. North, J. Brockner, and G. Grote. "Self-affirmation increases reemployment success for the unemployed," *PNAS* 120, no. 37 (2023): e2301532120.

256   satisfy the fundamental human need for meaning: L. J. Kray, L. G. George, K. A. Liljenquist, A. D. Galinsky, P. E. Tetlock, and N. J. Roese, "From what *might* have been to what *must* have been: Counterfactual thinking creates meaning," *Journal of Personality and Social Psychology* 98 (2010): 106–18.

256   experience our vision more deeply: Carton et al., "How can leaders overcome the blurry vision bias?," 2106–29.

256   recalling an experience with power makes us physiologically more calm and psychologically more confident and authentic: A. D. Galinsky, D. D. Rucker, and J. C. Magee, "Power: Past findings, present considerations, and future directions," in J. A. Simpson, J. F. Dovidio (assoc. eds.), M. Mikulincer, and P. R. Shaver (eds.), *APA Handbook of Personality and Social Psychology, Vol. 3:*

Interpersonal Relations (Washington, DC: American Psychological Association, 2015), 421–60.

258 their co-led groups were much *less* effective than their solo-led ones: E. Anicich, F. C. Godart, R. I. Swaab, and A. Galinsky, "The Costs of Co-Leadership in Fashion Houses, Mountaineering Teams, Qualitative Reports, and the Lab," *Academy of Management Proceedings* 2017, no. 1 (2017): 11655.

258 a brilliant strategic thinker and marketing genius, but he lacked engineering skills: J. Goodell, "Steve Jobs in 1994: The Rolling Stone Interview," *Rolling Stone*, https://www.rollingstone.com/culture/culture-news/steve-jobs-in-1994-the-rolling-stone-interview-231132/.

258 he lacked ambition and a strategic vision: "Steve Wozniak," The Heinz Awards, 2001, https://www.heinzawards.org/pages/steve-wozniak#:~:text=Wozniak%2C%20who%20never%20did%20join,time%20for%20the%20past%20decade.

260 "And as I sat there brooding on the old, unknown world, I thought of Gatsby's wonder when he first picked out the green light at the end of Daisy's dock": F. S. Fitzgerald, *The Great Gatsby* (New York: Charles Scribner's Sons, 1925).

Index

About the Author

ADAM GALINSKY IS the Paul Calello Professor of Leadership and Ethics at the Columbia Business School. He received his PhD from Princeton University and his bachelor's degree from Harvard University.

Adam has published more than three hundred articles on leadership, negotiations, diversity, decision-making, and ethics. He coauthored the bestselling book *Friend & Foe*, which offers a radically new perspective on conflict and cooperation, and received uniformly positive reviews from the *New York Times*, the *Financial Times*, and the *Economist*, among other publications. His TED Talk, *How to Speak Up for Yourself*, has over 7.5 million views. Adam has conducted executive workshops for and consulted with hundreds of clients across the globe, including Fortune 100 firms, nonprofits, and local and national governments.

His research has received numerous national and international awards from the scientific and pedagogical community. In 2016, Adam received the Career Trajectory Award, given to one social psychologist each year for "uniquely creative and influential scholarly productivity at or near the peak of one's scientific career." *Poets & Quants* selected Adam as one of the World's 50 Best B-School Professors in 2012. In 2022, Columbia University honored him with its prestigious Mentoring Award for demonstrating "an exceptional commitment to faculty mentoring through work with tenure-track and mid-career faculty in developing their careers." He has received teaching awards at the Kellogg School of Management at Northwestern University and Princeton University.

Adam has served as a damages expert in numerous defamation trials involving reputational damage, including *Dominion Voting Systems v. Fox News* and *Bacon v. Nygard*. His expert reports and testimony have generated more than $1 billion in verdicts and settlements for clients.

He is the executive and associate producer on many award-winning documentaries, including *Horns and Halos* and *Battle for Brooklyn*, which were both short-listed (final 15) for Best Documentary at the Academy Awards.

Adam is an enthusiastic participant in life who embraces new experiences, from learning skiing and scuba diving in his thirties to sampling local cuisines when he travels. He is married to the remarkable Jenny O, whose intellectual curiosity, understated elegance, and curation of near and far experiences lift him up and expand his horizons. His favorite experience is being a dad; he finds no greater joy than just spending time with his boys as they discover the world and themselves.